# The Stalin Years

# The Stalin Years

## A Reader

EDITED BY

## CHRISTOPHER READ

First published 2003 by
PALGRAVE MACMILLAN
Houndmills, Basingstoke, Hampshire RG21 6XS and
175 Fifth Avenue, New York, N.Y. 10010
Companies and representatives throughout the world

PALGRAVE MACMILLAN is the global academic imprint of the Palgrave Macmillan division of St. Martin's Press, LLC and of Palgrave Macmillan Ltd. Macmillan® is a registered trademark in the United States, United Kingdom and other countries. Palgrave is a registered trademark in the European Union and other countries.

ISBN 0–333–96342–3 hardback
ISBN 0–333–96343–1 paperback

This book is printed on paper suitable for recycling and made from fully managed and sustained forest sources.

A catalogue record for this book is available from the British Library.

Library of Congress Cataloging-in-Publication Data

The Stalin years: a reader / edited by Christopher Read.
      p. cm.
   Includes bibliographical references and index.
   ISBN 0–333–96342–3 – ISBN 0–333–96343–1 (pbk.)
      1. Soviet Union – politics and government – 1917–1936. 2. Soviet Uniion – Politics and government – 1936–1953. 3. Stalin, Joseph, 1879–1953. I. Read, Christopher, 1946–

DK267 .S6937 2002
947.084′2–dc21                                                     2002035909

10   9   8   7   6   5   4   3   2   1
12   11   10   09   08   07   06   05   04   03

Typeset in Great Britain by
Aarontype Ltd, Easton, Bristol

Printed and bound in Great Britain by
Creative Print and Design (Wales), Ebbw Vale

*To Paul, Monica, Nick, Tom, Liz and Matt*

# Contents

# Preface

The aim of the present collection is twofold. First, it provides a self-contained journey through the Stalin years, focusing in detail on the main events. Second, it gives an opportunity for those readers interested in the period who do not normally have access to the main research journals and monographs to sample the new historiography emerging, for the first time, from the Russian archives. Items have been selected not only for their outstanding quality but also for originality in opening up new areas of topics and, in particular, balancing the impact of central politics with the day-to-day lives of ordinary Russians. It is in this last sphere that the historiography of the post-Soviet has been most illuminating. The items selected cover a wide range of themes and topics which could not be explored in earlier generations. Social policy, the experiences of the provinces, the role of local party institutions, new ideas about exactly how Stalin governed, new documents on foreign policy, the importance of cultural revolution as well as the economic, social and political revolutions – these are some of the themes emphasized by the contributors. Overall, these themes provide a basis for a fuller, more complex understanding of the Stalin years.

The items included are presented in their entirety as far as the text is concerned with the exception of minor cosmetic changes to standardize spelling and the addition of occasional explanatory parentheses for unusual terms. The notes have, however, been greatly simplified. Items likely to be unavailable to the majority of readers of this selection – notably archive references and Russian language materials – have been edited out. English language items have been retained. A glossary has been added to further assist the less-specialized reader. It should be emphasized that there has certainly not been the slightest 'dumbing-down' of the texts. Some of the items require careful, concentrated reading and serve to remind us that real scholarship necessarily has to be complex at times and cannot be reduced to soundbites and samples.

Finally, there are no articles about the knotty subject of how many victims of Stalinism there were. The issue is dealt with in the introductory chapter and elsewhere and extensive references are given to the main items in this controversy. The question has not been avoided. However, to include articles devoted to the question would have invited criticism of blatant bias (if only one article from one side of the debate had been included) or of stifling the other topics (if two or more selections had been included).

# Acknowledgements

The editor and publisher wish to thank the following for permission to use copyright material:

The American Association for the Advancement of Slavic Studies, for the extracts from the following: 'Stalin, Grain Stocks and Famine of 1932–3' by R. W. Davies, M. B. Tauger and S. G. Wheatcroft in *Slavic Review, 54* (1995); and 'Building the "Soviet Detroit": the Construction of the Nizhnii-Novgorod Automobile Factory, 1927–32' by Kurt S. Schultz, in *Slavic Review, 49* (1990). Reproduced by permission of the American Association for the Advancement of Slavic Studies.

Blackwell Publishing Ltd, for the extracts from 'How the Mice Buried the Cat: Scenes from the Great Purges of 1937 in the Russian Provinces' by Sheila Fitzpatrick, in *The Russian Review, 52* (1993). Reproduced by permission of Blackwell Publishing Ltd.

Palgrave Macmillan Ltd, for the extracts from the following: 'The Objectives of the Great Terror' by Oleg Khlevnyuk, in J. Cooper, M. Perrie and E. A. Rees (eds), *Soviet History, 1917–1953: Essays in Honour of R. W. Davies* (1995); and 'Soviet Women at War' by John Erickson, in J. and C. Garrard (eds), *World War Two and the Soviet People: Selected Papers from the Fourth World Congress for Soviet and East European Studies, Harrogate, 1990* (1993); © International Council for Soviet and East European Studies, and John and Carol Garrard. Reproduced by permission of Palgrave Macmillan Ltd.

Taylor & Francis Ltd, for the extracts from the following: 'The Modernization of Russian Motherhood, 1917–37' by Elizabeth Waters, in *Europe–Asia Studies* (formerly *Soviet Studies*), *44* (1992); 'The 1929 Congress of the Godless' by Daniel Peris, in *Europe–Asia Studies* (formerly *Soviet Studies*), *43* (1991); 'Moscow and the Marshall Plan: Politics, Ideology and the Onset of the Cold War, 1947' by Geoffrey Roberts, in *Europe–Asia Studies, 46* (1994); and 'Stalin's Cabinet: the Politburo and Decision Making in the Postwar Years' by Yoram Gorlizki, in *Europe–Asia Studies, 53* (2001). Reproduced by permission of Taylor & Francis Ltd (journals website: http://www.tandf.co.uk/journals).

University of California Press, for the extracts from *Magnetic Mountain: Stalinism as a Civilization* by Stephen Kotkin, copyright © 1997 the Regents of the University of California. Reproduced by permission of University of California Press.

# Glossary

| | |
|---|---|
| *agitprop* | Agitation and Propaganda Department of the Central Committee |
| *akty* | affidavits |
| Amtorg | Soviet-American Trading Agency (based in New York) |
| Avtostroi | State Automobile Construction Agency |
| *babka* | village wise woman |
| *Bezbozhnik* | *The Atheist* (a newspaper) |
| *bezkul'ture* | lacking in culture |
| *boevaya podruga* | female fighting companion (loosely 'Amazon') |
| *Cheka* | secret police |
| *chetverka* | group of four |
| Comecon (CMEA) | Council for Mutual Economic Assistance (a body set up to coordinate the national economies of the Soviet bloc countries) |
| Cominform | Communist Information Bureau (a scaled-down version of Comintern) |
| Comintern | Communist International (a body which attempted to co-ordinate policies of communist parties around the world from 1919 to 1943) |
| Commissar | Minister |
| Commissariat of Enlightenment | Ministry of Education |
| CPSU | Communist Party of the Soviet Union |
| *dacha* | house in the country |
| *devushki-pulemyotchitsy* | girl machine-gunners |
| *devushki-snaipery* | girl snipers |
| *devyatka* | group of nine |
| *Ekonomicheskaya zhizn'* | *Economic Life* (a newspaper) |
| *frontoviki* | front-line fighters |
| *glasnost'* | openness |
| GKO | State Defence Committee |
| *gorkom* | city committee of party |
| *gosfond (gosudarstvennyi fond)* | state fund |
| Gosplan | State Planning Commission |

| | |
|---|---|
| *kolkhoz* | collective farm |
| *kolkhoznik* | collective farmer |
| Komsomol | Communist Youth League |
| *Komsomol'skaya pravda* | *Communist Youth League Pravda* (a newspaper) |
| Komzag | Agricultural Collections Committee (which supervised grain collection nationwide) |
| *krai* | region, province, county |
| *kraikom* | regional (*krai*) party committee |
| *Krest'ianskaya gazeta* | *Peasant Gazette* (a newspaper) |
| *kulak* | a rural entrepreneur; controversially, Leninist thought equated this category with 'rich peasants'. |
| *kul'turnost'* | level of culture |
| *limit(y)* | limit(s); quota(s) |
| Metallostroi | a soviet construction agency |
| *mobfond* (*mobilizatsionnyi fond*) | mobilization fund |
| MTS | machine and tractor station |
| *narkom* | people's commissar (abbreviation) |
| Narkomsnab | People's Commissariat for Supply (in charge of food distribution) |
| Narkompros | Ministry of Education |
| Narkomyust | People's Commissariat of Justice |
| *narodnoe opolchenie* | people's militia; Home Guard |
| NEP | New Economic Policy; a controversial partial restoration of market relations from 1920 to the First Five-Year Plan |
| *nepfond* (*neprikosnovennyi fond*) | untouchable fund (i.e. final reserve fund) |
| *nepmen* | small-scale traders who flourished under the New Economic Policy (NEP) |
| *nevidimiye zapasy* | invisible stocks |
| NKVD | secret police (formerly OGPU and *Cheka*) |
| *obkom* | provincial (oblast') committee of party |
| *oblast'* | province |
| OGPU | secret police (formerly *Cheka*) |
| *Okhmatmlad* | Subdepartment for Protection of Motherhood and Infancy of the Commissariat of Health |
| *okrug* | region |
| *okrugkom* | regional committee of party |
| Orgburo | Organization Bureau (of Communist Party) |
| Osoaviakhim | Association for National Defence and for Aviation and Chemical Construction |

| | |
|---|---|
| *osobye papki* | special files |
| *perekhodiashchie ostatki* | transitional stocks |
| *perestroika* | restructuring (esp. during 1985–91) |
| *pokazatel'nyi sud* | show trial |
| Politburo | Political Bureau (of Communist Party): in effect the main component of Soviet government |
| *pood* | 36 pounds (weight) |
| *popovshchina* | attack by clerics |
| *prazdnik* | a festival |
| Proletkul't | The Proletarian Cultural-Educational Association |
| *pyaterka* | group of five |
| *rabfak* | workers' faculty |
| *Rabotnitsa* | *Working Woman* (a newspaper) |
| *raikom* | regional (*raion*) party committee |
| *raion* | district |
| *samizdat* | self-published writings, i.e. unofficial typescripts |
| *sel'kory* | rural correspondents |
| *sel'sovet* | rural soviet |
| *smychka* | alliance; specifically of peasants and workers in Lenin's testament |
| *snaiper-nastavnik* | master sniper instructor |
| *Sovkhoz* | state farm |
| Sovmin | Council (Soviet) of Ministers |
| *Sovnarkom* | Soviet of People's Commissars (loosely the Soviet Cabinet) |
| *spetsy* | specialists trained in pre-Soviet times who were kept on in their specialities by the Soviet authorities. They included former tsarist army officers. |
| *sploshnya kollektivizatsiya* | total collectivization |
| *spravka(i)* | inventory, inventories |
| STO | Council for Labour and Defence |
| *troika* | group of three |
| *trudoden/trudodni* | labour day(s) (unit of payment on a *kolkhoz*) |
| TsIK | Soviet Central Executive Committee |
| VATO | All-Union Automobile and Tractor Association (a government agency which supervised the automobile and tractor industries) |
| Vesenkha | Supreme Council of the National Economy |

| | |
|---|---|
| *vidimiye zapasy* | visible stocks |
| *voenkomat* | military command centre |
| *voennyi zapas* | military stocks |
| *vozhd'* | leader, boss (term often applied to Stalin) |
| *Vsevobuch* | universal military training |
| *Za industrializatsiiu* | *For Industrialization* (a newspaper) |
| *zhenotdel* | Women's Section of the Communist Party |
| *zhenshchiny-voiny* | women soldiers |
| *znakharstvo* | herbal medicine |

# Notes on the Contributors

**R. W. Davies** is Emeritus Professor and Senior Fellow of the Centre for Russian and East European Studies at the University of Birmingham.

**The late John Erickson** was Professor of History at the University of Edinburgh.

**Sheila Fitzpatrick** is Bemadotte E. Schmitt Distinguished Service Professor in the Department of History at the University of Chicago.

**Yoram Gorlizki** is a Lecturer in the Department of Government at the University of Manchester.

**Oleg Khlevnyuk** is a Senior Research Fellow at the State Archive of the Russian Federation, Moscow.

**Stephen Kotkin** is Associate Professor of History at Princeton University.

**Daniel Peris** is a Securities Analyst at Argus Research Corporation, New York City. He was formerly Assistant Professor of History at the University of Wyoming.

**Christopher Read** is Professor of History at the University of Warwick.

**Geoffrey Roberts** is Statutory Lecturer in History at the University of Cork.

**Kurt S. Schultz** is Managing Editor of *Russian Review* and teaches in the History Department at Iowa State University.

**M. B. Tauger** is Associate Professor of History at West Virginia University.

**Elizabeth Waters** teaches at University College Medical School, London. She has taught Russian and Soviet history at universities in the UK and Australia, and is currently Visiting Academic at the Kazakstan–UK Centre, Middlesex University.

**S. G. Wheatcroft** is Associate Professor of History at the University of Melbourne.

# Stalin's Life and Times

### 1879–1905

Born in Gori, Georgia (9 December 1879); attends Tiflis (Tbilisi) Seminary. Expelled for political (probably nationalist) activities (1899); spends next few years in revolutionary work in Caucasus and South Russia, mainly among the predominantly Muslim oil-workers of Baku.

### 1905–17

Following failure of 1905 revolution Stalin takes his first steps up the Bolshevik party hierarchy. Represents Georgia and South Russia at party conferences in Tammerfors (Finland) and Stockholm in 1905 and 1906. Co-opted onto Central Committee of party at Lenin's initiative and becomes editor of *Pravda*, the party newspaper (1912). As a result he is arrested by the Tsarist authorities and exiled to Siberia until March 1917.

### 1917–22

Active as organizer in central party apparatus. Specializes in nationalities questions. Becomes Commissar for Nationalities in first Soviet Government. Key figure in Worker Peasant Inspectorate. Also an active commander in the Civil War but recalled by Lenin after a dispute with Trotsky in 1919. Becomes General Secretary of Party in 1922.

### 1922–7

Crucial years in Stalin's rise. Partly through his own manoeuvring and partly through the mistakes and ineptitude of his chief opponents, Stalin emerges as the leading figure in the party, though by no means in complete control. Succession dispute with Trotsky (1923/5) and then with Kamenev and Zinoviev (1925/7). Stalin controls 1927 Party Congress which expels his principal rivals.

### 1927–8/9

Crucial turning point. War scare (1927); collapse of NEP. Decision taken to indusrialize at full speed. Five-Year-Plan adopted (1928). Collectivization begins in autumn 1929. Defeat of Bukharin and Right Opposition who resist these initiatives.

**1928/9–32/3**
First Five-Year Plan. Collectivization. Cultural Revolution. Stalinist system of centrally planned economy and police state emerges. Famine.

**1933/4**
A short period of apparent 'thaw'

**1934–9**
Murder of Kirov, December 1934. The Great Terror and Show Trials (1936–8). Beria becomes head of secret police (1939).

**1939–45**
Nazi–Soviet Pact signed (August 1939). Second World War begins (September 1939). Military action against Japan (in Mongolia and North China), 1938 and 1939. Occupation of Eastern Poland and Baltic States (autumn 1939–40); Winter War against Finland (1939/40). Germany invades USSR (22 June 1941). Battle of Moscow (December 1941). Siege of Leningrad (1941/3). Battles of Stalingrad (1942/3) and Kursk (1943); Belorussian Campaign (1944). Soviet troops take Warsaw, Prague, Bucharest, Sofia, Belgrade, Vienna and Berlin by early 1945. Manchurian campaign cut short by Japanese surrender (August 1945).

**1945–53**
Cold War and internal reconstruction. Stalin dies 6 March 1953.

# I   Main Currents of Interpretation of Stalin and the Stalin Years

## DURING STALIN'S LIFETIME

One of the best known, most improbable-sounding but actually highly accurate descriptions of Stalin appears in N. N. Sukhanov's eyewitness account of the Russian Revolution. There Stalin is described as 'a grey blur'. At the moment of high drama in 1917, when the Bolshevik party was in the process of transforming itself from an obscure sect into the rulers of one-sixth of the earth, Stalin was a hazy figure even to those, like Sukhanov, who were closest to the action in the leadership of the Petrograd Soviet. What did fellow party members think of Stalin? How was he perceived in wider society? Stalin's story would never have become important were it not for the fact that he had one, crucial, admirer – Lenin. At all stages, it was Lenin's hand that guided Stalin to high office. It was Lenin who picked him out as a rising star in the 1905–6 revolution. It was Lenin who had him appointed to the Central Committee, to the editorship of *Pravda* in 1912. Above all, his appointment as General Secretary in 1922 was at Lenin's behest. We have many quotations from Lenin about his 'splendid Georgian', but he also said in 1922 that 'that cook will prepare nothing but peppery dishes'.[1] Lenin's selection of Stalin as General Secretary crystallized what Lenin admired in Stalin. The post was primarily administrative. Stalin suited it because, unlike the more ideological members of the leadership – notably Trotsky and Bukharin but also Kamenev and Zinoviev – Stalin was happier to do as he was told, providing it was Lenin who was doing the telling. He was Lenin's most trusted associate in practical matters even to the responsibility, while Lenin was ill, of guarding the poison phial Lenin had to hand in case his illness deteriorated and he thought it necessary to end his own life.

On a more mundane level Stalin supervised the running of the party, ensuring the dilution of the oppositions that were emerging, and main-taining the centre's tight control of the party apparatus. Lenin trusted Stalin to get the job done as he wanted it done. In a sense, it was Stalin's very responsibilities which brought about his one and only, near fatal in terms of Stalin's career, clash with Lenin. Lenin heard that Stalin had had a furious row with Lenin's wife Krupskaia because she was, it appeared, not following doctor's orders and allowing Lenin to work too much. Lenin demanded Stalin's apologies which were immediately forthcoming. However, the doubts escalated and political clouds began to darken the Lenin–Stalin relationship though Lenin relapsed before the outcome was settled. Trotsky has since claimed that Lenin planned to remove Stalin from his post but we will never know for sure if Lenin's judgement was simply impaired by his illness (as Stalin's supporters have always argued) or whether the dispute might have blown over – remembering that Lenin had been at much more serious loggerheads with Trotsky, Kamenev and Zinoviev at various points in the past – or whether Lenin might have finished off Stalin's career.[2] What we do know is that in his political testament Lenin said Stalin was 'too rude', by which he probably meant crude, unsophisticated and unsubtle, and that he would not always use his power wisely and as a consequence he should be removed from the position of General Secretary. In a document which pointed to shortcomings of all the other leaders, including Trotsky who was described as being 'too preoccupied with the administrative side of things', what Lenin wrote about Stalin did not add up to total condemnation. According to Stalin's close aide Molotov, 'After Lenin, Stalin was the strongest politician. Lenin considered him the most reliable, the one whom you could count upon. But he criticized him, too.'[3]

In contrast Trotsky had a long-standing, ever-deepening antipathy to Stalin. In the manuscript of his unfinished book about Stalin he described the emerging successor to Lenin in unflattering terms. To take one example he wrote that 'Stalin's slyness is essentially very crude and designed for primitive minds.'[4] This tied in with his view that Stalin represented the dregs emerging from the collapsing revolution. In a memorable statement of the mid-1920s, Trotsky claimed 'Stalin is needed by the tired radicals, by the bureaucrats, by all the worms that are crawling out of the upturned soil of the revolution. He speaks their language and he knows how to lead them.' Wherever two or three Trotsky supporters were gathered together, denigration of Stalin would be prominent. In his autobiography he summed up his views on Stalinism thus: 'Stalinism is, above all else, the automatic work of the impersonal apparatus on the decline of the revolution.'[5] Clearly, for Trotsky, Stalin was the personification of the revolution's degeneration. Most fatefully, on 25 October 1926 at a Politburo meeting in which Stalin introduced an attack on Trotsky and the opposition, Trotsky responded by pointing to Stalin and saying: 'The First Secretary poses his candidature to the post of grave-digger of the revolution!'[6] In saying this, Trotsky had gone too far and finalized the split between himself and Stalin, whereupon his most crushing statements about Stalin were unleashed over the next fifteen years. In particular, Trotsky developed what has become the most widely accepted view of Stalin as an undereducated, insecure man, envious in the extreme of his intellectual betters, looking everywhere for conspiracies and maintaining a vindictive attitude to the enemies he identified. At the same time, friends were supposed to assuage his inferiority complex through sycophantic adulation.

While Trotsky exaggerated these characteristics, they were also noted by others closer to Stalin and less hostile, most notably his daughter, Svetlana Alliluyeva. She noted a 'cruel, implacable nature' when given evidence of someone's treachery. 'Years of friendship and fighting side by side in a common cause might as well never have been . . . he could wipe it all out at a stroke.'[7] At the same time, she and others testify to another Stalin, a bluff, humorous, family man. With his second wife Nadezhda, Svetlana's mother, he presided over a friendly household at his *dacha* (country residence) outside Moscow. Many friends, colleagues and relatives participated in Stalin's hospitality. According to Svetlana it was 'a house that was sunny and gay, filled with the sounds of children's voices and cheerful, openhearted people This was the house my mother created and presided over, a house that was filled with her presence. In this house, my father was neither a god nor a "cult" but just the father of a family.'[8] Even after Nadezhda's tragic suicide in 1932 the atmosphere survived. A new *dacha* was built in 1934.

> I remember how the whole family came out to see the new house and how noisy and cheerful it was. . . . The house was as happy and full of people as it had been in my mother's day. Everybody brought their children. The children shouted and played, and my father enjoyed it very much. My mother's parents came too. It's not true that after my mother died her family repudiated my father. On the contrary, they all did their best to make him happier. They treated him with consideration and he was cordial and kind to them all.[9]

Indeed, the Alliluyev family had witnessed the human side of Stalin from early on. Recalling 1912 Anna Alliluyeva, Svetlana's aunt, had written: 'We now know Soso [Joseph] more intimately. We know that he can be simple and gay and that, although he is usually uncommunicative and reserved he can also laugh and joke boyishly and tell amusing stories. He sees the funny side of people and imitates them to such perfection that everyone roars with laughter.'[10]

But how did the other leaders see him? Kamenev and Zinoviev underestimated him. Bukharin, one of the frequenters of Stalin's *dacha*, turned against him, calling him 'Genghis Khan' in 1928, in secret conversations with Kamenev.[11] The perceptions of many of those around Stalin depended on their current political relationship with him. It is clearly not the case that, as the caricatural view would have it, Stalin was surrounded by people who simply feared him and followed his every whim. Many of his friends remained with him for decades and were prepared to argue with him over crucial issues. Talking long after Stalin's death, Molotov summed him up: 'I don't consider him a genius, but I think he was a great person. I called him great at his seventieth birthday. He was close to genius in tactics; in theory he was weaker. In our party I consider Lenin alone to be a genius.' In personal terms he was 'a simple, very sociable person. He was a good comrade.'[12]

A survey of Stalin's complex personality would not be complete without taking into account the wealth of personal material we have arising from the war, including reminiscences by commanders who worked with him on a day-to-day basis, foreign leaders and diplomats who encountered him at conferences and other official occasions and foreign communists who visited Moscow. A fairly consistent picture of a bluff, hard-working, well-informed and pragmatic figure emerges. In the words of one historian of the period:

> The two principal levels of military leadership where Stalin's strength impressed and surprised Western military men, diplomats and journalists concerned grand strategy and technical detail. With regard to the former it appeared to them that Stalin had an extraordinary grasp of war goals and major long-range plans for conducting the war and a talent for adjusting the conduct of military operations to political realities. While Stalin's judgement proved erroneous in a number of instances, it nevertheless evoked the admiration of his Allied partners. ... On the second level, that of technical expertise, Western observers were struck by Stalin's mastery of detail, his attention to the purely professional aspects of waging war. Their accounts are corroborated in the memoirs of Soviet commanders and industrial managers.[13]

The words of the most famous of those commanders sum up the situation. 'Stalin was conversant with the principles of organizing the operations of Fronts and groups of Fronts, and he supervised them knowledgeably.' Stalin possessed 'rich intuition and the ability to find the main point in a strategic situation.'[14] Incidentally, though mistakes are acknowledged, none of the memoirs, nor the subsequent primary research in formerly closed archives by privileged researchers such as Colonel General Dmitrii Volkogonov, has uncovered evidence that Stalin suffered a breakdown in the early days of the war as Khrushchev hinted in his so-called Secret Speech of 1956. After the early uncertainties he developed into a competent and confident war leader who let his generals have their head and intervened largely to clarify and arbitrate between their proposals. His style is shown by the famous story told by Rokossovsky and confirmed by others about the final decision over Operation Bagration, a decisive and massive military operation which coincided with D-Day. Operation Bagration was described laconically by one western historian as being 'ignored' in many western accounts of the war even though 'it dwarfs almost every other battle of World War II and was to prove more devastating than anything the Germans had so far experienced'.[15] Stalin argued for a single attack to open the campaign but Rokossovsky argued for a double thrust. After arguing over it, Stalin invited Rokossovsky to leave the room to think it over. Recalled twenty minutes later, Stalin asked if he was now in favour of a single point of attack. Rokossovsky replied that he still thought two would be better. Again he was invited to retire to a neighbouring room alone and think it over. As he pondered, Molotov and Malenkov came in to tell him he must change his mind and agree with Stalin. Rokossovsky returned to Stalin's presence and once again said he favoured twin attacks. According to one account by K. Nepomniashchii, 'at these words, that ominous silence set in which in this office usually preceded terrible outbursts of rage' but, after further pondering, Stalin agreed with Rokossovsky, reportedly saying 'When a commander is so determined he probably knows what is best.'[16]

The uneasy, ambiguous, frank but dangerous atmosphere of Stalin's circle was also memorably captured by the young Yugoslav communist Milovan Djilas who visited Moscow at the end of the war. The leaders were at their most unbuttoned at long suppers starting at nine or ten in the evening and going on until four or five in the morning. Djilas describes the scene:

> At these dinners the Soviet leaders were at their closest, most intimate with one another. Everyone would tell the news from his departments, whom he had met that day, and what plans he was making. The sumptuous table and considerable though not immoderate amounts of alcohol enlivened spirits and increased the atmosphere of cordiality and informality. An uninstructed visitor might hardly have detected any difference between Stalin and the rest [especially since Stalin never sat at the head of the table but always to the left of the head]. Yet it existed. His opinion was carefully noted. No one opposed him very hard. It all rather resembled a patriarchal family with a crotchety head whose foibles made his kinsfolk somewhat apprehensive.[17]

Djilas was undoubtedly right to say that 'a significant part of Soviet policy was decided at these dinners'[18] and 'It was at these dinners that the destiny of the vast Russian land, of the newly acquired territories and, to a considerable degree, of the human race was decided.'[19]

So far we have been looking at the perceptions of people who knew Stalin personally. For the greater public within and beyond Russia he remained, for many years, Sukhanov's 'grey blur'. Only once he emerged as leader of the party and embarked on the second revolution of 1928–38 did the rest of the world really begin to take notice. Unsurprisingly, perceptions of Stalin for the rest of his life were intimately tied up with the dominant political forces of the day, notably the rise of Nazism, the Second World War and the Cold War.

From the time Stalin began to make his mark on Soviet Russia with the great upheavals of collectivization and industrialization, opinions began to polarize. It was hard to remain neutral about such cataclysmic events, particularly since they appeared to suggest the Soviet Union was making rapid 'advances' at a time when, under the influence of the Wall Street crash, the rival capitalist world was moving into depression and prolonged crisis. Many foreigners began to admire the signs of Soviet achievement. Many of them were not especially political and had been brought into the USSR as contract workers employed by western companies keen to take advantage of any business that might come their way in the difficult conditions of the early 1930s. In the forefront of such observers was the American engineer John Scott who wrote extensively about his experiences. He describes his reasons for going to the Soviet Union:

> Something seemed to be wrong with America. I began to read extensively about the Soviet Union, and gradually came to the conclusion that the Bolsheviks had found answers to at least some of the questions Americans were asking each other. I decided to go to Russia to work, study, and to lend a hand in the construction of a society which seemed to be at least one step ahead of the American.[20]

Even after five years living deep within the Soviet Union he would still express sentiments that became rarer and rarer other than in the mouths of propagandists and party members: 'Socialism as it functioned in Magnitogorsk displayed numerous shortcomings, as did capitalism as operated in Gastonia, Dunkirk or Coventry. But Socialism in Magnitogorsk did well enough so that I am convinced that many valuable lessons can be learned from a study of it.'[21]

While some might dismiss Scott as a youthful romantic (he was 25 when he left Magnitogorsk), more seasoned observers could still look relatively objectively at what was happening in Soviet Russia. In the forefront was the journalist and historian William H. Chamberlin. In the late 1920s he produced a thoughtful, carefully observed and considered picture of the current situation in his book *Soviet Russia*. Explaining his aims for the book he wrote in the introduction:

> I can hardly expect that my book will satisfy those extreme partisans in opposed controversial camps who regard Bolshevism as either the greatest calamity or the greatest blessing which ever befell mankind. I hope, however, that it may be of some service to those people who feel that an honest effort at understanding is a

more useful form of approach to the complicated problem of the Russian revolution than are rhetorical exercises in eulogy and denunciation.[22]

Of course, Chamberlin and Scott were writing before the worst horrors of the thirties had happened or become known, though both were aware of the collectivization of agriculture if not of the precise magnitude of its human cost.

Perhaps perversely, however, the 1930s saw the growth of a much more vociferous, adulatory and politically committed group of foreign supporters composed of foreign communists and fellow travellers. The history of the fellow travellers is sufficiently well known not to require extensive further elaboration here. A few examples from the leading account of the topic will give the flavour.[23] In the 1920s the journalist M. Philips Price described Stalin as 'one of the big minds in Russia today.' A decade later Anna Louise Strong found 'His eyes were kind yet grave, giving rest and assurance.' Stalin was 'a man to whom you could say anything; he knew almost before you spoke; he wished to know more clearly and to help'. Even scholars like Bernard Pares could be adulatory. Stalin 'has shown that his heart is in his own country, that he has set his reputation on a purely practical object of vast scope, radical transformation for the benefit of all'. In 1945 Hewlett Johnson, the so-called 'Red Dean of Canterbury', said of his meeting: 'Stalin was calm, composed, simple. Not lacking in humour. Direct in speech, untouched by the slightest suspicion of pomposity. There was nothing cruel or dramatic ... about Stalin's face. Just steady purpose and a kind geniality.' None of these commentators was a communist. Party members were even more sycophantic, attending great Soviet public events, accepting high honours and producing fulsome praise, especially after the rise of Hitler, of all things Soviet.

Obviously one of the most important factors in encouraging the fellow travellers was the looming menace of fascism across Europe and of Nazism in Germany. The Soviet Union was, in the mid-1930s, the only major power to stand up resolutely against Nazism and to throw all its weight into an effort to create a united front against Nazi Germany with the participation primarily of Britain and France as well as the United States if at all possible. Indeed, driven by a common hostility to the equally threatening rise of an expansionist Japan, the USSR finally joined the League of Nations on 19 September1934 and shortly after was officially recognized for the first time by the USA. In the eyes of anti-Nazis, the credentials of the USSR as the main rock of resistance were confirmed by Soviet action to support the Republican Government in Spain against the Francoite rebels who were heavily backed by Fascist Italy and Nazi Germany. In the circumstances, few people in western Europe wanted to see the increasingly apparent black side of events in the USSR. A number of voices spoke out against Stalin and his government. Predictably, Trotsky was in the forefront, producing his most coruscating indictment of the Soviet government's policies in his 1936 publication, *The Revolution Betrayed.*

Trotskyite polemic not only appeared to have little effect but was, in some senses, counterproductive in that much soundly based criticism of the USSR was dismissed precisely because it appeared simply to be opposition rhetoric. This meant that some of the earliest warnings about the black side of Soviet rule were disregarded. A prime example is that of the revolutionary Victor Serge, released from the Gulag as a result of a concerted campaign by western intellectual sympathisers. It was in response to a direct request by one of them, Romain Rolland, that Serge was released. Despite his first-hand knowledge of the situation, he had an uphill struggle to make his voice heard among left-wing circles in the west. In Serge's words:

> For years there would be this struggle of no more than a handful of individual consciences against a total suppression of the truth, in the face of crimes which were beheading the Soviet Union and would soon bring about the downfall of the Spanish Republic. Often we felt like voices crying in the wilderness.[24]

Even more extraordinary, his 'saviour', Rolland, distanced himself from Serge. In a letter of 1938 he wrote to a friend that 'I regret not being able to share your confidence in the vindictive diatribes of Victor Serge' even though he shared, in private, many of Serge's views about the burgeoning dictatorship and prison system.

There were also other warnings. Many visitors to the Soviet Union had had wind of the famines of 1932–3 but were often inclined to minimize their extent. Among the exceptions were Ewald Ammende and Malcolm Muggeridge who wrote extensively about widespread deaths and even reports of cannibalism. Some former fellow travellers reached breaking point, most notably André Gide who wrote the most famous recantation of the period in *Retour de l'URSS* (*Return from the USSR*). In Britain the independent voice of George Orwell refused to go along with casuistic half-truths about Russia. In his journalism and then in his account of the Spanish Civil War, *Homage to Catalonia*, he put forward uncomfortable truths about Stalin's purges and their destructive effect on the fight against fascism in Spain.

Inevitably, once the Soviet Union was invaded, all anti-Nazi forces took a more positive view about Stalin. Many were simply cynical, like Churchill who, when questioned about his apparently softening attitude to Stalin memorably replied that to help the war effort he would make a favourable reference to the devil and Hell if needs be. For a few years, friendlier relations prevailed and greater information about each side of the divide circulated in the other. Dora Russell mentions in her memoirs her experiences of producing a newspaper about Britain for circulation in the USSR. It was called *Britanskii soiuznik* (*British Ally*) and was set up in August 1942 and continued until the Foreign Office abandoned it in August 1950.[25] A Soviet equivalent, *Soviet Weekly*, was set up which continued to publish up until the last years of the USSR. However, in most respects the moment passed quickly once the war was over and it was back to official hostility on both sides.

# COLD WAR, THE DEATH OF STALIN AND THE RISE OF THE TOTALITARIAN THESIS

As the above testimony indicates, the authorities (on both sides) had been extremely careful to ensure that the tiny 'thaw' of the war years did not get out of hand. On the Soviet side, a clampdown on cultural pluralism, known as the Zhdanovshchina after its chief promoter, Andrei Zhdanov, restored a grey and heavy-handed ideological orthodoxy. In the USA the developing Cold War atmosphere, which peaked with McCarthyite hysteria, cast a lesser pall over American and western intellectual life. Historians were quickly enlisted in the struggle to defend the self-styled free world. In 1949 the President of the American Historical Association, Conyers Read, called on historians to abandon their traditional 'plurality of aims and values' and accept 'a large measure of regimentation' because 'total war, whether hot or cold, enlists everyone and calls upon everyone to assume his part'.[26] It is at this point that the interpretation of Stalinism and the USSR entered a phase which is still working itself out. Dominant historical analysis began to revolve around the 'totalitarian thesis' and the people associated with it were sometimes thought of as 'Cold Warriors'.

Briefly defined, the totalitarian thesis argued that, in certain conditions, the state came to absorb the rest of society – the state became 'total'. Later on, in an important modification, some argued that even if the state did not achieve total control it would qualify as totalitarian simply by aspiring to such control. The word itself was coined, with pride, by Mussolini and his supporters in Italy and was developed primarily through analysis of fascist states which were seen to penetrate and dominate the whole of society. They did this through establishing single-party control, usually under a dictatorial leader, sustained by conventional and secret police forces and special legislation. There was also a massive propaganda apparatus which demanded – and this was another crucial feature – not just passive acceptance of the ruling party but active association with it and with its goals. Having developed it in this way, using the term to describe the USSR as well was too good an opportunity for western propagandists to miss. A chief attraction, which remained effective for decades, was that it tarred the Soviet Union with the same brush as Nazi Germany by pointing to the undoubted similarities between the two systems. The cost of the operation was that it overlooked or ignored the equally significant differences, of which the most notable was Nazi reliance on racism which was never a fundamental component of the Soviet outlook.

The intellectual energy for the new ideas was generated by two classic texts. In 1948, Hannah Arendt decided, perhaps influenced by the rising Cold War atmosphere, to add sections on the Soviet Union to her almost completed book, *The Origins of Totalitarianism*.[27] Even though the additions were comparatively under-researched and under-analysed, giving them a kind of bolt-on feel, the book as a whole was a tremendous success once it was published in 1951. It launched the notion of lumping the USSR in with Nazi Germany, almost as analytical twins, since seeking similarities was the order of the day while differences were overlooked. The second, less directly influential volume, was part of a trilogy by J. L. Talmon, not completed until 1980.[28] The first volume, *The Origins of Totalitarian Democracy*, traced a dictatorial line in various forms of prescriptive and utopian political thought from Plato via Rousseau's idea of the General Will interpreted by the Lawgiver, through to Marx and, in particular, Lenin's conception of the vanguard party. A third book, not dissimilar in scope to Talmon's, was produced in 1950 by Karl Popper entitled *The Open Society and its Enemies*.[29] Mention should also be made of the seminal volume by Friedrich Hayek entitled *The Road to Serfdom* of 1944 in which he argued that planned, socialist economies led to authoritarian, unfree societies while free markets were the bedrock of free democratic societies.[30] Having been banished to the fringes by the hegemony of postwar Keynesianism in the advanced capitalist world, Hayek's ideas had a strange resurrection in the 1980s in the form of Reaganism and Thatcherism even though the Soviet example would suggest Soviet-style planning arose from dictatorship rather than the other way round.

From these roots political scientists began to develop more detailed theories. Carl Friedrich organized a conference at Harvard in 1953 which resulted in a series of papers and a volume edited by Friedrich himself.[31] In 1956 Friedrich and Zbygniew Brzezinski produced their influential volume *Totalitarian Dictatorship and Autocracy* while Brzezinski himself wrote *The Permanent Purge: Politics in Soviet Totalitarianism* in the same year.[32] Before Friedrich's conference, one of the few things the pioneer writers like Talmon, Arendt, Popper and Hayek had in common was that they were not specialists on the Soviet Union and few of them even knew Russian. Not surprisingly, the first, and perhaps classic, application of the concept by a leading scholar of the Soviet Union was more nuanced than that of the ideologues. In his immensely influential *How Russia is Ruled*, Merle Fainsod did not go the whole way in absorbing the totalitarian thesis. In particular, as Abbott Gleason pointed out in his masterly study of the evolution of the concept of totalitarianism, Fainsod laid more emphasis on the peculiarly Russian roots of the Bolshevik system, putting many of its characteristics – cult of the leader, authoritarianism, centralization, bureaucratization – in the wider Russian context. He also argued that the faults of tsarism in keeping Russia backward and unfree helped shape the Bolshevik movement.[33] Other leading Sovietologists, as they were coming to be known, also modified the doctrine. In his extremely important works, such as *The Communist Party of the Soviet Union*, Leonard Schapiro argued that Bolshevism's problems arose from its Russified Marxism developed by Lenin which came to dominate the party and project it into what later became known as its 'leading role' in society. Although he wrote a short book discussing the term, Schapiro did not use the word 'totalitarian' very much. Rather, in one of his key works, he talked about *The Origin of the Communist Autocracy*.[34] In addition, there were influential writers on the Soviet Union such as E. H. Carr and Isaac Deutscher who rejected the totalitarian thesis out of hand. In his preface to the first volume of his history of Russia since the revolution, published in 1950 before the totalitarian thesis was even formulated, Carr was distancing himself from its central assumption:

> Books written in Great Britain and the United States about western or central Europe are often marred by the unconscious assumption that the policies and institutions of, say, France, Italy or Germany, can be understood in the light of British or American analogies. No sensible person will be tempted to measure the Russia of Lenin, Trotsky, and Stalin by any yardstick borrowed from the Britain of MacDonald, Baldwin, and Churchill or the America of Wilson, Hoover, and Franklin Roosevelt.[35]

Nonetheless, the overwhelming majority of academics who worked on Soviet history and politics were close to the totalitarians. Analysis of the leadership in the USSR was, by and large, deemed to be sufficient to understand the society as a whole. The idea that there could be deep-rooted divisions in Soviet politics or society or the thought that the leadership could be influenced from below were dismissed from the outset. Not surprisingly this led to many errors in analysing Soviet realities. Mainstream observers completely missed the impact the regeneration of communism in Prague in 1968 and in western Europe in the era of Eurocommunism had on an important minority in the Soviet party. Such ideas fed into Gorbachev's reforms, a turn of events for which the totalitarian thesis had no explanation in its own terms. Similarly, the comparison constantly led Cold Warriors into equating Soviet foreign policy with Nazi-type expansionism. This led to catastrophic misinterpretation of the early post-Stalin years when the Cold War might have been reined in. It continued through the near-disastrous Cuban missile crisis to the fateful decision to shower arms on Islamic fundamentalist terrorists in Afghanistan, including Osama bin Laden and al-Qaedha, with the aim of embarrassing the Soviet-backed government. Indeed, Margaret Thatcher explicitly compared Soviet foreign policy to that of Nazi Germany and any effort to improve relations with the USSR was instantly branded as 'appeasement' by hard-line Cold Warriors throughout the period.

Developments of this nature were all the more extraordinary since the totalitarian thesis had a number of vulnerable points. In the first place, it was coming into predominance, in the period 1953–6, just at the time when the USSR was moving away from full-blown Stalinism. In 1956, Khrushchev denounced many aspects of Stalin's rule. The process of destalinization he began had no comparator in Nazism. Dehitlerized Nazism was inconceivable. However, the gurus of the totalitarian concept were unconcerned. It was also clear that there was a contradiction between the classic formulations of the concept – based on a heavily centralized state and party apparatus, an ubiquitous political police, mass repressions, the extermination of civil society and the all-embracing command economy controlling agriculture as well as industry, transport and so on – and the different periods of Soviet history. The system in the civil war differed from that of the 1920s. The twenties differed from the thirties. Even the late Stalin years were not identical with the first decade and the war was also different. Clearly, to specialists and neutrals (if there were any) Khrushchev's Soviet Union was significantly different from Brezhnev's and both were far from the 1930s, not least in that the scale of political imprisonment had fallen from millions to thousands. Only with difficulty could all these experiences be fitted within the 'one size fits all' concept of totalitarianism. To extend it, without serious modifications, to other communist states, as diverse as Hungary and Vietnam, Poland and China, Cuba and Kampuchea, was to fly in the face of reality. However, even though the term fitted awkwardly with the actualities of the situation and dragging in comparison with Nazi Germany and Fascist Italy concealed as much as it revealed, it did serve a major political purpose. It blocked off serious public discussion of the west's perceived enemies – since such discussions often degenerated into trying to turn all critics of the prevailing orthodoxy into 'communist sympathizers' or 'appeasers' in the case of, for example, groups pointing out the dangers of proliferation of nuclear weapons. Having noted that, however, the term itself could not have had the impact it had without having some grain of truth. Although many analysts were critical of the unmodified concept, the idea that the Soviet system and many of those modelled on it, were distinguished by their attempts to exert an unprecedented degree of control and direction over the society they ruled, was, in itself, in accordance with the basic realities. The point was, however, that fully-fledged totalitarians tended to assume that Soviet-type systems did achieve 'total' control over their societies whereas, in practice, none was particularly successful in achieving such goals. However, to ignore such niceties, plus the nuances and differences mentioned above, discredited the whole notion in the eyes of a rising generation of historians.

## THE RISE OF REVISIONISM

In the 1960s, in a well-known reaction to two decades of conservative stuffiness and material expansion, thrown into a menacing light by the unedifying spectacle of the Vietnam war in which the world's most powerful country could only have defeated a poor peasant country by destroying it, new challenges emerged to the Keynesian centrist consensus. In particular, the Cold War appeared to need reappraisal. The Vietnam war focused on two salient issues for its critics. In the first place no one ever had a clear or credible idea of why the United States was so committed to it. Secondly, it appeared to show the US as an aggressor, not as a country which only responded to direct threats to its existence as standard Cold War ideas suggested. In this light, revisionist ideas swept the field of Cold War analysis and soon began to affect interpretations, first of the Russian revolution and then of the Stalin period. While the former is not our direct concern we do need to note that the underlying reassessment centred on suggesting that the October revolution was not a simple coup from above and that Lenin and the Bolsheviks did have a certain amount of popular support. For some, the deformations in the early Soviet regime were not the inevitable result of the application of Marxist principles, as suggested by Talmon, but rather they were the result of the conditions under which the regime was born – notably economic collapse, civil war and political intervention by all Russia's neighbours and all the great powers. The regime's minority status was rarely noted by revisionists as an additional reason for its growing dictatorship. Lenin's Russia was not, so it was argued, totalitarian in the classic sense. In particular, there was a variety of currents in leadership ideology, not just one, and a degree of pragmatism was detected in, for example, the abandonment of war communism and the adoption of a very partially restored market in the form of the New Economic Policy (NEP). Most revisionists were careful to distinguish Leninism from Stalinism.[36]

However, it was only a matter of time before an even more controversial form of revisionism began to attempt a reassessment of Stalinism. Works by Sheila Fitzpatrick, as a leading example, began to identify a social base for Stalinism in the form of its beneficiaries in the 1920s, notably the rapidly educated workers-turned party members-turned managers of society and industry.[37] Further work even seemed to suggest that such people formed a left-leaning pressure group that practically forced the leadership into the radical initiatives of the first five-year plan, collectivization and cultural revolution in the period from 1928 to 1932. For quite some time the weight of scholarship focused on support for these initiatives.[38]

Support for such initiatives no doubt existed but it took another decade or two for these writers to begin to give full weight to the much larger number of opponents.[39] Overlooking, notably, peasant opposition for so long may be an indication of the revisionists' long-standing lack of interest in Russia's peasant majority compared to its small working class. Be that as it may, an even more controversial group began to demolish the totalitarian model as applied to the worst features of Soviet life in the 1930s, the purges. Historians such as J. Arch Getty, Gabor Rittersporn and Robert Thurston questioned the extent, impact and motivation of the purges.[40] Whereas the overwhelming consensus was that Stalin was almost single-handedly responsible and terrorized the entire country, Getty, Rittersporn and Thurston argued that, while Stalin was obviously a major player, the initiatives of the centre were distorted and exaggerated by local actors using the purges to settle their own scores. One major point that came out of their argument was that the Soviet state in the 1930s was not, as totalitarians suggested, a fiendishly efficient machine supposed to maintain total control of politics, the economy, religion, culture and everything else. Instead it was a rather loose, dilapidated and ramshackle affair in which the centre was often ignorant of what was happening at the periphery and the periphery deceived and manipulated the centre about what they were actually up to. Thurston in particular attacked the totalitarian thesis head on by arguing that, to a degree unacknowledged by the totalitarians, everyday life in Stalin's Russia went on as normally as possible. People worked, played, married, had parties, went to the cinema and theatre, as best they could and did not all crawl around in fear as the hard-line totalitarians had suggested. While, for almost everyone, such interpretations went too far, they did, nonetheless, contain a corrective grain of truth in pointing to the *dis*organization of Soviet institutions and the selective rather than universal impact of the terror.

The Getty revisionists were, of course, reacting to the totalitarian thesis in general but that school had increasingly become associated with one remarkable champion, the English poet turned historian, Robert Conquest. Conquest constituted practically single-handed a neo-totalitarian school which dominated popular discourse on the Stalin years but which had much less support among those who also studied the sources carefully. During the 'Second Cold War' of the Reagan/Thatcher years, Conquest enjoyed wide access to the media to spread his views on Stalin as did his counterpart on the history of the revolution and the Lenin years, Richard Pipes, Reagan's special adviser on Soviet affairs and member of the National Security Council. Conquest's career as a historian was remarkable. For many years a privately funded researcher he wrote book after book, mainly on the period from 1930 to 1938. The famine of 1932–3 was a 'terror-famine'. The murder of Kirov in 1934 was the 'crime of the century'. Above all, his reputation stands or falls mainly on his mammoth account of *The Great Terror*, first published in 1968, and republished, little-changed except for an 'I told you so, I was right all along' preface in the anti-communist, triumphalist atmosphere of 1990. The image of the purges given by Conquest is undoubtedly one of Stalin in total control (daily signing long lists of death warrants at the peak) and of an entire country atomized in fear. Very high estimates for the victims – Conquest's assessment of 20 million has become consensual in the non-academic discourse and was taken for granted in post-Soviet Russia – confirmed its massive and uniquely malevolent impact. Grisly debates were fired up about the exact numbers of victims. For twenty years half the career of one scholar, Stephen Wheatcroft, has been occupied in attempted dialogue with Conquest over his figures though the exchanges between the two have been somewhat frosty to say the least. So far the better-grounded late and post-Soviet figures have suggested much lower totals for the number of victims but they have had little impact on public as opposed to specialist discourse. If recent exchanges are anything to go by, they have had even less impact on Conquest who sticks by his original calculations.[41] Underneath the issue of precise numbers – important though they are in their own right and out of respect for the, in any case, totally unimaginable and unjustifiable, human cost – lies a macabre 'competition' to crown Stalin rather than Hitler as world champion of twentieth-century brutality and thereby tarnish all forms of Marxism and socialism by implication. As a result, ideas derived from the totalitarian thesis long remained a stock-in-trade of right-wing hegemony. Even organizations like the British Labour Party – whose tradition for anti-communism goes back at least to its role in being an enthusiastic founder of NATO – were accused of supporting 'Eastern-European style' regimes. It is perhaps no coincidence that the crisis of the traditional European and American right, comprising Republicans, Conservatives and Christian Democrats, in the 1990s coincided with the disappearance of their communist bogeyman, as Jesse Jackson pointed out in television interviews the day Clinton won the Presidency. Be that as it may, the calculation of numbers remains distastefully political and polemical as much as academic, as the attention given to and the argument surrounding *The Black Book of Communism*[42] has shown in recent years. In any case, deaths in the Second World War, undoubtedly consciously precipitated by Hitler, are excluded from the calculation although, ironically, Soviet war victims are sometimes added to Stalin's 'death count'. For the time being, the most careful calculations suggest figures appalling enough but considerably lower than those of Conquest. For the purge years (1936–41), almost a million executions and some two million prisoner deaths in camp and exile appear to have taken place.

One important side effect of this debate was a significant change of emphasis. In the early revisionist years, there was far more discussion about the revolution and civil war than about the 1930s which were largely considered relatively impenetrable given the lack of access to archives and other sources. However, in the late 1970s and early 1980s, the emphasis changed from the revolution to the Stalin years. This tendency was emphasized by the sensational turn of events in the Soviet Union in 1985.

## PERESTROIKA AND AFTER

One of the astonishing consequences of Gorbachev's emergence as Soviet leader was, for the first time, Russian and other Soviet writers and historians playing a full and unfettered part in the debate over their own country's history. The first step in this direction preceded Gorbachev's emergence by more than a decade. It came in the form of Roy Medvedev's magisterial account of Stalin's life entitled *Let History Judge*.[43] Interestingly, Medvedev came from the same rather narrow and, at the time, misunderstood, overlooked even, reformist tendency in Soviet Communism influenced by the democratic adaptations of Dubcek's 'socialism with a human face' and Eurocommunism to which Gorbachev himself belonged. It was, of course, impossible at the time for Medvedev to work openly and obtain full research access to sources in a normal way. Nonetheless, drawing on earlier studies, personal experience, oral history and such written sources as were available to him, Medvedev produced a formidable indictment of Stalin's misrule and of the gross distortions of his 'cult of personality'. Medvedev was able to enjoy the limited freedom he had compared to others because, although he was a dissident, he was a reform communist. The main point he made in his lengthy account was that Stalin had grossly distorted Lenin's democratic and revolutionary principles. It was, he argued, necessary to rescue Leninism from the disasters imposed by Stalin in order for Russia to make progress along its socialist path.

His conclusion stung his fellow dissident and former camp inmate, Alexander Solzhenitsyn, into arguing that there was no such thing as Stalinism or Leninism, only one Bolshevism based on an unchanging set of utopian and dictatorial principles. Solzhenitsyn's main contribution to the debate was a massive compilation of accounts of victims of terror from the early prisons such as the Solovetsky Island monastery dating from the Lenin period to the massive, postwar system in which Solzhenitsyn himself was entrapped between 1945 and the era of major releases beginning in 1954 which resulted in almost all political prisoners being let out of the camps. Through Solzhenitsyn's work, some of which was even published in the Soviet Union, most notably his story of *One Day in the Life of Ivan Denisovich*, a worldwide audience became familiar with the horrors of the Gulag system. A whole genre of camp memoirs emerged to complement the scanty accounts largely by released foreigners which already existed. *Ivan Denisovich* was not the only example of history dressed up as fiction. Partly in an attempt to beat the censorship, many novels and stories, few of which were published in the decaying USSR, dealt with aspects of life in the Stalin era. Solzhenitsyn produced *Cancer Ward* and *The First Circle*. Vassili Grossman's *Forever Flowing* was published abroad but it was only with perestroika that his great *Life and Fate*, an epic of life in the thirties and forties, saw the light of day. Extraordinarily, Vladimir Voinovich broke the shell of seriousness and even used the holy of holies, the experiences of war, as material for a humorous novel, *The Life and Extraordinary Adventures of Private Ivan Chonkin*, about the eponymous private who was sent to guard a crashed German aircraft early in the war and was then forgotten about. The book is famous for one of its parables which illustrates one of the deep contradictions of the time. The village party secretary phones the regional party secretary to report that the villagers have gathered together seeking news of the dramatic crash. The regional secretary asks, did the people gather spontaneously? On being told that they had he instructs the local secretary to disperse them and then report back. The local secretary breaks up the gathering and reports back asking what to do next. The regional secretary tells him to immediately convene an emergency general meeting of the villagers! A number of these works not only discussed life in the Stalin years but also took time out to muse on its dominant character. In *The First Circle*, Solzhenitsyn portrays a broodingly malevolent, lonely and somewhat pathetic Stalin imprisoned in his own dictatorship, moving between two identically furnished rooms, one his Kremlin office, the other in his *dacha*. In another unusually satirical variant blending black comedy and farce, the Abkhazian writer Fazil Iskander poured ridicule on the great leader and his cult of personality. In one of his stories the central character, Uncle Sandro, gets his long johns wet wading in a mountain stream to help

Stalin fish while he is on vacation. As Sandro changes his wet clothes a secret service man creeps up to him in the bushes with a present, a pair of Stalin's long johns:

> Uncle Sandro took the long johns, marvelling at their fluffy lightness. Forgetting to thank the departing secret service man, he began to pull them on, feeling the unusual lightness and warmth of the wool. ...
> 'What amazes me,' Uncle Sandro went on, 'I've been wearing these long johns ever since and they're still like new. They must be a special kind of wool.'
> 'Secret sheep,' Tengiz remarked.[44]

Once perestroika got underway the valuable trickle of dissident and samizdat (self-published, i.e. illegally circulated) material turned into a flood. Perhaps without knowing exactly what he was letting himself in for, Gorbachev called, in November 1987, for there to be no more 'blank pages' in Soviet history. A legion of historians, journalists, novelists, short story writers, dramatists, cinema directors, memoirists and ordinary people in the street heeded his call. First Stalin and then, more tentatively, possibly at prompting from above, Lenin were debunked. A torrent of material emerged. In a striking comment one observer said history was 'running in the streets'. Through 1988 and early 1989 the Soviet Union was mesmerized by the historical debate and the rehabilitation of old demons. Works not only by Bukharin but even by Trotsky were published. Small groups brought out works by anarchists such as Kropotkin and Bakunin. Robert Conquest's major works were translated and lapped up. By and large, the totalitarians were undisputed brand leaders among foreign analytical imports. Russians did not want to hear that things had not been so bad, they seemed to want them to be worse. The greater the suffering depicted the more the Soviet public seemed to like it. This was ironic given that, at that very moment and for the first time, Soviet researchers were finding ways of compiling the more reliable, and apparently lower, figures for the victims of Stalin. Only specialists took note. For a while, there were no limits. The Soviet Union had the world's freest press, uninhibited by libel, custom, law or government interference. Organizations were set up dedicated to rediscovering the past and granting respect to its victims. Informal memorials began to appear. A rock from an outlying part of the gulag was placed in a flower bed in front of the KGB headquarters. Rough wooden crosses were erected near the Kremlin commemorating Russia's 'lost' political parties of 1917 – Socialist Revolutionaries, Liberals, Mensheviks and Anarchists. An organization called *Pamiat'* (Memory) sprang up as a focus for research and as a pressure group for setting up permanent memorials. It was not only the memory of the centre and left that was reviving. Monarchists and people dressed in the uniforms of the

White Armies also gathered at public meetings. Confusingly, a small antisemitic, Russian nationalist group also called itself *Pamiat'*.

From this torrent one item in particular needs to be mentioned because it impinges on our enquiries. One of the most influential accounts of Stalin in these years came in the form of a conventional history by a general whose career had been primarily in the Army's political-educational apparatus, Dmitrii Volkogonov. He produced the first serious Soviet-period history of Stalin in the form of a massive four-volume tome based on a wide (but no means complete) range of archival and personal sources. If anything, Stalin emerged as less monstrous than his fictional and western biographers had become used to. While it contained vast amounts of new material the project was undermined by its greatly uneven coverage of the subject matter. Stalin's actions in the war played a much greater part in the book than analysis of the terror. However, it was undoubtedly a milestone in the Russian historiography of the Stalin years and pointed the way to the final, post-perestroika, accounts of the topic.

The final collapse of communism in 1991 brought radically new conditions for scholars to work in. Sources were more readily available and openness of discussion was the order of the day. The archive service was reorganized with each archive operating independently. Even so, the situation was not ideal. State sponsorship of archives was vastly reduced and they were thrown onto an uncertain sea of partial self-financing. Preservation conditions for the materials got worse as buildings and, as scholars also noted, heating systems deteriorated. To save money archives shortened their hours. Also a desire to prove the worst replaced the official task of proving the best which had dominated the Soviet years. Either way, objectivity was threatened. Despite these negatives, however, the scene was set for a new flourishing of research based on access to formerly unavailable sources. A more detailed account of the Stalin years began to emerge. In particular the mechanisms of the society and its real impact on the masses of people began to be much better understood. The role of Stalin, in the context of his fellow leaders and in the wider set-up, was depicted with more certainty. One of the plus points was the emergence of memoirs of former leading figures in the Stalin regime. Although, like all memoirs, they have to be treated with caution, they were of immense value, none more so than those of the extraordinary Viacheslav Molotov and Andrei Gromyko. Molotov had been an intimate part of the Soviet leadership from before Lenin's return until after Stalin's death. He had been Stalin's closest associate more or less throughout his leadership career. His memoirs, in the form of conversations he had with a largely sympathetic journalist over a number of years, were published in Moscow in 1991 and were soon translated. They rank as a prime source even above those of Khrushchev, published in the 1970s, since he was such a vital figure for such a long time. Unsurprisingly, Molotov's overwhelming tone was one of self-justification. He stressed the leadership's view that they were, in the mid-1930s, surrounded by enemies and potential enemies who had to be destroyed. If a few innocents got mixed up with them, too bad but it was, in the leaders' view, a war.

Elsewhere, more detailed accounts of the thirties have been produced. Relying on unparalleled access to sources and to localities, since virtually the whole of Russia was opened up to foreign visitors, monumental local studies were produced with Stephen Kotkin's *Magnetic Mountain* in the forefront.[45] Some scholars appeared to have made major changes in their views of what was happening. Leading anti-totalitarians now urged us to concentrate on the awfulness of the Stalin years and to understand the opposition to it. Of course, in the true totalitarian thesis, the existence of opposition was considered near-impossible so they were not giving in to their opponents but they were sharing large parts of their analysis of a potentially ubiquitous and uniformly evil dictatorship.

A further development was the emergence of Russian scholars as full-scale analysts of the Lenin and Stalin years. Curiously, interest in past issues has waned since the late perestroika upsurge and, perhaps as a result of an understandable surfeit of histories, bogus or otherwise, of the Soviet period, interest has declined and more remote periods or escapism of various kinds have become more prominent. Interestingly, the war remains the focus of official respect and a massive memorial park commemorating victory was opened in Moscow for the fiftieth anniversary of VE (Victory in Europe) Day.

All these factors combine to produce a historiography of unparalleled authenticity and of unprecedented multiplicity of competing schools and approaches. The present selection aims to bring something of this excitement to its readers. With that in mind, let us begin our exploration of the Stalin years through the works of the most recent generation of researchers.

NOTES

1. Quoted, for example, in L. Trotsky, *Stalin: An Appraisal of the Man and His Influence*, vol. 2: *The Revolutionary in Power* (London, 1969) p. 187.

2. M. Lewin, *Lenin's Last Struggle* (London, 1969); R. Service, *Lenin: A Political Life*, 3 vols (London, 1985, 1991, 1994).

3. A. Resis (ed.), *Molotov Remembers* (Chicago, 1993) p. 156.

4. L. Trotsky, *Stalin: An Appraisal of the Man and His Influence*, vol. 2, p. 250.

5. L. Trotsky, *My Life: An Attempt at an Autobiography* (Harmondsworth, 1975) p. 528.

6. I. Deutscher, *The Prophet Unarmed: Trotsky, 1921–1929* (London, 1970) p. 296.

7. S. Alliluyeva, *Twenty Letters to a Friend* (London, 1967) p. 86.

8. Ibid., p. 32.

9. Ibid., pp. 26–7.

10. D. Tutaev (ed.), *The Alliluyev Memoirs* (London, 1968) p. 139.

11. S. Cohen, *Bukharin and the Bolshevik Revolution: A Political Biography, 1888–1938* (London, 1973) p. 291.

12. A. Resis (ed.), *Molotov Remembers*, pp. 166, 177.

13. S. Bialer (ed.), *Stalin and His Generals: Soviet Memoirs of World War II* (London, 1970) p. 35.

14. Marshall G. Zhukov, *Reminiscences and Reflections* (Moscow, 1974) p. 174.

15. Albert Axell, *Stalin's War through the Eyes of His Commanders* (London, 1997) p. 97.

16. Accounts of the incident, in English, can be found in Axell, *Stalin's War*, pp. 99–100 and Bialer, *Stalin and His Generals*, pp. 459–61.

17. Milovan Djilas, *Conversations with Stalin* (Harmondsworth, 1963) p. 64.

18. Ibid., p. 63.

19. Ibid., p. 65.

20. J. Scott, *Behind the Urals: An American Worker in Russia's City of Steel* (Bloomington, 1973) p. 3.

21. Ibid., p. 249.

22. W. H. Chamberlin, *Soviet Russia: A Living Record and a History* (London, 1930) p. viii.

23. The most informative source is still D. Caute, *The Fellow Travellers: A Postscript to the Enlightenment* (London, 1977) to which I am indebted for the quotations given here. See pp. 86, 89 and 131.

24. Victor Serge, *Memoirs of a Revolutionary, 1901–1941*, trans. by Peter Sidgwick (Oxford, 1963) p. 331.

25. Dora Russell, *The Tamarisk Tree*, vol. 3: *Challenge to the Cold War* (London, 1985) pp. 10–110.

26. Conyers Read, 'The Social Responsibilities of the Historian', *American Historical Review*, January 1950, pp. 282–3, quoted by Stephen Cohen in *Rethinking the Soviet Experience: Politics and History since 1917* (New York, 1985) p. 13.

27. H. Arendt, *The Origins of Totalitarianism* (New York, 1951).

28. J. L. Talmon, *The Origins of Totalitarian Democracy* (London, 1952), *Political Messianism: The Romantic Phase* (London, 1960) and *The Myth of the Nation and the Vision of Revolution* (London, 1980).

29. Karl Popper, *The Open Society and its Enemies* (Princeton, 1950).

30. F. A. Hayek, *The Road to Serfdom* (London, 1944).

31. C. Friedrich (ed.), *Totalitarianism* (Cambridge, Mass., 1954).

32. Carl Friedrich and Zbygniew Brzezinski, *Totalitarian Dictatorship and Autocracy* (New York, 1956); Zbygniew Brzezinski, *The Permanent Purge: Politics in Soviet Totalitarianism* (Cambridge, Mass., 1956).

33. M. Fainsod, *How Russia is Ruled* (Cambridge, Mass., 1953). Abbott Gleason, *Totalitarianism: The Inner History of the Cold War* (New York and Oxford, 1995) pp. 122–3.

34. Leonard Schapiro, *The Communist Party of the Soviet Union* (London, 1960), *The Origin of the Communist Autocracy: Political Opposition in the Soviet State: The First Phase, 1917–22* (London, 1965) and *Totalitarianism* (London, 1972).

35. E. H. Carr, *The Bolshevik Revolution 1917–23*, vol. 1 (Harmondsworth, 1966) p. 5.

36. See, for example, the discussion of the historiography of the Russian Revolution in Christopher Read, 'The Russian Revolution After the Fall of Communism', *The Historical Journal*, vol. 40, no. 4, 1998, pp. 1127–34.

37. S. Fitzpatrick, *Education and Social Mobility in the Soviet Union, 1921–1934* (Bloomington, 1979).

38. See, for example, Lynne Viola, *Best Sons of the Fatherland: Workers in the Vanguard of Soviet Collectivization* (Oxford, 1987) and Hiroaki Kuromiya, *Stalin's Industrial Revolution: Politics and Workers, 1928–32* (Cambridge, 1988).

39. A very different tone prevails in S. Fitzpatrick, *Everyday Stalinism* (Oxford, 1999) and Lynne Viola, *Peasant Rebels under Stalin: Collectivization and the Culture of Peasant Resistance* (Oxford, 1996).

40. J. A. Getty and Roberta Manning (eds), *Stalinist Terror: New Perspectives* (Cambridge, 1993).

41. Issues relating to calculation of victims are numerous and complex. Here are some major contributions. See the exchange in *Soviet Studies* between S. Rosefielde (in vol. 33, no. 1, January 1981, pp. 51–87) and Stephen Wheatcroft (in vol. 33, no. 2, April 1981 and vol. 35, no. 2, April 1983). Subsequently Wheatcroft revised his estimate of famine victims upwards, having the good grace to accept that his earlier calculations were no longer sustainable – something none of the other interpreters has, up to the present, been prepared to do. See S. Wheatcroft, 'More Light on the Scale of Repression and Excess Mortality in the Soviet Union in the 1930s', in J. Arch Getty and Roberta T. Manning (eds), *Stalinist Terror: New Perspectives* (Cambridge, 1993) pp. 275–90. On terror victims see A. Nove, 'Victims of Stalinism: How Many?', in Getty and Manning (eds), *Stalinist Terror: New Perspectives*, p. 271 and Edwin Bacon, *The Gulag at War* (London, 1994), S. G. Wheatcroft, 'Victims of Stalinism and the Secret Police: The Comparability and Reliability of the Archival data – Not the Last Word', *Europe-Asia Studies*, vol. 51, no. 2, 1999, pp. 315–45 and R. Conquest, 'Comment on Wheatcroft', *Europe-Asia Studies*, vol. 51, no. 8, 1999, pp. 1479–83.

42. S. Courtois, *The Black Book of Communism* (1999), claimed that some 100 million people had fallen as victims of communism. Even some of the contributors distanced themselves from the final, sensation-seeking, product.

43. R. Medvedev, *Let History Judge: The Origins and Consequences of Stalinism* (London, 1971).

44. Fazil Iskander, *Sandro of Chegem* (Harmondsworth, 1985) pp. 270, 272.

45. Stephen Kotkin, *Magnetic Mountain: Stalinism as a Civilization* (Berkeley, 1995).

# II Cultural Revolution

## SOCIAL MODERNIZATION

Modernization is one of the key themes of the Stalin years. In Isaac Deutscher's ringing phrase Stalin found Russia using the wooden plough and left it using the atomic reactor (*Russia after Stalin*, p. 55). Out of the maelstrom of the Stalin years there emerged, among many other things, the world's first welfare state. Thus it is fitting that we should look at a crucial example of modernization – the approach to motherhood.

In Elizabeth Waters' article there are three collective actors. These are the mothers, the doctors and the state authorities, all in ever-changing relationships with each other. The mothers were suspended between traditional beliefs and practices embodied in rural and folk midwives (wise women) and the new scientific, hospitalized childbirth preached by doctors. The doctors themselves were torn, partly over differing ideas of good practice, as is the case with medical people everywhere, but mainly over their role in the new society. Traditionally, doctors, especially those who served poor rural communities, were driven by a certain populist streak; that is, they tended to follow the nineteenth-century intelligentsia code of serving the people as a matter of conscience and moral duty. In the new scheme of things they were being bound more and more closely to the authorities and their much-prized professional independence was being undermined. The third party, the state, also had its own difficulties. The relatively tranquil years of relaxation between the end of the civil war in late 1920 and the upheavals embarked upon by Stalin from 1928 onwards had not been long enough for a stable, competent and organized state apparatus to form. Instead, there was a ramshackle mixture of old civil servants, new radical firebrands, conservative academics and a handful of brilliant researchers all trying to influence social policy in areas where no state or party had gone before. As in all areas of activity the authorities were driven by a confusing combination of primary impulses. On the one hand, there was the attempt to implement the principles of socialism. A major problem here was that practical socialism had to be invented as the authorities went along, there being no blueprint. Second, there were pragmatic impulses just to keep things going. Finally, there were the already formative influences of productionism with its attendant evils of careerism and bureaucratism.

Put briefly, productionism was a response to the peculiarities of the Russian revolution which had produced a Marxist, proletarian government in an economically underdeveloped peasant country. Even though one might argue about the level of Russia's development before 1914, it was beyond question that, by 1921, it had lost a vast chunk of its industry, its skilled personnel and its international connections after six years of international and revolutionary war. Industrial production collapsed to around ten per cent of prewar output and the number of factory workers had fallen dramatically. In other words, Russia was the site of a proletarian revolution without a proletariat. Whether they fully believed it or not, Lenin, and still more Trotsky, had explained to their followers that, being a backward country, Russia could not build or sustain socialism on its own. There would have to be socialist revolutions in western Europe to help the fragile Russian revolution. In their speeches in October 1917 both Lenin and Trotsky had said that the aim of the Russian revolution was to spark off revolutions elsewhere. Without them it would not survive. Of course, we now know that those supporting revolutions were destined never to take place. It became increasingly obvious that the Russian revolution would remain isolated. As early as 1918 Lenin, though never abandoning the hope of international revolution, began to develop a siege mentality of defending the Russian revolution at all costs and instigating an early version of 'socialism in one country'.

It is not our concern to follow this in detail but rather to examine its consequences for our period. In the forefront was the emergence of productionism. If Russia was backward then Marxist socialism, which needed advanced industries to exist before it could be built, was not possible. As a first step to constructing socialism backwardness had to be overcome and an advanced industry had to be developed. Therefore, the first task of the revolution was to industrialize and overtake capitalism. The methods involved in this, to which we will return later, might be as much pragmatic as socialist but it meant all efforts were to be focused on maximizing economic production. Not only industry and agriculture but education and medical and social services were to be centred around this overarching goal. In order to achieve the goal, and to keep the minds of people focused on the distant mountain tops of socialism and communism, the party had become increasingly authoritarian and had assumed what was later to be called 'the leading role in society'. Party groups increasingly dominated every aspect of life in the factory, the army, the sports club, the school, the housing block and, least effectively, the village. This leadership function meant the party was stretched in all directions. It needed, in Maoist terminology, people who were both 'red' and 'expert' – committed communists and technically competent. There were very few such people. As a result, party jobs were often taken up by half-hearted 'communists' more interested in the fruits of office than in building a new world. These people became known as careerists and, given its centralized, authoritarian nature arising from its ubiquitous leading role, the apparatus in which they worked became 'bureaucratized', that is driven from above by the leaders not from below by the people. Lenin and Trotsky's efforts to deal with these deeply structural deformations of the Russian revolution were all totally inadequate. Under Stalin, they developed to an unprecedented degree.

Elizabeth Waters' article brings out these themes. In the twenties the authorities temporarily set aside the far-reaching goals of specifically communist transformation and, instead, settled for a form of modernization they could share with the doctors, notably developing health along with other forms of education in order to spread scientific ideas in place of folk traditions and herbal remedies. The stepping up of pace under Stalin brought crude productionism to the fore. This meant, for example, providing childcare less to relieve mothers of its burdens but rather to release them into the burgeoning industrial workforce. Notions of gender also changed and the party, even more than the medical profession, waged war on traditional stereotypes of women's behaviour and occupations. These last were demonstrated in the posters Dr Waters used as key sources in her research.

## 1 Elizabeth Waters: 'The Modernization of Russian Motherhood, 1917–37'

In a famous speech delivered during the First Five-Year Plan in 1931, Stalin exhorted his people to greater efforts in the construction of socialism.

> To slacken the pace would mean to lag behind; and those who lag behind are beaten ... Russia ... was ceaselessly beaten for her backwardness ... For military backwardness, for cultural backwardness, for political backwardness, for industrial backwardness, for agricultural backwardness.[1]

The phraseology had a novel bluntness, but the underlying message – that the country must modernize if it were to maintain its status in the Western community of nations – went back to Peter the Great. In Stalin's Russia, catching up and overtaking the West meant above all achieving higher levels of production, but it was also recognized that before the workers and peasants could transform the economy they themselves must be transformed: the new Soviet Man must be neat and efficient, literate and cultured, hygienic and healthy. The health of the next generation, of infants and young children, had from early in the nineteenth century been a matter for national concern, and campaigns for modern mothering dated from that era. Enlightenment propaganda aimed to inculcate the ideas of modern medicine on pregnancy, childbirth and infant care current across the industrializing world from Paris to New York and Sydney. In post-revolutionary Russia, this transmission of knowledge was effected through clinics, public lectures and the mass publication of popular literature, the same methods of propaganda employed elsewhere. Also, as elsewhere in the Western world, both before and since, the campaign for modern mothering was coordinated by the medical profession, which presented itself as the guardian and practitioner of the new knowledge and instructed mothers to turn to doctors rather than to wise women for advice and aid.

As well as these similarities, this modernization of Russian motherhood exhibited a number of special characteristics. It was rather late in starting, and slow to get off the ground. At the end of the nineteenth century, child care manuals were circulating in the cities, and urban clinics had opened their doors, but not until the 1920s and 1930s did the new medical knowledge begin to make an impression on the villages, and even then changes were sporadic and uneven. Because of the sharp gulf, historically, between society and the people in Russia, and the small size of the middle class, this shift from traditional to modern was resisted with unusual vigour. It took place at a time of revolutionary upheavals, at a time when ideas of freeing women from the 'cross' of motherhood were proclaimed, a circumstance which might have been expected to place the doctors, who were not radical socialists by any means, in opposition to the regime, and to some extent it did. However, the tradition of public service to which the obstetricians and gynaecologists subscribed predisposed them to take in their stride the notion of state-organized and communally oriented care. Moreover, the more radical ideas of social restructuring – the withering away of the family and the household – were shelved in the early 1920s as the New Economic Policy was introduced and the discipline of the market accepted. This moderation of Bolshevik aims made possible an alliance between the medical profession and the party based on their shared belief in the need for modernization, an alliance further cemented by the party's willingness, once the principle of state control had been asserted, to allow doctors a certain amount of autonomy. Like other alliances made in the 1920s, though, this one did not survive the First Five-Year Plan. When the country, with Stalin at the helm, plunged towards industrialization, all professional groups, including the doctors, lost status and social influence. While the messages on mothering remained constant in content, their context was transformed: it was politicized, and harnessed in the cause of economic targets. The regime in the 1930s expected women to reproduce and produce for its convenience, with only the barest of welfare provisions.

Ironically, it was in these years of extreme hardship for mothers that their image was adopted by the political iconographers. In a society living under extraordinary pressure, in constant flux, the sense of continuity offered by the maternal image, its suggestion of intimacy and solace, had therapeutic possibilities. With the disappearance, one after the other, of those institutions mediating between the family and the government – political factions, voluntary organizations, (relatively) independent unions and press, and the *zhenotdel* (women's department) – the iconic conflation of mother and motherland, family and state served to humanize and legitimize the party.

*Enlightenment propaganda: content and form*

Mothercraft was coordinated in the post-revolutionary period by a sub-department for the Protection of Motherhood and Infancy (usually known by its abbreviations, Okhmatmlad or OMM) under the Commissariat of Health. By 1925 it was operating over 200 clinics in the Russian Republic (RSFSR)[2] for pregnant women and around 400 for mothers with young babies. Women were advised to make regular visits from the time they discovered their pregnancy until the child was two years old, when it became the responsibility of the regular health clinics. Okhmatmlad had its own publishing house and between 1926 and 1927 brought out more than 170 titles, in a total of over 1.5 million copies. The written word could not be relied upon solely in a country with a high female illiteracy rate, and was complemented by radio programmes, slide shows and public talks, and most importantly by the posters that decorated the clinics and the *zhenotdel*, and the women's corners and displays in clubs and libraries, and that were the subject of frequent special exhibitions. These posters covered all aspects of modern mothering in a manner designed to be striking, comprehensible and persuasive.[3]

'Look After the Mother', a poster produced in the 1920s for a peasant audience, comprised two scenes of pregnant women doing heavy work – carrying wood and a pail, and bringing in the harvest – and one of a mother engaged in feeding livestock, a task considered appropriate to her condition. The husband is told he must free his wife from unsuitable work, such as lifting weights. 'The master of the house', the text notes wryly, 'looks after his mare and his cow, but not his pregnant wife.'

If the medical profession had something to say on the responsibilities of family members to the mother, it focused mainly on the numerous and weighty responsibilities of the mother to the child. These included providing the right environment – a room that was clean, full of light and well ventilated. 'Sun is the baby's best friend', advised one poster. 'Cleanliness is the guarantee of health', taught a second. Breast feeding was another of the mother's responsibilities. 'Nature has its iron laws', wrote one doctor, 'and punishes for the slightest failure to observe them. Breast feeding of the baby by the biological mother is one of these iron laws of nature which cannot be broken without serious consequences.' The consequences were graphically spelled out in a poster entitled 'Mothers, Breast Feed Your Babies', which featured a bottle-feeding mother, inset against a cemetery, and a breast-feeding mother beneath a scene of healthy little children playing games.

Just as infants could be endangered by their mothers' ignorance of the rules of feeding, they could be put at risk if sleeping arrangements were incorrect. 'How to look after your baby' included, as one of its five panels, a picture of a hanging cradle and a text below, enumerating its dangers, 'The cradle is very harmful. The cradle stupefies the baby. Do not rock [the baby] either in a cradle or in your arms'. Another panel warned the mother against taking the infant to bed with her because of the risk of accidently smothering it, or of passing on infection. In the final panel a baby sleeps peacefully in a neat and clean crib, illustrating the moral of this story, reiterated by the text: 'Buy a linen basket and your baby will have a cheap and healthy bed!'

'How to look after your baby' also included instructions on swaddling, a practice still customary in Russian towns, as well as in the countryside. Strips of cloth were wrapped around the baby, restricting its movement, and thus keeping it out of mischief, and saving the mother from having to tend it constantly or worry for its safety. While swaddling was not linked by the doctors to high rates of infant mortality, it was thought to prevent normal physical development and hence occupied a prominent place in the list of 'don'ts'. 'Do not swaddle the baby and do not dress it in a bonnet indoors', the poster commanded. 'Do not wrap it up tightly either in winter or summer. The swaddling bands prevent the child from breathing and growing and encourage various rashes. Dress the child so that it can move its arms and legs freely.' The text is not essential for comprehension. The chubby-faced infant clad only in a short vest, content and comfortable in its cot, was designed to warm a mother's heart, just as the drawn and distressed face of the swaddled mite was guaranteed to prick her conscience. This same contrast between pleasure and misery, between the baby who cries and the baby who smiles, is employed by the artist A. Komarov in another poster, this time exclusively devoted to the theme, 'Do not swaddle infants and do not dress them in a bonnet'.

In their attempts to gain and hold attention, the posters used a variety of techniques. Babies were shown in a number of life-threatening situations: Komarov, for example, drew a baby, alone in a rough-hewn sailing boat, buffeted between rocks that were labelled with incorrect mothering practices: 'stuffy, stale air', 'dark room', 'poor care', 'dirty environment' and 'cow's milk'. They were shown making demands on their mothers in a series of posters of babes and toddlers holding banners and demonstrating for correct care; in one case, animated and militant, they are attending a meeting to listen to a nightgowned peer making a speech, and waving placards that proclaim, among other things, 'midwives, not wise women', 'mother's breast', 'protection from flies', and 'dry, clean, nappies'.

Texts were didactic and authoritarian in style, a characteristic of all enlightenment propaganda produced in this period (and indeed of the literature on mothering produced in other Western countries also). The tone adopted by G. N. Speransky in his popular *Azbuka materi* (*ABC of Motherhood*) which went through several editions in the 1920s, was typical. 'If they tell you that without swaddling-bands the legs will be crooked, don't believe it', he wrote; 'it's absolute rubbish'. His comments on such matters as breast feeding and diet were equally short and sharp. It was not that the medical profession lacked arguments, rather it appears to have felt that Soviet mothers should be prepared to take on trust whatever advice it saw fit to offer.

The medical profession had emerged in nineteenth-century Russia, recruiting from the small, educated elite, and its members were often critics of tsarism, anxious to do something to change their society. It was not uncommon for men and women who had been active in radical movements to choose a career in medicine and a job in the countryside, with the aim of improving the lot of the peasants. For all their good intentions, perhaps precisely because of them, the doctors never doubted that they had a right to teach, to enlighten, to remake the lives of 'the people'. Mothering, the enlightenment propaganda emphasized, was not a matter of intuition, or something the woman would pick up as she went along; it was a craft that had to be learned, and learned from those who knew best. As experts on the subject of modern medical knowledge, the doctors felt that it was their task to teach and command, and the duty of women to listen and obey. Because their own lives and experiences were so removed from those of their patients, they tended to dismiss with contempt traditional methods of mothering. This high-handed approach was no doubt also fuelled by a sense of isolation. In the 1920s only 5 per cent of births were attended by trained medical personnel, such was the shortage of doctors. And whereas in other Western countries urbanization, print culture and education had created fairly favourable conditions for the wide reception of modern mothering among all sections of the population, and middle-class women especially were willing converts to its cause, Russia was still rural and unschooled, and the pool of educated women from whom help could be expected was tiny.

Moreover, the system of traditional care was still well entrenched. Every Russian village had its *babka*, a woman wise in magic spells and herbal medicine (*znakharstvo*), who attended at childbirth and gave advice to young mothers. The medical profession remained combative in the face of this formidable resistance to its messages. One doctor called for a 'struggle against *znakharstvo*, which still holds our Russian woman firmly in its tenacious paws'; another wrote of the necessity of 'completely destroying the remnants of darkness and superstition'. In the 1920s and 1930s, as the regime was consolidated and the villages were gradually caught in the orbit of state institutions, the opportunities for organizing such a struggle improved. All methods of propaganda were pressed into service. Short stories cast the *babka* as villain, plays examined the fatal influence she could have on the young and unsuspecting, and posters illustrated the positive benefits that accrued from avoiding her. One poster contrasts a rude peasant hut with a bright and shining hospital, and the wise woman's ignorance – she is old, gnarled and clutching a new born baby in a dirty rag – with the doctor's expertise. 'Give birth in a hospital, the wise woman ruins your health', reads the text. The damage the wise woman can do to health is the focal point of another poster: leaning on a stick, a peasant woman hobbles painfully about her business, clearly a victim of the wise woman, who lurks in the background, old, unclean and menacing. Modern medicine is represented by a young woman clad from head to foot in white, who points to a notice which reads 'hospital' and to a row of neat and spotless beds. The written text confirms the message of the visual images: 'With the wise woman's help you will soon give up the ghost. Without the midwife you will suffer pain'.

## Doctors and the party: the making and the breaking of an alliance

If this bid to transform the social relations of motherhood – the replacement of traditional healers by professional experts – was typical for countries travelling the path of modernity, it occurred for the first time against the background of a political revolution that identified itself as socialist, a coincidence that was not without impact on the manner in which the messages about mothering were conveyed. Bolshevik enlightenment propaganda in the immediate post-revolutionary years made reference to the emancipation of women and the triumph of the October revolution over exploitation and oppression. A poster produced in Saratov in 1920 linked the provision of child-care facilities with the creation of a socialist society. In its top left-hand corner, a bloated, top-hatted capitalist greedily clasps to his bosom the chains of women's unfortunate destiny, while his victims huddle below, in the shadow of a reformatory, a brothel and various nightspots, which signify the system of social and sexual oppression under which they live. On the right-hand side of the poster we are shown the socialist future, a world of creches and nurseries, in which women, unfettered and joyful, gather under a banner proclaiming, 'All hail the 3rd Communist International'.

The first head of the administrative board of Okhmatmlad, Alexandra Kollontai, was well known for her radical views on women and the family. She was confident that the revolution would usher in equality and freedom for women, and would provide the most favourable conditions for the 'combination of work and motherhood'. While capitalism forced women to work right up until childbirth in conditions of poverty and neglect, and to experience motherhood as a 'cross', socialism, she promised, would do everything in its power to assist women with their mothering, and would accord them the high status that was their due. Motherhood, Kollontai emphasized, was a social rather than a private matter, and child care ought to be communal rather than domestic. During the period of 'war communism' such views had considerable currency. A resolution passed in 1918 at the First Congress of Worker and Peasant Women advocated a system of social education for children from birth to 16 years of age. The following year, at the First Congress on the Protection of Childhood, one delegate argued that the state alone was able to create the necessary educational environment for the development of the communist personality, an opinion echoed by V. Golubeva, a *zhenotdel* organizer, in her paper at the first Okhmatmlad conference in 1920. Nadezhda Krupskaya remembered how during the civil war she and her colleagues in the Commissariat of Enlightenment believed social upbringing to be both 'essential' and 'feasible'. Another educationalist, Anna Kalinina, described how her department 'sought out' children for communal institutions and 'carried out propaganda among the parents'.

There were some who worried that parents were usually assumed to be female: 'We organise talks at clinics and schools for women only, instead of for parents', wrote an Okhmatmlad organizer, 'invite only wives and not husbands or parents to the abortion commissions, organize childcare circles for "future mothers" and "for girls", and do not encourage boys to be involved in these activities'. The young communist paper, *Komsomol'skaya pravda*, criticized the idea that wives must take all the responsibility for looking after their babies, and their husbands none at all. *Rabotnitsa* on one occasion appealed to men to take a greater part in child care, and on another published a short fictional piece about a man who stayed home to look after his baby, supported by alimony from his ex-wife. Early *zhenotdel* leaders, in particular Inessa Armand and Alexandra Kollontai, were careful to use ungendered words when referring to the child minders of the future, or to include men as well as women in their number. This challenge to sexual stereotyping, though, was weak and hesitant, and found no broad support among party activists, let alone enthusiasm among the masses.

Nor were efforts to substitute public for private child care successful. To be sure, communal alternatives to family upbringing grew in number at a rate initially undreamed of by even their most enthusiastic supporters. The number of children in homes rose from just under 30,000 in 1917 to 400,000 in 1920, and to over half a million in 1922. However homes were crowded with children who had been deserted and orphaned by war and revolution and their aftermath, who came out of necessity; they fell far short of the ideals of cleanliness, comfort and communist socialization. The lofty purpose of childcare institutions – the education of citizens for a new world – was not quite forgotten, but the mundane issues of everyday crisis management held centre stage: instructions during the civil war noted the importance for the emancipation of women of the 'combination of mother-hood and work', but then turned to the question of fixing water mains and to the need for the 'closest attention' to 'the struggle against flies'.

In the economic and social environment of NEP – the streamlined industry, the high female unemployment, the reduction of welfare bud-gets – talk of emancipating women through the transformation of the family and the socialization of child care was seen as increasingly inappropriate. There was neither the political will nor the funding for the construction of a comprehensive network of communally run services to replace the private household. The family was recognized to be, for the time being, the safest and best environment for the child, and with the relegalization of fostering and adoption in the mid-1920s the children's home became the last resort, even for the orphan. The creche and the nursery, too, were luxuries beyond the party purse. Manuals on mother-ing in the 1920s rarely mentioned the public alternatives to family care. Even the journal *Okhrana materinstva i mladenchestva* (*Protection of Mother-hood and Infancy*), designed primarily for Okhmatmlad organizers, was devoting almost half of its pages to the purely medical aspects of mother-hood and infancy by 1927.

The Bolshevik rejection of the more radical aims of 'social upbringing' further disposed the medical profession to make peace with the regime. Especially as the doctors were themselves inclined, by and large, to favour a certain measure of public care. They believed most women to be ignorant and in need of tutelage, and had few qualms about intervention in the families of 'the people'; they viewed the creche and the nursery as excellent channels for the dissemination of modern ideas on mothering. While the doctors may have thought it right that their own wives should stay at home, they took it for granted that most women would work outside the family. Domesticity was not as universal an ideal as it was elsewhere in the West.

A second bone of contention between the doctors and the Bolsheviks had been the question of power. In the first months after the October revolution the patty's position was insecure, and it took what measures it could to pre-empt oppositional challenges. As early as December 1917 one of the pre-revolutionary mothercraft organizations, the Council of Children's Shelters, was abolished, and the All Russian Guardianship (*Vserossiiskoe Popechitel'stvo*), a charitable body set up by tsarist directive in 1913 to supervise child welfare, was ordered to hand over its property and equipment to the recently formed Okhmatmlad. These moves to deprive the medical profession of its organizational role aroused deep resentment. Over this issue, too, an acceptable compromise was soon reached. The Bolsheviks had no option but to rely on the expertise of the 'bourgeois specialists' (there was no other kind available), and were willing to recognize, in return for cooperation, a certain amount of professional autonomy. Doctors were invited to sit on committees and draft proposals; their learned societies, disrupted by the uncertainties of the civil war, resumed activity. Business for the medical profession proceeded much as usual. An issue of *Zhurnal akusherstva i zhenskikh boleznei* (*Journal of Childbirth and Gynaecology*) in 1927 dedicated to A. V. Markovsky was accompanied by a photograph of the professor, smart in jacket, tie and pin-striped trousers, very much the gentleman-physician. The journal *Okhrana materinstva i mladenchestva*, honouring the 25 years of service to the profession of another eminent specialist with a biographical essay, saw no need to mention the October revolution or the Soviet regime, so little apparently did the political upheavals impinge on medical careers.

However, a few years later the alliance between the party and the doctors came to an end. In 1931 the January issue of *Okhrana materinstva i mladenchestva* appeared under a new editor and with a fresh orientation. The previous leadership was criticized for its 'isolationism' (*otorvannost'*) and 'its distance from the basic tasks of socialist construction' and its 'rather apolitical approach'. From now on, it was stated, the journal would take a greater interest in the political issues of the day, and reject the (alleged) narrow-mindedness, sentimentality and elitism of the old editorial board. As evidence of this determination to change direction, the format of the journal was altered, social and political articles, of which there were far more than before, were placed first, while medical matters were dealt with briefly, and at the back. In these years of cultural revolution the whole range of enlightenment propaganda came under scrutiny. Posters were examined closely for ideological errors, certain mothering manuals were denounced as 'bourgeois' and their withdrawal from circulation advised. The methods and relationships of mothering remained unchanged; it was their political context that underwent restructuring. The state was intent on establishing its control, and did so without too much difficulty, through a mixture of bullying, intimidation and intervention. The professional organizations of gynaecologists and obstetricians, as well as their editorial boards, came under attack, and one of the most serious blows to the profession's power and prestige, paradoxically, was the vast expansion and dilution of its ranks by an ill-educated, and largely female, student body.

There was, during the period of the First Five-Year Plan, a resurgence of interest in the creche and the nursery. The promise of rapid industrial development and communist construction encouraged the re-emergence of the utopian ideas of the post-revolutionary years, including predictions about the withering away of the family and the household. This time round, though, the interests of the economy were given a priority they had not had before, as the posters of the time clearly demonstrated. One, issued in 1930, proclaimed the message: 'By strengthening the protection of motherhood and childhood, we help the working woman to be an active constructor of socialism', and illustrated it with a large red woman in factory clothes, a kerchief round her head and a hammer in her hand, against a distant background of creche buildings. This lack of proportion – large working women, small communal facilities – is a feature of a number of posters of the period; so too is the productionist bent of their slogans:

> By organising creches, children's playgrounds, factory kitchens, canteens and mechanised laundries we will provide 1,600,000 new working women for the completion of the Five-Year plan.

> The broad development of the network of creches, nurseries, canteens and laundries guarantees the participation of women in socialist construction.

These posters did not hide the fact that the creche was the means to an end; the provision of child care would increase the number of women working in the economy and their productivity in factory and field. Also, childcare provision would make it possible for women to have more children, a crucial consideration for a government that kept a worried eye on the birth rate. 'Children are our future', claimed a poster produced shortly after abortion was banned in 1936; it depicted a woman sitting at home with a baby on her lap and a child at her side and advised its audience 'not to deprive themselves of the joys of motherhood'. Women were to be both workers and reproducers, whatever the cost – and the cost to maternal and infant health, to the psychological and social well-being of the mother and child, in the 1930s was very high indeed.[4]

## Motherhood and nation

Soviet political iconographers, in their attempts to provide a population ravaged by rapid industrialization, forced collectivization and famine and the purges with a sense of self, with the cement of identity and unity, began to employ images of motherhood. Historically, maternity had a firm place in the Russian visual lexicon. Icons of the Mother and Child were, in the pre-revolutionary period, regularly carried with armies, taken on demonstrations and used to decorate the home and the work place, as well as the church. In the posters on mothering produced after October 1917 there were some echoes, suitably secularized, of the composition and style of the Orthodox *Bogomater'* and the Catholic Madonna: women held their babies close to their bodies or sat them on their laps; often mother and child were positioned against a blank or ornamental background, or isolated by distance from society.[5] These posters, though, had limited circulation and were mostly confined to female spaces, to the walls of maternity clinics, *zhenotdel* offices and 'women's pages'. In public and political iconography women and children were conspicuous by their absence. Despite its professed commitment to women's emancipation, the Bolshevik regime saw change in terms of factory and production, reference points that were primarily masculine; the hero was the male industrial worker and it was his image that stood for revolution and socialism.

At the time of the First Five-Year Plan this male hegemony was challenged. The state, in need of an increasing supply of workers, elevated maternity to an issue of national resonance. Posters on Okhmatmlad were displayed in public places;[6] mothers and children featured for the first time on postage stamps; women participated in gymnastic parades, wearing narrow, mid-calf skirts, and holding aloft bouquet-bearing children.[7] In search of unifying symbols the state twinned motherhood and nation. A political poster produced in the mid-1930s shows a mother and girl-child cowering helplessly before the Nazi menace; the two figures, painted in a realistic style, draw attention to the dangers which individual women and children face, but they clearly also represent the nation that has to be defended against fascism. During the Great Patriotic War this conflation of family and state and their representation by motherhood became commonplace. The middle-aged woman holding up in urgent entreaty a copy of the 'military oath' in Iraklii Toidze's famous war poster '*Rodina-mat'* zovet (*The Motherland-Mother calls*) is both real mother and motherland. '*Za rodinu-mat'* (*For the Motherland*) another of the most ubiquitous posters of the period, depicts five soldiers in battle-like poses beneath the towering figure of a woman, draped in red, with a banner raised in her right hand, her free arm round a small (male) child; she combines the qualities of both the martial female heroines of Russian folklore and the maternal stereotype. She is *Matushka-Rossiya* (*Mother Russia*) personified. Viktor Koretsky's '*Voin krasnoi armii, spasi!*' (Soldiers of the Red Army, save us!) – a mother and (male) child threatened by an enemy bayonet – evokes, in its realism, the loved ones left behind and, in its composition, the Mother of God, symbol of faith and nation. Gigantic reproductions of this poster were pasted up in Soviet streets, as if it were an icon affirming the holy nature of the struggle against Germany.

The shift of Soviet ideology towards traditional themes, particularly Russian nationalism, is often dated to 1941, and certainly the frequent depiction of motherhood in poster art during the war attests to their growing importance; but the appropriation by public iconography of mother and child began earlier, as the Stalinist regime sought to bolster its legitimacy through a semblance of patriarchal stability.

### The modernization of motherhood

Over the past 20 years a substantial sociological and historical literature on the impact modern medicine on motherhood and infant welfare has been published.[8] While earlier work in the field chronicled the development of the medical profession and listed its achievements, the more recent literature has examined critically the benefits and drawbacks of modern mothering and its wider significance for society and culture. The transformation of motherhood from a social into a medical event has been described, following the emergence, beginning from the eighteenth century, of the medical profession and its successful claim to supervise birth and infant care. In many cases, control passed as a result of this process from women to men – from female healers, friends, relatives, neighbours and from mothers themselves, to male doctors; everywhere decision making passed from individuals and their communities to the experts. Modernization thus comprised not only new knowledge about the birth process and a set of instructions on mothering but also, and more importantly, a range of new social relationships.

In Russia, by the end of the nineteenth century, gynaecologists and obstetricians were already well organized in the cities. Lectures were held and manuals published to preach the virtues of modern mothering; in major urban areas the medicalization of childbirth was far advanced, with over 60 per cent of births in St Petersburg and Moscow taking place in maternity shelters and wards by 1914. The Bolsheviks, when they came to power, criticized the tsarist regime for the timidity and inadequacies of its reforms, and condemned the philanthropy and class inequalities of the past, but they did not make fundamental changes to the programme of modernization embarked upon by the pre-revolutionary doctors. The Soviet government was happy to sponsor campaigns that exhorted women to bath their children with soap and water and buy them cribs to sleep in, happy to see wise women denounced. The official notion of modernization, in this instance, fitted well with the one subscribed to by the professional intelligentsia. Bolshevik socialism, even in its Utopian moments, provided few resources for prefiguring contemporary criticisms of the medicalization of motherhood and contemporary concern with the mother's loss of control over the processes of pregnancy and birth and the father's lack of participation in parenting. The Bolsheviks shared the faith of their era in technology and expertise; and at the same time, and again in tune with their times, they paid homage to nature and did not question the maternal instincts of women or seek to emancipate them from their monopoly on the nurturing role.

The Bolsheviks set out to do things bigger and better, but not differently. The modernization of motherhood after 1917 continued along pre-revolutionary lines and it conformed to patterns of development observable everywhere in the Western world. Modernization in the Russian context did have its specificities. The country was vast and rural, which put brakes on the spread of the new knowledge on mothering, both before and after 1917. The professional classes were tiny and isolated, and inclined as a consequence to accept collective, state-orchestrated solutions to the problems of maternal and infant welfare. And finally, the weakness of civil society and of democratic political traditions in Russia propelled the state, rather later than was fashionable in most Western countries, to employ motherhood as a political icon.

NOTES

[Reorganized and renumbered from the original.]

This article is based on a paper presented to the First Meeting of the International Federation for Research in Women's History at the 17th International Congress of Historical Sciences, Madrid, August 1990. I would like to thank Susan Gross Solomon and Elizabeth Wood for comments on this earlier version.

My research on motherhood in post-revolutionary Russia has been made possible by a British Council Scholarship to the USSR in 1981–83 and a place on the Australian National University exchange with Moscow University in 1989–90. I am also grateful for grants from the ANU Faculties' Research Fund in 1989 and 1990. I would like to thank the curators of poster collections at the Hoover Institution, Stanford University, the State Lenin Library, Moscow, the State History Museum, Moscow, the State Museum of Revolution, Moscow, and the State Saltykov-Shchedrin Library, Leningrad, for their generous assistance.

1. Quoted in I. Deutscher, *Stalin: A Political Biography* (Harmondsworth, 1972), p. 328.

2. Okhmatmlad had branches in all the republics of the USSR and the process of modernization was in many respects uniform across the country. However, there were cultural differences, which need to be addressed separately. The focus here is on the RSFSR and Russian motherhood.

3. For a discussion of enlightenment propaganda see my 'Teaching Mothercraft in Post-Revolutionary Russia', *Australian Journal of Slavonic and East European Studies*, 1:2 (1987), pp. 29–56. The instructional images of Soviet motherhood posters are analysed in my 'Child care Posters and the Modernization of Motherhood in Post-Revolutionary Russia', *Sbornik: Study Group on the Russian Revolution*, 13 (1987), pp. 65–93.

4. In the early 1930s infant mortality rates increased, the number of foundlings rose and the proportion of working women provided with creche and nursery places for their children fell.

5. Two posters produced for 'Motherhood and Infancy Protection Weeks' in 1923, one in Moscow, the other in Georgia, show mothers and children against a plain background, unrelieved, or in the Georgian case broken only by stylized flowers and the branch of a tree. The emblem of Okhmatmlad featured in the foreground a mother with a baby on her lap and a toddler at her side, and far in the distance the urban skyline of the socialist future.

6. W. A. Rukeyser, *Working for the Soviet: An American Engineer in Russia* (London, 1932), p. 83.

7. For a photograph of such a parade see G. Shudakov, *Pioneers of Soviet Photography* (New York, 1983), p. 155. It was taken in Red Square by Ivan Shagin in 1937, the year after the ban on abortion was introduced, and contrasts sharply with one from 1930 by the photographer Arkadii Shaikhet of determined women gymnasts in shorts and t-shirts, striding out unencumbered.

8. See Nancy Schron Dye, 'History of Childbirth in America', *Signs*, 1 (1980), pp. 97–108; Judith Walzer Leavitt, 'Under the Shadow of Maternity: American Women's Responses to Death and Debility Fears in Nineteenth Century Childbirth', *Feminist Review*, 1 (1986), pp. 129–54 Barbara Ehrenrich and Deirdre English, *For Her Own Good: 150 Years of the Experts' Advice to Women* (London, 1979); Ann Oakley, *Women Confined: Towards a Sociology of Childbirth* (Oxford, 1980); J. Lewis, *The Politics of Motherhood: Child and Maternal Welfare in England 1900–1939* (London, 1980); E. Shorter, *A History of Women's Bodies* (New York, 1982); Ann Oakley, *The Captured Womb: a History of the Medical Care of Pregnant Women* (Oxford, 1984); Philippa Mein Smith, *Maternity in Dispute. New Zealand 1920–1939* (Wellington, 1986).

# TOWARDS THE 'NEW SOVIET PERSON': THE ASSAULT ON RELIGION

Cultural themes are often passed over in analysis of the Stalin years. They should not be. Culture was central to the Soviet project. That is why this collection has opened with two articles on cultural questions. Why is culture so important? At heart, the goal of communism was not only to reform institutions but to change the human personality. In the Stalin years there was much talk about 'The New Soviet Person' who would be produced as socialism advanced. Where bourgeois society needed greedy, selfish individualists socialism would bring out the inner generosity of people and build up their need for co-operation and community spirit. From the early days of the revolution there had been disputes about exactly what the characteristics of the new person would be and, even more complex, how such people would be produced. A special organization, The Proletarian Cultural Educational Association (usually referred to as Proletkul't for short), was set up shortly before the October revolution. Its stormy early history led to the curtailment of its autonomy in 1920 after which it became little more than a part of the growing propaganda apparatus. However, the drive to create the new person lived on. One fundamental characteristic which no one in the party criticized was that science and a scientific view of the world would be at the heart of the new person's outlook. In the early stages of the revolution the 1919 Party Programme stated that the Party would help 'the toiling masses to liberate their minds from religious prejudices' by 'organizing on a wide scale scientific-educational and anti-religious propaganda'. But, the programme continued, it was 'necessary to avoid offending the religious susceptibilities of believers, which leads only to the hardening of religious fanaticism.'

During the 1920s direct confrontation with religion, and particularly the Orthodox church, had given way to more subtle tactics. A group, known as the Living Church broke away from the mainstream of Orthodoxy and professed support for the social aims of the revolution. It was not notably successful either in winning over believers or placating left-wing militants for whom Lenin's intolerant snort – 'to prefer a blue devil to a yellow one is a hundred times worse than not saying anything about it at all' – expressed their own feelings. As the twenties progressed, the atmosphere gradually developed into the rising confrontational mentality of the thirties. In the mid-twenties militant groups had tried to seize control over the field of literature. They achieved a partial victory in 1925 when a resolution called for closer party supervision of literature. However, for the moment, non-communist writers thought to be sympathetic to the revolution, the so-called 'fellow travellers', were allowed to continue to publish. Journals such as *Novyi mir* (*New World*) and *Krasnaia nov'* (*Red Virgin Soil*) continued with relatively liberal publishing policies.

However, the left-wing groups, such as the Russian Association of Proletarian Writers, continued to put pressure for a narrower definition of what was acceptable. The late twenties saw a growing clamour from ultra-leftist militants to such an extent that some observers believe pressure from below was instrumental in setting off the new revolution of 1928–32 which embraced cultural, industrial and economic spheres. However, that belief has waned somewhat in recent years and even its apparent proponents seem to disclaim it. We will return to the issue of the precise reason for the adoption of the 'great turn' in 1928 later on but for the moment it is only necessary to note that an avalanche of utopian ideas, some of which were a revival of concepts from the period of the revolutionary wars (1918–21), began to gather momentum. Extreme thinking had never been abandoned. The fanciful plan for a colossal 'House of Soviets' had begun to be implemented with the blowing up of one of Moscow's most prominent, and ugliest, cathedrals in 1931. Reality had clicked in too late when it was discovered that the geological formations of the area would not bear the weight of the proposed super-skyscraper. The big hole left by the demolition was converted into an open-air swimming pool until, in post-Soviet times, the cathedral was, contro-versially, rebuilt. A number of buildings, including the Lenin Mausoleum on Red Square and the scattering of workers clubs and houses in Moscow by Konstantin Mel'nikov, were constructed according to radical principles. After 1928, however, utopian ideas had their head. Architecture remained an area in which extravagant plans for Soviet homes and Soviet cities were drawn up. The homes would have communal facilities for cooking, eating, washing and childcare to replace private ones. This meant apartments without kitchens. Attempts were made to design cities appropriate to the new values. A proposed linear city, crossing the entire country, was intended to fulfil the demand of the *Communist Manifesto* that the distinction between town and country should be abolished.

In all areas of cultural life battles between 'fellow travellers' and party moderates on one hand and leftist militants on the other were waged. Philosophy, history, music art, literature, education, science were turned into left/right conflicts. Increasingly, the slogan 'There is no fortress the Bolsheviks cannot storm' was taken literally by the militants. Bolshevik will was deemed to be all that was necessary to achieve a task. Failure in such a task was, therefore, attributed mainly to weakness of will. In a manner imitated by Maoists in 1966, 'objective' constraints (that is, whether something was practically possible or not) were dismissed as bourgeois illusions. Anything, it seemed, could be achieved if it was willed sufficiently strongly. This phase of ultra-leftist utopianism lasted until 1931–2 when more conventional ideas began to reassert themselves.

Not surprisingly, however, in the utopian wave, the issue of religion came to the fore. In his article, which was later incorporated in a book on the topic, Daniel Peris shows in detail the way one major anti-religious organization, the League of Godless, operated. Relative moderates set the organization up in the first place but in 1929 their positions were attacked by extremists intent on taking it over. Peris hints that the differences included a significant generation gap with most of the militants being younger than the moderates. They also tended to focus on organizations like the Communist Youth League (*Komsomol*) referred to several times by Peris. Typically, the left militants were repulsed at the Congress itself but, in effect, took the leadership into their hands shortly after anyway. They renamed it the League of Militant Godless and jacked up the pace of its activities, ruthlessly following their goals and claiming the mantle of party authority for their aggressive intolerance. Similar organizations were set up across the intellectual spectrum which attempted to be the self-appointed guardians of party orthodoxy in literature, academic life and the sciences.

The author presents his study of the congress as an exemplar of the practices of the time, illustrating the moderate/extremist clashes, which we have already seen in action in Elizabeth Waters' account, and many other aspects of the struggles of the period. One of these was the growing cult of Lenin, whose posthumous authority was sought by both sides who traded Lenin quotes in an attempt to outdo each other. Stalin has an ambiguous presence in Peris's account. He is rarely referred to in the congress discussions, though he is mentioned as the leader, it being the case that the downfall of Bukharin (who did address the congress) and the party right was already evident. An invitation was extended to Stalin to address the congress and thereby pronounce on its differences. Stalin's rejection of the invitation seems to have disappointed all the delegates. Nonetheless, a cult of Stalin was not yet evident. However, a culture of searching for 'deviationists', whether they were groups or hapless individuals like Galaktionov who was pilloried at the congress, was already well entrenched by this time and was to burgeon in the later years.

## 2 Daniel Peris: 'The 1929 Congress of the Godless'

Among the many social campaigns launched in the Soviet Union in the 1920s, the effort to counter the pervasive influence of religion was among the most visible. Examining how the Bolsheviks sought to introduce atheism into Holy Russia sheds light not only on Bolshevik strategies for planned secularization, but also on the evolving Soviet political culture. Both of these subjects can be approached through analysis of the stenographic report of the June 1929 Congress of the League of the Godless (*Soyuz bezbozhnikov*), the quasi-governmental organization charged with eradicating religion. This document serves as a window through which we observe the repeated clashes of two distinct and opposed camps promoting conflicting views on how the anti-religious campaign ought to be run. More importantly, the stenographic report highlights the shared assumptions and rhetorical conventions of the coalescing political culture in which the congress occurred and which qualitatively altered the character of the anti-religious debate.

This article first reviews the 12 years of anti-religious history prior to the congress. It then examines the divisions at the congress along ideological and institutional lines. The third section discusses those elements of the emerging political culture evident in the debate; finally, the conflicts in the anti-religious camp are linked to the broader political and social transformation engulfing Soviet society on the cusp of Stalin's revolution.

## Anti-religious agitation from the revolution to 1929

The stage was set for conflict at the congress by 12 years of experience which had yielded no certain method of pursuing anti-religious agitation and had created substantial ill-will among the institutions responsible for anti-religious affairs.[1] Indeed, the Soviet struggle against religion had evolved through two broad and generally contradictory stages. The initial phase, covering the first six years of Bolshevik rule, relied on legislative dismemberment of the Orthodox Church and selective repression of religious leaders. A second phase, beginning around 1923, increasingly employed propaganda and education with the goal of combating popular religious beliefs and practices. Thus, by 1929 two distinct and often conflicting models of anti-religious agitation had been employed. We shall explore each in turn.

Upon taking power, the Bolsheviks immediately disestablished Eastern Orthodoxy. They nationalized church property and transferred church-run educational institutions to the Commissariat of Enlightenment. Registration of births, marriages and deaths, acts formerly handled by the Church, were also given to civilian authorities. The constitution adopted by the Russian Soviet Republic on 10 July 1918 guaranteed freedom of religious and anti-religious propaganda, as well as the freedom to profess any religious creed. Rules eventually issued by the Commissariat of Justice allowed believers to retake possession of churches rent-free, but the frequent clarifications emanating from the Eighth Department (the division of the Justice Commissariat charged with overseeing the legal aspects of religion) during the early years of the Soviet regime seem to indicate a failed effort at achieving a smooth and uniform separation of church and state.[2] While the administrative body of the Orthodox Church was effectively suppressed through a variety of laws and extraordinary measures, there was little the new regime could do immediately to change popular behaviour. Bolshevik concessions to the continuation of religious expression sought to make a virtue of necessity – in this case, the undeniable pervasiveness of religion in Russia.

Factors other than legislation also contributed to church–state relations in this early period. First, the Civil War added its own measure of confusion and contradiction to Bolshevik policy. Although most clergy were sympathetic to the Whites, the Bolsheviks had to avoid alienating the peasantry, and this required some sensitivity in their handling of popular religious expression. The 'Church valuables' crisis in 1922 constituted a second moment in this initial period of church–state relations. Difficulties in responding to the famine in the Volga region in late 1921 and 1922 led the Bolsheviks to demand that the Orthodox Church sacrifice its collection of treasures, including sacramental vessels, to import grain. Despite wide contribution of non-sacramental treasures by the Church, the Bolsheviks initiated a general collection campaign in 1922 resulting in popular riots, the arrest of Church leaders, including Patriarch Tikhon, and the execution or imprisonment of numerous churchmen. In general, the first six years of Bolshevik rule were hard on the church. It was a period of legal dismemberment, overt repression, and direct, often violent, intervention against the body of the Church and its leaders. Dire circumstances and an ideology bitterly opposed to religion, and so far unmellowed by practical experience, formed the basis of anti-religious efforts during these years.

A second broad period of Bolshevik policy commenced in 1923. While legal and physical pressures continued on the clergy and what remained of the church's administrative body, new efforts relying on extensive propaganda and education sought to influence the everyday thinking and behaviour of believers.[3] One manifestation of this shift to a more systematic anti-religious effort was the creation of the League of the Godless in 1925, which will be discussed below. Another was the appearance of an array of anti-religious propaganda serials, pamphlets and books. This new orientation offered anti-religious lectures, museums, displays, 'evenings', a 'Godless' corner at the factory or village reading hut, and conspicuous display of anti-religious slogans. It is difficult to assess what impact, if any, these actions had on believers, but they constituted a significant part of the new anti-religious package.

Why had six years passed before the Bolsheviks turned to socializing the masses in a fundamental tenet of the ruling ideology? In its initial enthusiasm, the Bolshevik leadership may have laboured under the illusion that it could legislatively efface religion from the Russian landscape. Then the Civil War intervened and prevented systematic propaganda efforts. Even when the battlefields fell silent in late 1920, the Bolsheviks did not turn immediately to religious matters. The roll-back of the Bolsheviks presence in the countryside associated with the X Congress in March 1921 left the party in a weak position to influence everyday behaviour, particularly in the countryside where religion was strongest. The new direction in policy from 1923 onward reflected not only the lack of insurmountable obstacles to launching an anti-religious campaign, but also the growing realization that religion was not going to expire of its own accord once the administrative body of the church had been crushed. Both the XII (1923) and XIII (1924) Congresses called for systematic and careful anti-religious propaganda, but Bolshevik leaders remained concerned about alienating the population of the countryside, in which they were weakly represented. Hence, it is most reasonable to conclude that this shift in methods occurred at the first convenient opportunity, when the nation was no longer at war, when the Bolsheviks realized religion would not simply disappear, and when they could begin to give at least some attention to what they wanted to make out of the enormous country they had come to rule. In practical terms, this meant 1923 and later.

Yet another source of potential conflict at the congress stemmed from an ambiguous experience in the adminstration of the anti-religious effort. In the first period, the Commissariats of Enlightenment and Justice, the *agitprop* (agitation and propaganda) section of the Party Central Committee, the Central Committee's Anti-religious Commission and the Cheka, all participated in the management of religion, yet none of the institutions initially involved took the lead during the 1920s, and one that should have, the Komsomol, shied away from the task.[4] The resulting void in the management of anti-religious activities meant that the shift to a more propagandistic mode was not accompanied by clearer lines of authority. Despite occasional directives emanating from the Central Committee, the party did not take direct responsibility for a nationwide effort. While previous, small-scale propaganda efforts might have been arranged by the local party, Komsomol or trade union committee, or in the military, no broadly based, coordinated campaign existed.

Even the foundation of the League of the Godless in 1925 did not completely resolve the administrative difficulties facing anti-religious activists. The League had evolved out of a body formed in 1924, The Society of Friends of the Newspaper *Bezbozhnik* (*The Atheist*), which incorporated itself in April 1925 as the League of the Godless. Though the establishment of the League marked a watershed in Soviet anti-religious efforts, the organization remained weak. Its activities, under the direction of its leader and motivating force, Emil'yan Yaroslavsky,[5] concentrated primarily on the creation of a publishing empire, including serials, monographs, brochures and methodological tracts. In addition, the *Bezbozhniki* arranged specific campaigns, agitated against observance of religious holidays and rituals, sought to introduce new holidays and rituals, trained activists and held meetings and lectures on anti-religious themes. Despite these efforts, the League before 1929 appears to have been ineffective in its efforts to overcome religion. In 1929 membership jumped rapidly to 1 million, according to a League spokesman at the congress. This fourfold increase in the League's size from 1928 strongly suggests that the impressive strides made in membership did not necessarily indicate a sudden eradication of religion. Many delegates spoke of having only formally organized cells or councils by 1928, a refrain that could be heard from delegates such as Adel'berg from Siberia, Shchepkin from the Urals, and the delegate from Kirgizia, Abramson. The overall impact of the League's efforts is hard to assess, but we may safely conclude that by 1929 it had not achieved a comprehensive transformation of popular religious life.

The birth of the League of the Godless was not accomplished without difficulty. Battles over turf and ideology among the newly formed League, Moscow-based anti-religious activists, Ukrainian cadres and the Red Army characterized the early history of the League. These conflicts spilled into the central party press in 1925 and 1926 and were certainly not forgotten by 1929. The congress provided yet another opportunity for them to resurface.

To appreciate the developments at the 1929 congress it is crucial to understand this mixed and often contradictory legacy of 12 years of anti-religious experience. We have already noted how two different methods of anti-religious work had been employed. To this we must now add the factor of an uneasy institutional order administering the campaign. Latent divisions between the Komsomol and its supporters on the one hand and the League Central Council on the other characterized this order and would reappear at the congress.

## Ideologies and institutions

When the Godless delegates gathered on 10 June 1929 in Moscow at the House of the Red Army, the central issue of the congress was the implementation of an effective anti-religious campaign. Gone were the days when one could still believe religion would disappear naturally. In this sense, everyone gathered at the congress advocated an active, aggressive stance, but there existed two distinct groups characterized by qualitative differences over how this should be achieved.

One group, centred in the League Central Council and Narkompros, emphasized the cultural and social sources of religion and argued that it was not solely a political matter to be handled by the secret police. Adherents to this position distinguished between what they acknowledged as the consciously anti-Soviet leadership of religious groups and the more uninformed, uncultured mass of toilers who should not be considered plotting counterrevolutionaries. The problem lay in a lack of proper consciousness and '*kul'turnost*' among the believing masses. Yaroslavsky declared: 'All the same, it we take our peasantry ... then we see that *bezkul'tur'e* still plays an enormous role'.[6] These activists, whom I call 'culturalists', were quick to acknowledge the importance of what was labelled open, politically subversive activity by priests and kulaks, already *de rigueur* in Soviet discourse by mid-1929, but their arguments revealed an equal or greater emphasis on the cultural bases of religion.

Approaching religion from the culturalist perspective entailed important consequences for the forms and methods of anti-religious activity. It meant a policy of education, systematic propaganda and a concerted effort to change the behaviour and attitudes of the populace. It rejected forceful intervention to close churches or remove priests unless sufficient, genuine, popular support had been built beforehand. To do otherwise would mean, in Yaroslavsky's words, entering 'a bitter battle with at least 60–70 million toilers. Is that correct? No!'. This position was aired frequently during the congress. Lunacharsky, Commissar of Enlightenment, linked changing the consciousness of the rural masses to the establishment of socialism, which, he said, could not be achieved without extensive cultural work. Careful not to deny the relevance of administrative measures or compulsion when circumstances warranted, Lunacharsky criticized as politically unwise measures that would be perceived as violent, unwelcome attacks by a hostile regime: 'We should not undertake to make priests martyrs and have peasants turn against us'. The culturalists believed that the inculcation of communist morality would follow logically from anti-religious propaganda. As Lunacharsky declared, 'to destroy religion but not to replace it with a Marxist worldview – that is a slogan from bourgeois freethinkers', and Yaroslavsky rejected as ideologically unsound the charge that 'our task is not to replace religion, but to destroy it'.[7]

The most visible culturalist target was the Komsomol, and culturalist criticism of that organization indicates to what degree institutional or turf battles also played a role in the congress debates. Yaroslavsky complained that no one from the Central Committee of the Komsomol was in attendance at the congress; he also intimated that the popularity of some Christian youth groups reflected weak Komsomol influence and that ideological work was necessary among Komsomol members. He berated Komsomol superficiality in anti-religious work, and noted that the Komsomol representative on the League Central Council did not attend meetings. More was needed from the Komsomol, he continued, than efforts twice a year at Christmas and Easter. Yaroslavsky ended his main report by rejecting statements in *Komsomol'skaya Pravda* that criticized the replacement of Easter by May Day.[8]

The opposing camp placed culture second to politics in its analysis of the causes of religion and advocated a much more aggressive, volunteerist stance. This group, the 'interventionists', was centred primarily in the Komsomol, but it also enjoyed support from the Moscow League organization and other delegations. Central to the interventionist argument was that religion, as an expression of the former class structure, posed a direct political threat to socialism. A delegate from the Komsomol clearly articulated the interventionist position when he argued that religion was the ideology of our class enemy, and that among other measures, we must in the clearest, sharpest manner uncover the class essence of religion, prove that the church is a political organization of the class enemy and that the church's primary weapon is deception of the masses.

This threat was manifested through domestic enemies such as priests, religious organizers sympathetic *kulaks* and former Whites, and foreign enemies through protestant sectarians in Russia who maintained contacts with organizations abroad. A leading interventionist, I. Bukhartsev, attacked the League for not focusing on the class basis of religion. League leaders, he continued, paid lip service to the political element of religion, but in their actions they failed to link the battle against religion to the battle against class enemies. To a reformed League Bukhartsev offered the carrot of mass Komsomol enrolment:

> If you clearly frame the issue of anti-religious propaganda, if you sharply come out against atheistic lisping, against liberal methods of battle against religion, you will receive a fresh cohort of young workers and peasants, and the support of the Leninist Komsomol.

The activist position articulated by Bukhartsev was buttressed by the promulgation in April 1929, only two months before the congress, of a law further restricting religious expression, and one month later, in May 1929, by removal from the Soviet Constitution of the right to promote religion.

The interventionist camp placed greater emphasis than the culturalists on the dialectic of rising tension in society as the Soviet Union approached socialism. For example, a writer for *Komsomol'skaya Pravda* inveighed against Lunacharsky, now the radicals' favourite target and an embattled figure by 1929, for failing to realize the import of this new period which called for 'class-based criticism of religion on live, concrete, contemporary material'. Although all the delegates spoke in terms of the 'attack' of socialism and the 'counterattack' of religion, the radicals of Bukhartsev's stripe were eager to place all expressions of religious faith in terms of political subversion, and were equally quick to invoke military metaphors to justify an 'assault' on religion.

The interventionists were also less interested in distinguishing between the followers and leaders of religious groups and less prepared to apply different methods of anti-religious work to separate religious creeds. Even sectarian communes employing progressive agricultural methods were rejected out of hand. The interventionists also derided enlightenment and welcomed application of administrative measures. Speaking of the latter, one Moscow radical declared, 'it is impermissible to renounce and be afraid of them'. Administrative measures should be used to indicate the 'dictatorship of the proletariat'. One of the Komsomol radicals argued that they were necessary to give an 'irreconcilable, Bolshevik, clear, class rebuff to the assaulting *popovshchina*' (Clerical assault).

Fuelled by such impassioned debate, the conflict nearly got out of hand. At one point Bukhartsev directly indicted Yaroslavsky for overstating the cultural factor. Quoting Yaroslavsky on the 'enormous role' played by 'unculturedness', Bukhartsev countered, 'to me it seems that this does not capture the significance of religion at our stage'. Bukhartsev's comments were met by hissing from the floor. He shot back: 'What are you cackling about; really, this is not a meeting of kulaks'. The text of the stenographic report notes that the ensuing noise in the hall cut off the speaker. Having been voted more time to complete his fusillade, Bukhartsev then criticized the League's understanding of religion in the period of socialist construction.

Clearly, conflict between two very different camps characterized the congress, but it would be incorrect to assume that each side was completely unified. In the first place, only a few delegates gave presentations coherent or long enough to separate them from the stream of say-nothing appearances that crudely mouthed Yaroslavsky's statements. The real debate occurred among a limited number of self-interested delegates who had the opportunity to set out distinct positions. Determining which of the delegates spoke authoritatively for which organization or viewpoint constitutes an important task in analysing this meeting. We can safely assume that Yaroslavsky's position represented that of the league leadership and that Lunacharsky reflected the attitudes of many highly ranked pedagogues, but beyond that, it is difficult to draw precise institutional boundaries. Most notably, many delegates from local League councils were highly critical of Narkompros and harped on the lack of anti-religious work in the schools.

Among the opposition, the Komsomol, the Moscow and the Ukrainian League organizations appeared unified in their interventionism, with the Komsomol playing the leading role. Yaroslavsky pointed out that certain towns like Nizhnii-Novgorod and regions such as the Ukraine had prevented the formation of Godless cells. He roundly criticized the Moscow party activists who refused to cooperate with the League's Central Council. M. Galaktionov, a writer for *Komsomol'skaya Pravda*, indicated that his criticisms of Lukachevsky, a prominent League figure, were based in part on what he had learned at a recent Moscow Region League Council meeting. At a minimum, the Moscow and Komsomol interventionists communicated with each other. Nonetheless, their cooperation was potentially tactical, extending little beyond a shared, intense dislike for them League's central apparatus. The Muscovite stance reflected, in part, its long-standing conflict with the League; a Moscow radical, Orlov, declared that the Moscow organization differed from the Central Council over those same issues as in its earlier clash with the League in 1925 and 1926. The Ukrainian organization framed its opposition to the League Central Council as much in terms of Ukrainian autonomy as it did in terms of specific methodological disagreements. Rogal' of the Ukraine warned against excessive centralization and argued that best results would be achieved only if national peculiarities were taken into consideration. Several Ukrainian delegates, however, spoke at cross purposes in regard to League strategy and centralization, and this should alert us to the dangers of assuming institutional or regional uniformity of views. These qualifications aside, the popularly recognized bastion of interventionism lay in the offices of *Komsomol'skaya Pravda*, whence came repeated shrill attacks which were supported by Ukrainian and Muscovite delegates.

In sum, the dominant institutional framework of the congress presented a radicalized, vibrant, impatient Komsomol, in league with smaller groups of oppositionists and radicals, arrayed against the staid and sober representatives of the Soviet bureaucratic apparatus. Ferment characterized the Soviet anti-religious activist body; the outlines of the cultural upheaval of the First Five-Year Plan period were clearly visible.

### Soviet political culture and the Godless debates

While on the level of ideology and institutions – measures prominent in the existing historiography – serious divisions existed among the Godless, examination of the congress in terms of the rhetoric employed to wage the above-mentioned struggles reveals a number of shared assumptions and oratorical conventions which shed light on aspects of Soviet political culture, including one which has until recently evaded analysis, language. At least four elements of this culture can be discerned in the congress debates – the delegates' self-justification in terms of Lenin, their calls for centralization, their method of criticizing individuals rather than institutions, and their avowed subordination to the party. All took place against the backdrop of a political discourse which served as an increasingly opaque medium of debate. While objective differences between the opposing camps existed, the debates occurred in the context of a dominant political culture that accorded as much importance to certain words, phrases and metaphors as to the ideas they articulated. The battle raged on a field, language, sought by both contenders. The terrain was pitted, however, with traps which could capture those who vied for its control.

Both the interventionists and the culturalists sought to justify their positions in the light of the already crystalized source of transcendent truth in Soviet political debate: the corpus of Lenin's writings. By 1929 Lenin had become apotheosized as the font of Bolshevik wisdom and political culture.[9] Thus, both sides professed obeisance to the true doctrine of Lenin and charged the other side with straying from Lenin's understanding of religion. The breadth of Lenin's written legacy, however, allowed almost any position to be buttressed by a significant quotation. Yaroslavsky frequently referred to Lenin, and in his closing speech to the congress, an emotionally charged rebuttal of the interventionists' criticisms, he declared:

> That's how Lenin understood (it): organisation and enlightenment of the proletariat will lead to the dying out of religion, but we should not throw ourselves into the *avantyura* (adventure) of a political battle with religion.

Yaroslavsky then repeated a well known statement by Lenin on the importance of cultural work.[10] Bukhartsev justified the interventionist position by citing Lenin's claim that 'it would be foolishness to think that in a society based on the endless oppression and coarseness of the working masses, it is possible to dispel religious prejudices through purely propagandist means'.

The efforts of the opposing camps to determine anti-religious policy relied upon carving a generally accepted position on religion out of this broad and vague official dogma. The Godless operated in the environment of absolute doctrines characteristic of Russian intellectual development, yet no particular 'ism' explicitly directed them in the creation of an atheist society. Marx provided no practical plans; Lenin's *State and Revolution* was of little use in this regard. Even Yaroslavsky's pronouncements did not enjoy the status of unchallengeable doctrine. No unassailable source of wisdom in this regard existed because such a social transformation had never before been fully thought out or experienced. However, while no well trodden path existed, the political culture demanded that at each stage of social development there exist absolute procedures and methods of social management, and so the leaders of the anti-religious debates acted as if an absolute plan existed. Their task was simply to have their own answer to 'What do we do next?' accepted as that of Lenin and the party. While the debates reflected real policy alternatives, the existence of 'better' or 'worse' approaches receded behind the importance of having one's own method designated as Leninist, and therefore *a priori* the only correct strategy. The debates at the congress revealed the subjectivity of this process and the tension between a constrictive rhetorical framework and widely divergent policy proposals.

Centralized organization complemented obeisance to Lenin and constituted another basic theme of the congress. In his opening report Yaroslavsky attributed the weakness of anti-religious activity in large part to organizational shortcomings. In particular, uncoordinated and ineffective agitation resulted from a lack of centralized leadership that left broad swathes of society unexposed to anti-religious agitation. Yaroslavsky argued that the level of organization determined the success of anti-religious activities, and consequently that the remedy for the League's difficulties was centralization around the League's Central Council. He presented administrative reform to strengthen the League's ability to direct the anti-religious effort nationally as a panacea for the campaign's weaknesses. Following Yaroslavsky's lead, delegate after delegate parroted the catechism: 'We need centralization'. Delegates from as far afield as the Army and the Caucasus linked the shortcomings of their organizations to lack of a strong hand in Moscow. A call for the strictest possible centralization by a delegate from Uzbekistan drew applause from the hall, and his description of decentralization's evils all but suggested that the persistence of religion in Central Asia could be significantly countered by putting local anti-religious cells on a short leash.

Some limits to centralization existed. An amendment to the resolution on the League's regulations that would have required confirmation of regional council elections by the Central Council in Moscow was rejected by the congress as risking 'extraordinary centralization'. More importantly, some delegates saw centralization as a means by which their dissenting voices would be silenced. Delegates from the Ukraine, where efforts at local autonomy had been prominent in one form or another since the Germans marched through during the First World War were particularly vocal in this matter. Although one Ukrainian delegate argued for a centralized, 'monolithic, battle-ready organization', another Ukrainian speaker, Petrov, all but declared that the Emperor had no clothes. He daringly charged that the Central Council was hiding behind calls for centralization. (The stenographic report notes disturbance in the hall after this comment.) Petrov observed that during two days of discussion not one delegate had criticized the Central Council. He offered an alternative proposal, that

> the work of the League of the Godless should be constructed with regard to centralized general ideological and organizational leadership from the C[entral] C[ommittee], L[eague] of the G[odless], guaranteeing, as well as a unified line, responsibility for its execution by the republic councils.

Petrov further suggested that the League Central Council should link all the regional councils, apparently as an administrative entity rather than the locus of active leadership, and should be separated from the large RSFSR League organization. This wording would have left far greater responsibility with the republican councils than Yaroslavsky desired.

The reliance on centralization included within it the possibility of invoking the charge of deviationism as a powerful rhetorical weapon. In the context of the congress, the radicals appeared successful at putting the culturalists on the defensive by implying that the latter held a deviationist line. Meanwhile, they portrayed themselves as protectors of the party line. The Komsomol official Rakhmanov warned in his speech that the line of the party must be the line of the League and that the Komsomol would fight against any deviations from this line. This assertion was greeted by 'stormy applause'. In an act of false magnanimity, Rakhmanov announced that the Komsomol Central Committee did not consider the League Central Council's line to be deviationist, but his words rang hollow in the context of the congress. For his part, Yaroslavsky warned of factionalism: 'most dangerous [for the League is the possibility], if in our own midst, unanimity on issues of conducting [anti-religious] work did not exist'.

Both sides frequently framed their criticism in terms of deviation by individuals from the correct institutional lines. We find the culturalists Stukov and Yaroslavsky trying to patch up relations with the Komsomol by arguing that Bukhartsev's position was not that of his organization, although *Komsomol'skaya Pravda* quickly closed ranks and denied any division. Yaroslavsky later blamed the poor state of relations between the Central League Council and the Moscow League organization on perhaps the congress's leading irritant, Comrade Galaktionov. Yaroslavsky noted that where disagreements existed, they reflected the mistakes of individuals, not of the entire League. Taking aim at the hostile Moscow organization, Yaroslavsky charged that if Galaktionov were to renounce his anarchical phrases, anti-religious work in Moscow would benefit. Another League leader, F. Putintsev, joined the fray by calling Galaktionov 'illiterate' in his work. He charged that Galaktionov was not a Marxist, and continued ranting until interrupted by cries from the floor, 'enough about Galaktionov'. Putintsev levelled a final charge against Galaktionov that in later years could be deadly: he claimed that Galaktionov's misinterpretation of sectarianism amounted to attacking a position of Comrade Stalin's voiced in 1925.

From the other side, the Komsomol Central Committee's representative to the Congress, Rakhmanov, adopted similar tactics. His threats to the League lurked thinly veiled, if at all, behind constructive criticism and presentation of an olive branch. Rakhmanov spoke of the 'unhealthy atmosphere' linking the League to the Komsomol and *Komsomol'skaya Pravda*: 'We think that the All-Union Congress of the League of the Godless will renounce any unhealthy attitudes held by individual delegates, and find a way to cooperate'. Rakhmanov charged that it was only logical to find errant individuals in such a large organization as the

League. He admitted that the Komsomol had such individuals and battled with them. The League, he argued, should welcome the Komsomol's assistance in correcting individual members' mistakes. Rakhmanov was careful also to criticize anti-religious zealots, and to condemn exclusive reliance on administrative methods. On this issue, he claimed, the League and Komsomol Central Councils were united. In a more partisan turn, Rakhmanov defended Bukhartsev and charged that the latter's speech had been rudely interrupted; Rakhmanov added that he was sad to find 'people [at the Congress] who were trying to persecute the Komsomol'. This method of criticism, part of the broader Bolshevik emphasis on self-criticism, suggests that, in the evolving Soviet political culture, institutions could never err; only individuals in those institutions, or even leading them, could stray. This convention permitted the system to continue operating without criticism while individuals were held ultimately responsible for institutional practices beyond their control.

Subordination to the party constituted yet another powerful factor in Soviet political dialogue, and one that was clearly in evidence at the congress. Countless declarations of fealty to the party by Godless delegates indicate that party control had become a given, an abstraction unquestioningly accepted and integrated into the prevailing rhetoric. Certainly this understanding of the League's function was implicit in the numerous demands that the party line be followed exactly. On the level of explicit subordination, Yaroslavsky spoke of the League working closely with, i.e. under, the agitation-propaganda section of the party Central Committee; at another point he argued that local League cells should be under the direction of party and Komsomol members. Rakhmanov's insistence that the line of the party be the line of the League implied subordination, and by their repeated calls for the League to be *plus royaliste que le roi* (more royalist than the king) the interventionists sought to have the party, rather than the all but bourgeois educators of the League Central Council and the Commissariat of Enlightenment, direct the activities of the League. Certainly the party was strongly represented at the congress, and the party fraction had nominated the slate for the congress's Presidium and the League Central Council.[11]

By mid-1929, then, many of the hallmarks of the Stalinist political culture were already in place. On this level we see the insistence on a single, Leninist policy, implemented by centralized, factionless institutions led by the Communist Party. On another level, however, we can identify the continued existence as late as mid-1929 of quite conflicting policy alternatives being debated within this narrow, and presumably ever narrowing, framework. This complex situation simultaneously reflected and paralleled broader developments in society that influenced both the disagreements over policy and the pressures affecting all delegates to the Godless congress to conform to a certain style of presentation. As for the policy differences, the legacy of past experience has already been discussed. More contemporary sources of conflict, with positions analogous to the ones held among the Godless, characterized the Soviet political realm.

The culturalist–interventionist debate mirrored the concomitant conflict at the apex of the political structure between the so-called Right opposition led by Nikolai Bukharin and the party line arbitrarily determined by Stalin. Bukharin favoured a more gradual, evolutionary transition to socialism, and his programme served as an analogue for the culturalists in the realm of high politics. In contrast, Stalin favoured a rapid social transformation according to the First Five-Year Plan. Stalin's vision of social change was highly politicized and, as such, it underpinned the zeal of the anti-religious interventionists.

This struggle for control of the party was raging exactly at the moment when the Godless convened their congress, and appreciation of the congress debates is impossible without understanding the backdrop against which they occurred. Immediately before the congress the Right had suffered a devastating setback.[12] At a combined plenum of the Central Committee and the Party Control Commission in April 1929, Bukharin was relieved of his duties as editor of *Pravda* and as Secretary of the Comintern. When Bukharin addressed the League of the Godless congress as the official representative from the CC and the Politburo (from which he would be removed in November 1929), his slide from power could not have gone unnoticed by the delegates. Although only a few references were made to Stalin during the congress, they identified him as *the* leader of the party, and a last-minute call for him to appear before the delegates resulted in their disappointment when informed that he could not attend.

While the development of the anti-religious campaign was closely tied to the political matrix in the party, it was perhaps even more dependent upon any decisions taken at higher levels on the direction of rural economic policy. Everyone at the congress knew that religion was primarily a rural issue. Whatever general policy the party adopted towards the countryside would directly determine the nature of anti-religious activity. Bukharin's vision of gradual evolution of private rural farmers into socialist producers corresponded to the culturalists' perspective. For the interventionists, an activist policy to collectivize agriculture would represent authorization to eradicate religion as they saw fit: Like the political battle, with which it was intricately, bound, the economic issue was being decided just as the congress met. The First Five-Year Plan as presented to the party in April 1929 envisioned moderate growth of cooperative and collective farms, but individual farming, with high taxes and other pressures brought to bear on the dreaded kulaks, was to have remained a major element in the rural economy. At the time of the congress in mid-June, official Soviet policy foresaw a pressured but still organic development of the rural sector where brute force would not be invoked to achieve social transformation. The threshold to a new policy of greater intervention seems to have been crossed at the *end* of June, some two weeks after the congress closed, when the Central Committee issued new policy guidelines that extended control over the peasantry and strengthened the collective farm movement. During that summer reports of forced collectivization initiated locally began to be received, but the *sploshnaya kollektivizatsiya* (total collectivization) was yet to come.[13] Thus, the April plenum and the Sixteenth Party Conference (on the economy) that immediately followed the plenum left the future of the countryside in some question. Even as these economic debates transpired, tension grew as forced procurement and the resistance of the peasantry resulted in a crescendo of violence. This was the uncertain and fluid context in which the League held its congress. The congress did not bristle with discussion of collectivization, and although the 'socialist offensive in the countryside' was on every delegate's lips, the exact form of this campaign, that is the degree of intervention, remained unclear.

Given these divisions in the political realm, and considering the inherited conflict within the anti-religious camp, the debates between the Godless become comprehensible. What is perhaps more interesting is that while these divisions continued to exist, the pressures acting on Bolshevik political culture to arrive at a Stalinist mode of consensus were also clearly in evidence, not just at the congress as indicated here, but throughout Soviet political society. For instance, in regard to 'deviationism', the Sixteenth Conference in April 1929 had announced a general purge of the party to remove anyone determined ever to have opposed the party's position on any issue. Less than two, months later, when the congress met, the press bristled with discussion of the purge, which had been expanded to include non-party individuals working in Soviet bureaucracies. Following closely after the Shakhty trial of 'wreckers' in 1928, discussion of the new round of purging during the summer of 1929 gave a particular potency to labels like 'deviationist' and 'appeaser'. Because the rules for purging were so broad and subjective, these labels became powerful political weapons distinct from any actual threat to the Soviet system.

The April 1929 Plenum also influenced how the delegates to the Godless congress perceived, or were supposed to perceive, the social transformation occurring in the Soviet Union. At this plenum Stalin launched his attack on Bukharin, in part for not understanding that as the Soviet Union neared socialism, hostile capitalist elements in society would redouble their subversive efforts. He pointed to the Shakhty trial as an example and warned of wreckers operating throughout society. Stalin's thesis of an 'intensifying class struggle' as socialism advanced served as the dominant rhetorical framework to explain the rising tension and open conflict in Soviet society. Although the policy implications of the April plenum remained potentially unclear to those below, the intensification thesis rapidly permeated the level of the Soviet apparatus represented by the Godless and set the tone for their congress less than two months later. The rapid adoption of this catch-all explanation for the difficulties facing Soviet society suggests that the existing political culture welcomed sophisms that, implausible as they might have been, offered complete and vivid explanations of social development.

The call for centralization repeatedly aired at the congress also reflected a similar strain in Bolshevik thought, both economic and political. The very essence of Bolshevik modernization plans meant centralizing the management of the economy to remove all elements of uncontrolled choice in production. Many delegates referred to integrating anti-religious activity into the five-year plan, to make anti-religious achievements as much a part of the plan as steel production. Centralization was also inherent in the Bolshevik political ethos. Lenin had insisted on centralized control of the party under tsarism, and once in power, the party had adopted an official plank forbidding intra-party factions at the X Congress in 1921. Stalin's outmanoeuvering of his opponents of the leadership during the 1920s was framed specifically in terms of observing party discipline. Factionalism constituted a serious breach of party unity, and Bukharin felt the potency of this weapon when, in addition to all his other sins, he was charged with contacting a former Bolshevik Party leader, Lev Kamenev, after the latter had been politically isolated.

The party's assumed control of the League indicates that the same totalist pretensions manifested by the party in regard to the economic and political spheres also extended to the realm of social policy, that is, beyond the party's preview narrowly defined. These totalist pretensions meant that the League of the Godless, an ostensibly private organization, would serve ideally as an extension of the party in an area of society not directly arrogated to itself. Whether the party achieved total control of the social sphere has been much debated, and so far the answer remains uncertain.[14] What is clear is that in regard to religion, the intention was there.

*Conclusion*

The conflict between the Komsomol and the League certainly involved many elements: a history of confrontation, institutional tension and genuinely differing understandings of religion and its role in Soviet society. When we consider these arguments in broader terms, however, we cannot but note a significant division among Bolshevik activists over the more general issue of, how Soviet society should be managed. To shed light on the meaning of the culturalist–interventionist division, one might return to the nearly parallel debate in the 1920s over economic growth between the 'geneticists' and the 'teleologists'.[15] Like the geneticists, the culturalists thought in terms of evolution, organic development, and a pace of change based on honest recognition of constraints – in this case, the existence of large numbers of potentially hostile believers. While the culturalists advocated a hands-on approach to governing by which interference in individuals' lives for the purpose of directing their thinking and behaviour, was justified, even demanded, by their ideology, this effort would employ the media of words, education, persuasion and propaganda. It recognized that production of genuine atheists would require diligent work and patience.

The teleologists and interventionists, however, were less interested in method than in achieving a particular goal. Saddled with the exclusive blinders of political ideology, the interventionists perceived the problem of religion in a more direct manner. To destroy religious sects, close churches and imprison priests would achieve the goal of an atheist society. Goal preceded method, even if this method harboured potentially destabilizing consequences. Like the culturalists, the interventionists justified interference in the lives of individuals, but unlike the culturalists, they would use force and violence. They recognized no limits, organic or other, except the *élan* of their activists. Limitless faith justified the use of any means to construct socialism.[16] In the end the teleologists prevailed in the economic realm as Stalin opted for nearly fantastic growth rates to the First Five-Year Plan, to be realized through rapid industrialisation and forced collectivization.

Who emerged victorious in the anti-religious debates? In light of Yaroslavsky's position, it comes as no surprise that the resolutions adopted by the congress tended to support the culturalist programme.[17] Upon reading them, one is struck by how formulaically they were crafted. Here too, certain conventions in the proclamation of policy had been adopted: loud opening statements in line with official dogma, followed several paragraphs later by carefully phrased qualifications and criticisms. The main resolution on anti-religious work opened with fire and brimstone: religious organizations were calculating counterrevolutionary groups actively seeking through devious machinations to depose Bolshevism. With only minimal contradiction, the resolution then hailed the progress made against religion in the Soviet period. These matters now aside, the rest of the resolution addressed specific issues such as combating religious holidays, propaganda work among women and youth, better training of activist, further development of propaganda forms such as art, film, lectures and museums – all points on the culturalist agenda. The congress' resolution on sects adopted a similar tack. The, opening points proclaimed that sects were the weapon of capitalist elements in society; next it noted the general success of socialism in overcoming sectarianism. The rest of the document reveals an approach to sects that incorporated the educative, propagandistic approach to combating religion, while still acknowledging the role played by administrative action. The other resolutions on agitation among national minorities, youth, peasants and women did not differ significantly from this pattern.

The culturalists may have won the battle at this congress, but ironically they lost the larger war. Changes in the legal status of religion in 1929 and the forced closing of churches and exiling of priests during collectivization and dekulakization struck a tremendous blow against popular religious expression. More broadly, the turmoil of the cultural revolution, in which the Komsomol played a leading role in undermining institutions and organizations it saw as bureaucratic and/or bourgeois, and the eventual full crystallization of Stalinism during the 1930s, meant that administrative measures and compulsion would ultimately play a key role in Soviet efforts to engineer a socialist society. The fate of the Godless in the 1930s is not our immediate concern, however. More important is what we can learn from this snapshot of the Soviet apparatus during the crucial summer of 1929.

First, ferment and division characterized the Soviet polity, but the causes of this situation are more difficult to identify clearly. Several have been suggested in the Fitzpatrick volume on cultural revolution.[18] Certainly generational factors may have played a role.[19] Although there is no indication of the ages of Galaktionov, Rakhmanov or Bukhartsev, they were hardly likely to be as old as Yaroslavsky, Lunacharsky (who were, respectively, 51 and 54 at the time of the congress), or other members of the central League leadership. An impatience among younger activists with the evolution of society in the NEP period could understandably have resulted in a determination to take matters into hand immediately and to reject the slower, education-based methods advocated by older revolutionaries. Whatever the source, the hostilities at the Second Congress of the League of the Godless revealed a divided activist body with opposing sides clashing in a highly charged atmosphere. This should provide further evidence that the cultural revolution of 1928–32 cannot be explained entirely as a phenomenon inspired and directed from above. While legal and constitutional changes in the status of religion in 1929 sent signals from the state to the activists below, there was clearly a movement already present within the anti-religious community for a shift towards a more directly interventionist, more openly political management of society. The state, defined here as the uppermost echelon of political authority, was either in accord with or encouraging its lower-level activists, especially the Komsomol, against its own middle-level bureaucracy.[20]

A second, closely related, conclusion concerns the nature of politics in the early Stalin period. The debate at the congress reveals that, despite the rapid internalization of certain political and rhetorical conventions later closely identified with Stalinism, the level of Soviet apparatus represented at the congress was not without its clashes and spirited debates. Nor do these debates portray a society moving inevitably towards collectivization and Stalin's dictatorship. While even a gathering such as this was dominated by important officials such as Yaroslavsky and Rakhmanov, the text of the stenographic report yields extensive, if less articulate, debate. Frenzy gripped the activist body, and its eventual outcome remained hidden from general view. There were no clear signposts to the future, and although each delegate heralded the rapid advance of socialism, their speeches did not assume the advent of Stalinism. Again, it is worth noting that a social transformation on the scale undertaken in the Soviet Union had never before been attempted. The acrimonious debates at the congress indicate that the activists did not share a vision of inevitable development (beyond vague conceptions of socialism) based on forced collectivization and a cult of the Leader. Their debates reveal, however, a political culture strongly predisposed to the dictates of a doctrine as expressed by the party line. Once articulated, these tenets would become unassailable, and the key challenge centred on being in the position to have one's interpretation of the party line generally accepted.

Thirdly, because the broad ideology motivating these activists insisted on the eventual eradication of traditional religious beliefs and practices, the debates over achieving this goal shed light on the process of secularization as part of a campaign of social engineering. As manifested at the congress, the preferred Bolshevik means to the end of an atheist society stood in stark contrast to the Marxist analysis of religion. Both culturalists and interventionists clashed on a theoretical level with orthodox Marxism that interpreted religion and culture as reflections of a particular mode of production.[21] Changes in the mode of production would result in changes in society and religion. The achievement of communism would spell the final demise of religion that had earlier served to distract workers from the class struggle. What the culturalists proposed to do in the 1920s represented a reversal of causality. They argued that attacking religion could be done independently of material circumstance and could even aid the construction of communal production. While Lunacharsky acknowledged that only the full implementation of socialism would result in the complete eradication of religion, he continued:

> This does not mean that we should say that, as long as we have not changed the economic conditions and everyday conditions from which religion grows inevitably, there is nothing for us to say about methods of cultural influence on

people who are the victims of religion, or political influence in the form of a most direct battle against those people who sow religious prejudices and who reap the harvest of their evil crops.

In this passage, Lunacharsky protected himself by justifying both cultural and political forms of agitation. Referring directly to Marx, Lunacharsky spoke of the need to change consciousness since it lagged behind the material structure, but 'sometimes it outpaces the speed of things'. Lunacharsky argued that changing consciousness through enlightenment and cultural work was a pressing need even after a workers' government had taken political control of the nation. To wait for socialism to destroy religion meant rejection of Leninism in favour of Menshevism. Here was the basic justification of propaganda work throughout the 1920s: consciousness was not dependent entirely on economic circumstances. In fact, the position of superstructure and base had been reversed.

Similar though less sophisticated explanations were advanced by the interventionists to justify their activism. They claimed that priests and religious leaders were deliberately undermining the reconstruction of the countryside and sabotaging industry. To expunge these harmful elements would advance socialism. This perhaps was the single point of agreement between the culturalists and interventionists. While both paid lip service to the importance of economic relations, both in fact followed agendas that posited the superstructure as more important. Both groups followed closely on the coat-tails of Lenin, who, in light of Russia's position in the international economic system and her particular development, had justified a political coup in a country that was unprepared in Marxist developmental terms for socialism. Twelve years later the country was still unprepared, and Soviet activists of varying persuasions were ready to advocate political or cultural methods of work. By this time, of course, industrialization had begun and the cooperative movement and collective farms were appearing in the countryside. These developments contributed to the contemporary justification for anti-religious activity by allowing the charge that the clergy and religious organizations were obstructing the building of socialism by opposing cooperatives and collective farms.

The delegates to the congress rallied around two distinct methods of overcoming religion, both broadly fitting into a Leninist framework, and both having rejected the traditional Marxist prescription for religion. Clearly, the Soviet view of the secularization process turned on highly engaged strategies, one employing education, the other favouring physical intevention. How do these methods compare with other efforts at secularization? As in the case of the USSR, the best opportunities to examine rapid, planned secularization campaigns are to be found in those instances when a government comes to power armed with an ideology hostile to religion. In modern history, this has necessarily meant a revolutionary situation such as occurred in France, China or Cuba.[22] While these revolutions were firmly rooted in their respective indigenous cultures, analysis of the stragegies employed to combat religion in these cases and in the USSR should further our understanding both of secularization and social engineering. Is there a similar pattern of anti-clericalism evinced in all these instances? Do the ruling revolutionaries in each case agree on the exact nature of the atheism to replace the inherited religion? To what extent does the culture of each nation influence or even determine the anti-religious strategies employed by revolutionaries? French anti-clericalism might parallel the position of the Soviet 'inter-ventionists', but the rapid creation of secular rituals in France and the genuflecting before the God of Reason exhibited several assumptions apparently shared by the 'culturalists'. Even without the comparative examples, the zigzag pattern of Soviet anti-religious policy up to 1929 should serve as a corrective against assuming a single, natural pattern of socially engineered secularization.

Finally, exegesis of the congress stenographic report reveals that the rhetoric employed during the debates did not entirely serve the instru-mental function of articulating ideological and institutional positions. It also played a crucial role in those debates as the important high ground which both sides sought to control. The frequent and indiscriminate use of Leninist rhetoric to fight internal battles alerts us to the subjectivity of this language. Certainly the battle for 'Lenin' represented genuine ideological differences, and the tenets of centralization and subordination to the party reflected very real historical conditions, but the struggle to control the meaning of words such as 'Leninist', 'socialist', 'the party line' and 'deviationism' provided the framework in which actual differences in policy were debated. While the divisions were real, their expression in vivid terms close to the heart of Bolshevism exaggerated those disagreements and altered the differences between policy alternatives. There existed a tension between the necessity to operate within a narrow framework and the desire to set out a distinct programme. Because justification of almost any partisan position could draw on a variety of statements by Lenin and the confusing legacy of anti-religious experience, the battle to determine Lenin's *real* position, the *real* party line on religion, etc., came to dominate the congress; hence the efforts to invoke Lenin's name, to declare one's loyalty to the party line whatever it might be and to charge one's opponents with deviationism.

There is no reason to believe that this tension between rhetorical constraints and the need to express differing policy views was limited to the anti-religious field. Indeed, all regime activists had to operate within this rhetorical framework. Whereas the Fitzpatrick volume on the cultural revolution has identified a number of professions in which tensions rose to the surface, we ought to consider returning and examining the early Stalin period anew to seek additional evidence of distinctive policy disagreements glossed over by a thin coating of rhetorically forged, ideological consensus.

More generally, the language of Soviet life and political development in the 1920s and 1930s provides a remarkably rich field for analysis. Our understanding of this period may well benefit from a closer examination of Soviet political and social discourse. The Soviet Union at this time offered a vast array of stunning images purveyed through a variety of media, such as photographs, rituals, portraits, parades and the daily language and practice of political life.[23] In one specific matter, the leaders of the League showed themselves aware of the power of images propagated through language. The proposal from a Northern Region delegate to change the League's name to the League of Militant (*voinstvuyushchikh*) Godless elicited no reaction at the time, but soon after the congress closed on 15 June 1929 the new name had been adopted as an appropriate title for a social organization embroiled in the cultural revolution.

NOTES

[Reorganized and renumbered from the original.]

I would like to thank Diane P. Koenker, Andrew Vernon and Benjamin Uroff for their comments on earlier drafts of this paper. My research was supported by a fellowship from the Russian and East European Center, University of Illinois.

1. No comprehensive study of the Soviet anti-religious movement in the 1920s exists. Numerous Western works have charted the course of the Russian Orthodox Church under Soviet rule, but far fewer have examined efforts to promote atheism in the first decades of Soviet rule. Although dated, the best introduction to the subject can be found in John Shelton Curtiss, *The Russian Church and the Soviet State* (Boston, MA, 1953). Richard Stites has a chapter on the Godless in his study of Soviet utopianism, *Revolutionary Dreams* (New York, 1989). Glennys Young, 'Rural Religion and Soviet Power' (PhD dissertation, University of California, Berkeley, CA, 1989), charts elements of the anti-religious campaign. Dmitri Pospielovsky's three-volume history, *A History of Soviet Atheism in Theory and Practice, and the Believer* (New York, 1987, 1988); vol. 1: *A History of Marxist–Leninist Atheism and Soviet Anti-religious Policies*, vol. 2: *Anti-religious Campaigns and Persecutions*; vol. 3: *Soviet Studies on the Church and the Believer's Response to Atheism*, focuses primarily on the post-Second World War but devotes some attention, and unsparing criticism to Soviet policy to the interwar period. See also Joan Delaney, 'The Origins of Soviet Anti-religious Organizations', in Richard Marshall, Jr., ed., *Aspects of Religion in the Soviet Union* (Chicago, IL, 1971); Gregory Massell, *The Surrogate Proletariat* (Princeton, NJ, 1974); Christel Lane,

*The Rites of Rulers* (Cambridge, 1981) and David Powell, *Anti-religious Propaganda in the Soviet Union* (Cambridge, MA, 1975).

Soviet coverage is extremely limited and concentrates on official proclamations and programmes rather than on believer response or continuing popular religious expression.

2. The legal framework and policy guidelines established in the first few years of Soviet power remained in force until the end of the 1920s. In 1928 the Commissariat of Enlightenment replaced its 'areligious education' policy with an 'anti-religious' policy. In April 1929 the decree 'On Religious Associations' further limited opportunities for religious expression; and just one month before the opening of the League of the Godless Congress, the Sixteenth Congress of Soviets altered the Soviet Constitution to remove freedom of religious propaganda from constitutional protection. See Joshua Rothenburg, 'The Legal Status of Religion in the Soviet Union', in Marshall, Jr., ed., *Aspects of Religion*, pp. 61–102.

3. In the mid-1920s several factions of clergy vied for administrative control of the Orthodox church. The 'Renovationists' Struggle', though it involved high church politics, did not constitute a new period in religious life as experienced at the parish level. See Curtiss, *The Russian Church and the Soviet State*, pp. 129–95, and Dmitri Pospielovsky, *The Russian Church under the Soviet Regime, 1917–1982* (New York, 1984), pp. 43–162.

4. The Komosomol presented itself as the ideal vehicle for anti-religious agitation. Inspired to recreate Soviet society and energized by young activists, the Komsomol should have taken the lead in such enterprises as secularization, and indeed it orchestrated burlesque Christmas and Easter Carnivals in 1922 and 1923. The carnivals included disruption of Christmas services and assaults on worshippers. This form of direct confrontation, however, was deemed by the party's anti-religious commission to be counterproductive and shortly thereafter ceased in its original form. Perhaps this early reining in of the Komsomol explains its failure to become the institutional centre of anti-religious efforts, but for whatever reason, when the Komsomol returned to the anti-religious debate as a vocal participant at the end of the 1920s, it advocated a radical, direct action approach.

5. Yaroslavsky (1878–1943), born Minei Izraelevich Gubelmann, played a key role in the appearance of Soviet anti-religious propaganda. He edited and penned numerous anti-religious propaganda oversaw the establishment of the League, controlled the Second Congress, and continued as the leading Soviet anti-religious figure into the 1930s. In addition to his anti-religious responsibilities, Yaroslavsky served on many editorial boards and wrote a number of histories of the Communist Party. As a member of the Party Control Commission, he appears to have been an enthusiastic inquisitor during the Purges in the 1930s.

6. Culture, or the lack thereof (*bezkul'tur'e*), is a frequently encountered term in debates in the 1920s and 1930s. It signifies something far broader than the English usage of words. Not limited to one's exposure to high culture, culturedness indicates a much broader measurement of development encompassing knowledge, behaviour and attitudes.

7. One sees here remnants of the Godbuilding controversy early in the century involving Lunacharsky, Lenin, Gorky and Bogdanov. See Christopher Read, *Religion, Revolution, and the Russian Intelligentsia, 1900–1912* (Totowa, NJ,

1979), pp. 77–95. Pospielovksy's rendition of the culturalist argument can be found in vol. 1, pp. 51–2.

8. For a description of the Komsomol's Easter and Christmas campaigns, see Pospielovsky, vol. 2, p. 44, and Stites, *Revolutionary Dreams*, pp. 109–10.

9. On this development, see Nina Tumarkin, *Lenin Lives! The Lenin Cult in Soviet Russia* (Cambridge, MA, 1983).

10. The Lenin quotation reads: 'the centre of gravity for us has shifted to culture building, to peaceful, organizational, cultural work' (p. 273).

11. According to Kobetsky of the Mandate Commission, of the 956 congress delegates, 460 were members or candidate members of the party, and 50 more belonged to the Komsomol (p. 336); we may presume that party representation in the Congress Presidium was even greater.

12. As early as 1928 Stalin had targeted the Moscow Party organization leader, Nikolai Uglanov, for removal because of his support for the right. It is of interest to note the contrast between Uglanov's alliance with Bukharin at one level and the hostile attitude of the lower-level Moscow anti-religious activists towards the gradualist League Central Council.

13. Moshe Lewin, *Russian Peasants and Soviet Power: A Study of Collectivisation* (London, 1968), p. 406. See also Lynn Viola, 'The Campaign to Eliminate the Kulak as a Class, Winter 1929–1930: A Reevaluation of the Legislation', *Slavic Review*, 45, 3 (Fall, 1986), pp. 508, 512, 522.

14. For a first step into this voluminous literature, see the discussions of Stalinism in *Russian Review*, 45 (1986), pp. 357–413, and 46 (1987), pp. 375–421.

15. See Alexander Erlich, *The Soviet Industrialization Debate: 1924–1928* (Cambridge, MA, 1960).

16. As one Bolshevik activist later recalled: 'With the rest of my generation, I firmly believed that the ends justified the means. Our great goal was the universal triumph of Communism, and for the sake of that goal everything was permissible ... And to hesitate or doubt about all this was to give in to "intellectual squeamishness" and "stupid liberalism", the attributes of people who "could not see the forest for the trees"'. Lev Kopelev, *To be Preserved Forever*, trans. Anthony Austin (Philadelphia, PA, 1971), p. 11.

17. For Pospielovsky's commentary on the congress resolutions, see vol. 1, pp. 55–60.

18. Sheila Fitzpatrick, ed., *Cultural Revolution in Russia* (Bloomington, IN, 1978).

19. Of 920 delegates, 18 per cent were less than 23 years old, 63 per cent were between 23 and 40, and 19 per cent were older than 40.

20. Sheila Fitzpatrick, 'Cultural Revolution as Class War', in Fitzpatrick, *Cultural Revolution*, p. 25.

21. David McLellan, *Marxism and Religion* (London, 1987).

22. On the example perhaps closest to the Soviet, see Mona Azouf's entry on 'Revolutionary Religion' in Francois Furet and Mona Azouf, eds, *A Critical Dictionary of the French Revolution*, trans. by Arthur Goldhammer (Cambridge, MA, 1989); Suzanne Desan, *Reclaiming the Sacred: Lay Religions and Popular Politics in Revolutionary France* (Ithaca, NY, 1990).

23. Lane, *The Rites of Rulers*, analyses Soviet rituals in the post-Second World War period but she discusses their appearance in the 1920s and 1930s. There is also the substantial work of Richard Stites in *Revolutinary Dreams*, 'Adorning the Russian Revolution: The Primary Symbols of Bolshevism, 1917–1918', *Sbornik of the Group for the Study of the Russian Revolution*, 10 (Summer, 1984), and 'Iconoclastic Currents in the Russian Revolution: Destroying and Preserving the Past' in Abbott Gleason, Peter Kenez and Richard Stites (eds), *Bolshevik Culture: Experiment and Order in the Russian Revolution* (Bloomington, IN, 1985).

# III   Industrialization and Collectivization

## THE DRIVE TO INDUSTRIALIZE

For his many admirers and supporters over the decades industrialization was Stalin's greatest achievement. Without it the Soviet Union would have been powerless before the Hitlerite onslaught and not only Soviet but European civilization would have been at risk. The negative features of the process – its inefficiency and waste but above all the cruelties associated with it in the form of collectivization, famine and the Gulag – were dismissed as 'mistakes' or, more significantly, unavoidable costs justified by the ultimate victory. We will return to aspects of this debate in later chapters, pausing only, for the moment, to comment that the argument presupposes that the 'collateral damage' of mass death somehow contributed to rather than endangered final success.

The fact that the Soviet leadership decided to embark on an industrialization programme is no surprise. In the first place, it rose out of the logic of productionism. If Soviet Russia had to become an advanced, wealthy country in order to create a basis for socialism, only industry could lift it up. The process would strengthen the crucial proletariat (working class) and weaken the private-property-loving peasantry who would also be attracted to socialism by the advantages of large-scale collective farming and the availability of the modern technique and equipment that modernization would bring. There were other practical imperatives, too. In the forefront of these was the fundamental administrative issue facing any Russian government, tsarist, Soviet or capitalist – defence of a sprawling territory with no natural borders. The urgency of the question was heightened, in Bolshevik minds, by the history of foreign intervention in the revolutionary wars of 1918–20. Germany, France, Britain, Austria-Hungary, Turkey, Finland, Poland, Japan and the United States had all sent in significant armed forces and controlled or helped themselves to slices of territory of the former Russian Empire. Around the tenth anniversary of the revolution in 1927 the fear began to grow in Moscow that the capitalist world might awake from its post-world-war hangover and make a renewed attempt to overthrow its upstart communist competitor. From the mid-1920s military chiefs were warning the leadership of possible weakness and, with rising threats from an unstable Germany to its west and a collapsing China, eyed hungrily by a resurgent Japan, in the east, urgent action appeared to be needed.

The question, then, was not 'should the USSR industrialize?' since all the ideological, political, economic and strategic indicators pointed in the same direction, rather it was one of 'how should the USSR industrialize?' and that was a very different one. In the 1920s Soviet Russia was the site of a vast and intriguing debate about just how one might go about such a challenging process. Strange as it may seem, the economic sphere in Soviet Russia in the 1920s was rent by arguments comparable to those we have just encountered in the realm of religious policy. As Peris mentioned in his conclusion, the debate between what he terms 'culturalists' and 'interventionists' (in other words, moderates and militants) 'nearly parallels' that of the 'geneticists' and 'teleologists' in the economic sphere. Geneticists stood for gradual, step-by-step transformation of the economy, teleologists for one big heave into socialism. Underneath these divisions lay the left/right split in the party which persisted despite the expulsion of Trotsky and his exile in 1929. It was also significant that, not least because of the shortage of qualified Bolsheviks, many of the leading voices in this debate came from former Mensheviks, Socialist Revolutionaries and non-committed experts like the Orthodox priest Pavel Florensky, a mathematical and scientific genius who worked in the economic apparatus. Tragically, despite their honest and conscientious contribution to the process, Stalin's cultural revolution, aimed at tightening up ideological orthodoxy, and the search for scapegoats to blame for problems made such people immensely vulnerable and by the late 1920s and early 1930s many of them found themselves in the camps.

Nonetheless, in the mid 1920s the debate raged. On the one hand there was Bukharin and his supporters. For them, the mixture of state domination of 'the commanding heights' of the economy – large-scale industry, finance, taxation, transport, foreign trade – with limited restoration of the market, especially for small-scale crafts and services and for peasant agriculture, was the route chosen by Lenin for dynamic transformation to socialism. Though slow – Bukharin, ill-advisedly, comparing the speed of transition to that of a peasant pony – it was sure. For the impatient party militants, particularly veterans of the initial revolutionary struggles when they appeared to have conquered the whole of the old Russian world, the pace was too slow. They pointed out that NEP encouraged the growth of anti-socialist elements. In the forefront were petty traders, known as Nepmen (though many were women), and supposedly wealthier peasants, known as kulaks about whom we shall say more later. The critics of NEP had plenty of ammunition to throw at Bukharin. The maintenance of the relationship was not easy and at times seemed to be diverting resources the wrong way in that state prices for grain had to be raised from time to time to stimulate peasants to market more agricultural products. This drained resources the left wanted to gamble on a rush for industrialization. Bukharin, also armed with the last injunction of Lenin, that the working class should not attack the peasantry again as it had done through war, communism and the requisitioning of grain, stood firm for his line.

However, encouraging peasants to 'enrich themselves' as Bukharin exhorted in 1925 did not excite the militants. They were also discontented with the apparent lack of ambition of the leaders in reconciling themselves to the fate of building 'socialism in one country' rather than the more intoxicating goal of world revolution. Bukharin scoffed at such critics pointing, quite rightly, to the decline of revolutionary potential around the globe as the instability of the postwar period receded, for a while at least. The left, however, pressed for a more energetic policy. Obviously, a key issue for industrialization was investment. Even socialism could not develop industry without primary accumulation of resources. In Russia's case, historically, there had been no spare capital to use. Where centuries of foreign trade had prepared Britain and France for industrialization Russia had always had a major shortage of capital. The tsarist regime had resorted to foreign loans but substantial foreign involvement in the Soviet economy was precluded by Soviet ideological fear of dependence on capitalism and capitalist reluctance to invest in its potential rival. In the event, there was significant foreign involvement in the Soviet economy at various times. Lenin himself had encouraged it saying that Soviet contracts would support capitalism in the way that a rope supports a hanged man. Nonetheless, no one believed it to be desirable even if it might be unavoidable. Looking for internal sources of capital the eyes of the left-wing economists, with Preobrazhensky in the forefront, fell on the perceived enemy – the peasants. The NEP system envisaged relatively gentle pressure on peasants both through taxation and through turning them into a market for industrial products such as fertilizers and tractors. The left, however, took a narrower view. In a much-quoted and much-misunderstood phrase, Preobrazhensky described peasants as 'internal colonies'. What he meant was that, where imperialists accumulated from their overseas possessions, Soviet Russia had to accumulate from its internal sources. While he was not advocating a full-scale colonial war against the peasants he, and the left in general (whose political leader was Trotsky) called for more energetic pressure to be applied to the peasantry so that great industrial projects could proceed.

Curiously, the political defeat of the left as a party faction, in 1927, and the ensuing expulsion of its leaders, Kamenev and Zinoviev as well as Trotsky, did not take the heat out of the debate. Advocates of rapid industrialization were just as vociferous in 1928, perhaps more so, than in 1926.

Alongside this debate was a parallel discussion of planning. It was assumed that some form of state planning would be needed to encourage the growth of industry. The logic was that socialism was supposed to be an economic system based on reason rather than the arbitrariness of the market and that planning was the instrument whereby reason would direct the economy. At the time, state planning was coming into vogue not only in Soviet Russia but also in western Europe under the influence of the experience of war economies, reconstruction and, later, financial instability. However, it was in Russia that the debate was pursued most energetically. As Peris mentioned, there were two schools here, 'geneticists' who believed in the gradual evolution of planning on an initially modest scale, and 'teleologists' who wanted a short, sharp shock, to break through the initial barriers of backwardness.

How did this complex of debates result in the process of industrialization as it unfolded? In the first place, Stalin, though he had frequently shown signs of impatience with non-party specialists, nepmen and kulaks, had not joined the left in denouncing NEP. In fact, 'socialism in one country' is a slogan inextricably associated with Stalin. Trotsky roundly denounced him for timidity. By 1929, however, industrialization was advancing at an even greater pace than that envisaged by Preobrazhensky. The transformation had come about through several factors interacting with one another. The 'war scare' of 1927 focused attention on the potential strategic weakness of the country and thereby raised the stakes for industrialization. Second, NEP itself appeared to be in trouble. Grain marketings in 1928 were insufficient and rationing had to be applied. The Bukharinite solution of yet another substantial rise in grain prices was a step too far for an increasing number of party members. Instead, experiments in forcing the pace of establishing collective farms were tried out in the Urals and western Siberia. The Politburo, riven by division between the Bukharinite right and the industrializing left, adopted the First Five-Year Plan in 1928, but it was only in 1929 that planning turned decisively in the direction of teleologists rather than geneticists. At the April 1929 Central Committee Plenum Bukharin was defeated and a new wave of rapid industrialization, collectivization and enforced cultural revolution began.

Ironically, however, the onslaught the country suffered from this triple whammy owed nothing to planning in any real sense. Instead, it had the format of an effort to raise oneself out of a bog by pulling on one's own bootstraps. In Bukharin's despairing words, the leadership were trying to 'build today's factories with tomorrow's bricks'. Kurt Schultz's article could not provide a better example of this plus the already-mentioned Bolshevik determination that 'there was no fortress the Bolsheviks could not storm'. Far from being a carefully-planned and thought-through process the First

Five-Year Plan years represented nothing so much as a military campaign, conducted by raising and exhorting cadres to carry through policies in an endlessly improvised fashion. Unrealizable targets were actually raised, making them even more remote, as the plan went on. Eventually, as with its sister policies in the cultural and agricultural spheres, the result was such chaos that the squads had to be reined in and a more modest regime of advance instituted.

However, a decisive breakthrough had taken place. While calculations today show the falsity of the claims made at the time there can be no doubt that there were substantial advances. For example, the labour force more than doubled. Production in key areas did make an upward surge. Large-scale, often military-related, industries grew fastest. The overall urban population more or less doubled from 16 per cent of the total population in the 1926 census to 33 per cent in the 1939 census. Argument continues about the precise measurement of the advances but there is no doubt heavy industry grew at a rapid pace. Schultz's article shows how these processes appeared on the ground in the key project of constructing a major car factory in Nizhnii-Novgorod (later called Gorky). In particular it provides a vivid illustration of the chaos surrounding the effort and the extreme, far-from-planned methods characteristic of Stalinist policies in operation.

## 3   Kurt S. Schultz: 'Building the "Soviet Detroit": the Construction of the Nizhnii-Novgorod Automobile Factory, 1927–32'

Recent literature on interwar Soviet society is changing the way we view the 'Revolution from Above'. Instead of focusing on high politics, the authors of this literature have cast their analytical nets more widely and have revealed a remarkably dynamic society that was anything but clay in the hands of Kremlin potters.[1] The history of the massive automotive complex at Nizhnii-Novgorod adds weight to the conclusions growing out of this scholarship and sheds light on the origins and implementation of the larger plan to industrialize the Soviet economy; it shows in microcosm the many problems that often bedevilled and sometimes defeated the grand designs dreamed up in Moscow.

Like the First Five-Year Plan, the decision to build the Nizhnii-Novgorod automobile plant was forged in the ideologically charged debates over economic development policy that sundered the Communist party in the late 1920s.[2] These debates had barely been resolved when a relentless campaign for faster tempos and greater results led to persistent bottlenecks at Nizhnii-Novgorod and internecine strife between hard-pressed officials who were scrambling for scarce resources. To overcome these problems, Moscow had to intervene in everyday decisions, assign priority to critical projects, and reallocate materials in short supply. This intervention encountered resistance in both the capital and the provinces, with results that often slowed progress, led to further intrusions from the top, and dislocated other branches of the economy that were essential to the smooth operation of high-priority projects. The history of Soviet 'automobilization' illustrates the spiraling cycle of local improvisation, central intervention, and All-Union bureaucratic warfare that character-ized the First Five-Year Plan as a whole.

Central planners constantly modified plans for developing a domestic Soviet automotive industry before finally approving the Nizhnii-Novgorod project in April 1929. Although the changes reflected the fluid political situation in Moscow, they also resulted from the fractured Planning Commission (Gosplan) and a more ambitious group of individuals in the Supreme Council of the National Economy (Vesenkha) offered competing visions of industrial development.[3] Initial drafts of the five-year plan, drawn up by Gosplan in 1926–7. made no provision for substantially augmenting the country's automotive capacity. Instead, existing facilities would be upgraded slightly to increase their combined capacity to 10,000 vehicles during the entire quinquennium, and a modest number of imports would supplement domestic production.

These projections brought a variety of complaints, but none as strenuous as N. Osinskii's. Head of the Central Statistical Administration in mid-1927, Osinskii was an old leftist who had opposed the New Economic Policy and was now advocating a much more concerted industrialization effort. In a series of articles he decried the 'catastrophically backward' state of Soviet automotive transport, ridiculed Gosplan's targets as 'mere handicraft', and demanded the construction of an automobile plant capable of producing at least 100,000 vehicles annually. When critics claimed that existing roadways, repair facilities, and mechanical expertise could not support such a large volume of production, Osinskii countered by pointing to developments in the United States, where the technical infrastructure had expanded along with production. He also reminded his critics of the military implications of the automotive revolution. An underdeveloped automobile industry could not meet the needs of Soviet military doctrine, he said, which envisioned massive mechanized and motorized armies. Nor could sufficient vehicles be imported in the face of an economic blockade. Should the Red Army have to use 'the Russian peasant cart against the American or European automobile,' Osinskii warned, it would be 'threatened with the heaviest losses, not to say defeats'.

Osinskii's dissatisfaction with the modest plan for the Soviet auto-mobile industry reflected deeper disagreements in high party circles over strategies of industrial development, differences that also penetrated the state's economic planning and administrative agencies. In 1927, S. G. Strumilin, S. D. Shein, I. A. Kalinnikov, and others on the right wing of the party tended to dominate Gosplan's subordinate committees and bureaus. They opposed overly optimistic industrial plans, and their opposition squared with decisions that had been reached at the recent Fifteenth Party Congress.[4] In other agencies, however, a more aggressive industrialization drive drew support from key officials, including Valerian V. Kuibyshev, who had assumed the chairmanship of Vesenkha on 5 August 1926. A protégé of Stalin, Kuibyshev promptly set his staff to work on a more ambitious plan than the one Gosplan envisioned, and even this plan seemed inadequate by mid-1928, when the Soviet Union's economic difficulties pushed Stalin and his allies toward a more intensive industrialization policy. As a result of this shift to the left, automobilization finally assumed its place among the priorities of economic development.[5]

As early as 1926, Soviet representatives in the United States had tried to interest automobile manufacturers in building a plant on Soviet territory. These overtures did not interest the Americans, who worried about Moscow's ability to guarantee long-term, profitable operations. By early 1928, however, Soviet economic policymakers had shifted their sights toward an agreement under which a firm from the United States would provide technical assistance in constructing a plant to be owned and operated by the Soviet government. With this goal in mind, officials of Amtorg, the Soviet trading agency in New York, approached several automotive companies with a project for building a Soviet factory capable of producing between 12,000 and 50,000 vehicles annually.[6] Later that year, when Osinskii travelled to the United States for talks with the Ford Motor Company, the target had been raised to 100,000 vehicles. Henry Ford had his own reasons for being interested in the Soviet offer and he soon countered with a proposal that came close to the contract that Amtorg would sign with Ford in late May 1929. At this point, however, the Soviet agency hesitated.

The delay apparently stemmed from a lack of unity in the top economic poliymaking agencies in Moscow, particularly in Vesenkha and the Council of Labour and Defence (STO). In early March 1929, on the eve of the Sixteenth Party Conference that formally approved the 'optimal' variant of the First Five-Year Plan, Vesenkha and the STO announced the government's decision to build an automobile plant that would turn out 100,000 vehicles a year. The announcement did not delight everyone. Despite their support for a rapid industrialization drive, some left-wing elements in Vesenkha worried that the automobile plant would divert resources from more important projects.

Opponents on the right went further, as became clear once the STO and Vesenkha created a new agency, Avtostroi, to oversee the plant's construction and organize production. These opponents somehow managed to dominate the committee of experts that Avtostroi established to draft a plan for the new enterprise. Within a week of the committee's appointment Osinskii was warning that its members, who were recruited from two of Vesenkha's industrial design bureaus, neither believed in the project nor wished for its success. His foreboding was confirmed at the end of the month, when the committee presented a draft that fell far short of its instructions. The new plant got short shrift in the draft, which called instead for expansion of the factories in Moscow and Iaroslavl', for the construction of a new plant to produce a limited number of heavy trucks, and for total production by 1933 of not more than 39,000 vehicles.

The very appearance of the draft project, which amounted to the same kind of 'handicraft' approach Osinskii had deplored two years earlier, points up the byzantine complexity of administrative politics in 1928–9. By April 1929 both the STO and Vesenkha had opted for 'mass-production' over 'handicraft', while the party and state's highest bodies were about to sanction an industrial development plan that the right considered impossibly optimistic. Despite the leftward swing in party politics and Kuibyshev's position at the head of Vesenkha, advocates of a modest automobilization effort had managed to secure a draft project reflecting their position. Clearly the opponents of all-out industrialization, if not numerous, still occupied key positions in the planning apparatus.[7]

By the time Vesenkha's presidium met on 2 April to discuss the draft, however, Kuibyshev, Osinskii and their allies had outmanoeuvered and defeated their opponents. Some members of the presidium still supported a modest production effort in the belief that the Soviet economy could not produce or absorb a large number of vehicles. The Commissariat of Internal Affairs, for example, estimated the total transport needs of all cooperative economic organizations at roughly 4000 cars and trucks. But more powerful authorities scoffed at this estimate. *Ekonomicheskaia zhizn'* (*Economic Life*) denounced the committee's report as 'utterly worthless'. Osinskii, who by now sat on the presidia of both Gosplan and Vesenkha, condemned the 'extraordinary caution' of the experts. Kuibyshev and I. A. Khalepskii, chief of the Military-Technical Administration, felt the same way. Led by Osinskii, they persuaded the presidium to reject the draft.

The presidium also briefly discussed the type of vehicle to produce and where to locate the new factory. A few members favoured Chevrolet designs, whereas Kuibyshev, Osinskii, and Khalepskii argued that Ford's models were less expensive and better suited to Soviet road conditions. Since a Soviet delegation had reopened talks with Ford in February, a decision probably had been reached on this matter before the presidium gave its formal approval. Much the same can be said of Vesenkha's decision to build the plant on the outskirts of Nizhnii-Novgorod, a city of 258,000 and the administrative centre of the overwhelmingly agricultural Nizhegorodskii krai. Although the presidium considered Moscow, among other Soviet cities, it voted to go ahead with a plant at Nizhnii-Novgorod, stating merely that labour was cheaper there and more readily available. Vesenkha's design bureaus were given one month to draft a new plan for a plant that would produce 100,000 vehicles based on the Ford Model A car and Model AA truck.

The presidium's meeting of 2 April 1929 was yet another step toward the triumph of such men as Kuibyshev, Osinskii, and other allies of Stalin, all of whom pushed their designs for rapid industrialization with single-minded determination. By mid-1929 the advocates of an all-out effort were in control of at least the top economic policymaking positions, while such right-wing figures as Nikolai Bukharin and Mikhail Tomskii were losing their formal positions of power and influence. This shift almost certainly explains Vesenkha's actions of early 1929. It had reopened discussions with Ford in February, well before any formal decision had been made, and had decided in April to build the automobile factory and to use Ford designs, even though no agreement with the company had been reached. Whether Kuibyshev was confident of the outcome or already had reached a decision cannot be determined; in any event, he was vindicated on 29 May 1929, when his protégé, Vesenkha Deputy Chairman Valerii I. Mezhlauk, signed a contract with Ford that closely followed the lines of the company's 1928 proposal.

Although the details of this contract have been discussed elsewhere, certain provisions merit our attention.[8] At a cost of $30,000,000, Avtostroi would purchase the components of 74,000 automobiles and trucks, which over four years would be shipped to the USSR for assembly in a recon-ditioned factory. It would also acquire the designs for both the Model A and Model AA, as well as those for all equipment used in their production, and would send fifty workers a year to study production methods in Ford plants. These arrangements would 'speed the automobilization of the country', Osinskii concluded, but ultimate success also depended on overcoming a host of obstacles. Avtostroi had to mobilize the labour, equipment and raw materials needed to construct the plant, which was scheduled to begin operations on 1 January 1932. It also had to train supervisory, technical and production personnel who would keep the plant running smoothly. Even then, the success of its operations at Nizhnii-Novgorod depended to a large extent on the creation or expansion of a host of related industries that would support the automotive complex.

Party officials in Nizhnii-Novgorod did not need such tutelage from the centre to set construction in motion. Once Vesenkha named Nizhnii-Novgorod as the site of the automobile factory, the local organizational committee established a subcommittee and technical bureau to assist the construction effort. It also instructed local planning bureaus, economic councils and construction, supply, and production enterprises to cooperate fully with Avtostroi's officials. If necessary, they were to 'reexamine their five-year plans – particularly the current year's plan' – to ensure that Avtostroi received the necessary raw materials and manufactured goods.

At the national level, meanwhile, Gosplan and Vesenkha tried to coordinate the activities of plants and the administrative agencies whose participation was essential for constructing the new factory. In early June 1929, Gosplan convened an interagency committee to determine construction and production schedules. The first order of business was to reequip the factory near Nizhnii-Novgorod where Ford components would be assembled. This work was to be completed by 1 April 1930, so that the supply of cars and trucks could begin well before the main production plant was brought on line. The final specifications for the main plant were to be ready for approval no later than 1 October of the current year. In the meantime, constituent organizations of the interagency committee were to devise plans for supplying the automobile factory with the products for which they were responsible, be they raw materials, semifinished goods or cadres of engineers, technicians and workers.

The June interagency meeting was the first of what would become an expanding series of conferences, all issuing a flood of directives all designed to rectify the disorganization and delay that rapidly overtook the project. Vesenkha did manage to secure factory blueprints in short order, but only because it parcelled out that task to Austin and Company, an engineering firm from Cleveland, Ohio. Confusion surrounded every other aspect of construction. Vesenkha contributed to this situation in mid-June, when the presidium approved Osinskii's proposal to increase the plant's annual production target to 130,000. Of more immediate concern, however, were the transportation bottlenecks that impeded the flow of supplies to the construction site and the wilful obstructionism of officials in agencies and factories that were supposed to be cooperating with Avtostroi. In the months ahead, Vesenkha, the STO and even the Central Committee in Moscow would issue decree after decree in the hope of bringing order to the chaotic situation, only to find their efforts thwarted at every turn by administrative agencies in Moscow and industrial enterprises in the provinces, all of which had their own interests to protect.

By early 1930 these agencies, which supposedly were 'subordinate' to Vesenkha, were actually fighting each other for control of operations at the plant and the resources being funnelled into it. The first sign of trouble came at a meeting convened in mid-January 1930 by the All-Union Automobile and Tractor Association (VATO), the agency responsible for production in this branch of the economy. Summoned by VATO to report on progress at Nizhnii-Novgorod, spokesmen for Avtostroi and Metallostroi, the trust chosen by Vesenkha to build the factory, engaged instead in an 'animal fight', trading insults and 'petty accusations'. Having previously received rosy reports of progress, VATO now discovered that 'bureaucratic foul-ups' had nearly brought construction to a standstill. Although the supply schedule called for two hundred railway cars to arrive at the site each day, wrangling between Avtostroi, Metallostroi and other national and local agencies had cut the flow to an average of twenty cars.

VATO laid the blame for these problems squarely on Metallostroi, which had refused to comply with a 'categorical order' to provide Avtostroi with a variety of construction materials. Avtostroi had calculated the costs of its supplies and was unwilling to pay more. Metallostroi had other ideas and demanded that Avtostroi buy a larger amount of goods at prices that would help Metallostroi meet its production and distribution targets. Without intervention from Moscow, Metallostroi would have been in an impregnable position because, like other supply and production entities, it was barraged with more orders than it could possibly fulfil. The abolition of capitalist market relations notwithstanding, Metallostroi enjoyed a seller's market, which under 'socialism' allowed it to act 'like a feudal prince'; as long as its own plan was fulfilled it could 'treat the needs of its consumers with the arrogance of a baron'.

The alarming situation prompted VATO to dispatch a delegation to Nizhnii-Novgorod to correct the situation. Soon thereafter, construction materials and other equipment began to flow a bit more evenly, although problems ahead would still force officials to improvise solutions to keep construction on schedule. In late March, for example, when a shortage of bricks threatened to halt all activity at the site, the party's local executive committee simply requisitioned 48 million bricks from a nearby silicate plant. This hand-to-mouth supply system attended every aspect of construction at the 'Soviet Detroit'. Lumber, gravel, cement, and steel beams often went straight from railroad boxcars into the plant's assembly shops, foundries, coke ovens and blast furnaces. Quite frequently, however, they languished in the rail yard because Avtostroi never received more than half of the locomotives and trucks needed for internal transport. As a result, Avtostroi had to rely on the most primitive means of transport, and even this was 'catastrophically reduced by the low supply norms of oats for horses'.

Throughout the summer of 1930, Vesenkha and the STO complained ceaselessly about the haphazard work at Nizhnii-Novgorod, and these complaints, combined with occasional direct intervention from Moscow, finally resulted in an increased work tempo and new reports of progress. Vesenkha maintained the pressure, however, attributing most of the progress to 'happy circumstance' and accusing both Avtostroi and Metallostroi of showing more interest in 'taking vengeance' upon each other than in fulfilling their obligations. Formal affidavits [*akty*] became 'the most popular form of communication between the two organizations'. Avtostroi even assigned its contingent of American advisers to work on them. According to Boris Agapov, a correspondent for *Za industrializatsiiu* (*For Industrialization*), Avtostroi wanted to eliminate Metallostroi from any role at the construction site and therefore launched a campaign 'to discredit the enemy'. To be sure, Agapov noted, Metallostroi had 'broken all records with regard to total disorder', but Avtostroi was also guilty of contributing to the chaos. He demanded an 'immediate resolution' of bureaucractic 'squabbling', lest the situation be reduced to the point where 'one will build a wall, and the other will tear it down'.

In late August the presidium of Vesenkha intervened once again, relieving Metallostroi of its obligations and granting Avtostroi total control of the site. The presidium then instructed the 'victors' to reorganize the administrative apparatus at the construction site and 'liquidate all stoppages' by 10 September. Vesenkha also convened yet another conference of administrative and technical personnel for 'exchanging experience' and outlining the steps necessary to complete construction on time. To add force to the reorganization, in early September the Central Committee in Moscow decreed that the factory's party organizations should assume greater responsibilities at the plant. To ensure the implementation of this directive, the Central Committee transferred thirty-nine party, trade union and Komsomol officials to the factory site on a permanent basis.

The injection of party stalwarts, coupled with a minor purge of the party apparatus at the factory and the naming of Sergo Ordzhonikidze as the new chairman of Vesenkha, brought only a momentary burst of activity. By early 1931, Agapov was warning again of an impending crisis that would delay production even if the plant were completed on time. Apparently, neither Avtostroi nor Stal', a trust that manufactured steel products, had made plans to provide Nizhnii-Novgorod with the speciality steels that were needed for various parts. Avtostroi had let the months slip by, 'waiting for something to turn up'; Stal' had delayed its planning until September 1930, only then to discover that none of its factories could supply the steel that Avtostroi required. Both agencies, Agapov complained, had been 'secretly cherishing hopes of importing steel'.

The chairman of VATO, M. S. Mikhailov, tried to refute these charges by admitting that shops already completed were not yet equipped but insisting, contrary to Agapov's reports, that the biggest task remaining was to finish construction, which was 'only 30 percent complete'. One can hardly imagine a worse line of defence. Not surprisingly, *Za industrializatsiiu* launched a full-scale assault on Mikhailov and VATO's administrative apparatus. Vesenkha, meanwhile, sent still another commission to investigate conditions at Nizhnii-Novgorod and summoned Avtostroi's chief of construction, the secretary of the party committee at the plant and the editor of the factory's newspaper to explain the situation. Their reports, and the commission's findings, drew an unsettling picture of serious delays in building and equipping the main shops. Much work had been accomplished, but Vesenkha was not satisfied with partial progress. It was more interested in learning why the heating plant was behind schedule, when the ventilation and sewage systems would be installed and whether VATO and Avtostroi would ever reach agreement with a variety of factories and trusts for the provision of ball bearings, starters, rubber, glass and other critical commodities.

In mid-February 1931, Vesenkha responded to the chaos by again reorganizing the chain of command at the factory, while the STO issued a detailed decree covering virtually every outstanding question of supply and future production. The decree gave VATO and Avtostroi until 1 April to calculate the total cost of bringing the factory on line and spelled out the obligations of every enterprise and bureau involved in construction. Although this was Moscow's strongest intervention to date, little came of it. A month later, *Za industrializatsiiu* reported that the STO decree remained 'suspended in the stifling air of bureaucracy'. VATO and Avtostroi were putting their final estimate together 'at a snail's pace'. In early March, officials from the trusts and factories responsible for supplying the automobile plant gathered to clarify delivery schedules and costs, but agreed to nothing. To be sure, an official of Vesenkha's Electro-Technical Association gleefully observed that with the STO decree in hand it was now possible to 'grab some people by the throat and get everything we need for production'. What he wanted, however, was 400,000 gold rubles to import machinery the association was supposed to produce itself.

In retrospect, it is amazing that Avtostroi completed even the most critical shops and assembly lines by the 1 November deadline. In a report of late March, Vesenkha's inspection commission cited as the greatest barriers to progress the same factories, trusts and industrial combines criticized months before. Decrees from the Central Committee in late April and from Vesenkha in late May intoned a familiar refrain of unfulfilled plans and obligations on the part of the same organizations.

In late August, despite insistent demands from Moscow, Vesenkha's inspectorate had to admit that all of the presidium's decrees since March 'were being fulfilled extremely unsatisfactorily'.

Reports of ongoing transport problems and 'innumerable losses' resounded in the press throughout the summer, complaints that were not addressed until late September and October. The mobilization of party cadres for work at Nizhnii-Novgorod played a role in this transformation, although the decisive event occurred on 10 September, when Ordzhonikidze and his deputy, Lazar Kaganovich, descended from Moscow to rectify the situation. Work proceeded furiously after their departure, and the main shops of the huge industrial enterprise were completed, for the most part, by the first of November. Avtostroi had only to install the remaining complement of sophisticated machinery and fill out its work force, whereupon the factory would be ready to start production.

Meeting these requirements, however, often depended on constant intervention from higher authorities in Moscow, particularly Vesenkha, and in some cases even this intervention was not enough to guarantee progress. As we have seen, the contract between Amtorg and Ford provided Vesenkha with drawings and specifications for all equipment related to the manufacture of Model A cars and Model AA trucks. Avtostroi received these designs, but the USSR's underdeveloped machine tool industry, Vesenkha's desire to begin production as quickly as possible and a general proclivity to take the easy route of imports all guaranteed that Avtostroi and its suppliers would rely heavily on foreign companies for equipping the automotive plant. The chief administrators in Vesenkha routinely fought this tendency; the drastic decline in Soviet export earnings in the wake of global depression led them to redouble their efforts. But the general policy of reducing Soviet imports did not always apply to Nizhnii-Novgorod.

Moscow attached a great deal of political and economic significance to the automobile factory. As one of the 'projects of first importance' it had to be brought on line 'no matter what the cost', ensuring that Avtostroi would receive whatever it needed, 'even if it be to the temporary disadvantage of other enterprises'. Such priority status, however, did not always provide a magical solution to the problems that occasionally blocked progress. Placing an order for American machinery did not guarantee that Amtorg's representatives would act promptly, avoid dickering over prices or make proper shipping arrangements. Nor could it overcome the effects of the Soviet Union's inadequate port facilities and overburdened railways, which delayed shipments to the factory, or of the overworked, hapless administrators at Nizhnii-Novgorod, who often lost track of equipment once it arrived. Officials of VATO and Avtostroi constantly complained

about these problems and constantly turned to higher authorities in Vesenkha, whose timely intervention and generous funding usually sufficed to
resolve them.

On the labour front, however, the shortages were too extreme and the
interests too diverse to permit desperate officials the luxury of complying
with orders from Moscow. Although Avtostroi sent at least 230 workers
and engineers to study at Ford's plants in the United States, this number
made up only a fraction of the skilled workers required at Nizhnii-
Novgorod, and some of those trained in the United States actually were
assigned to other plants under VATO's control. Like every other industrial
enterprise of the time, in other words, Avtostroi had to struggle against an
enervating shortage of skilled workers and fantastic rates of turnover in the
labour force.

Although problems on the labour front grew out of the increasing
demand for workers of every description, VATO and Avtostroi followed
policies that made a bad situation worse. As late as October 1930 neither
agency had bothered to determine how many workers the automobile
factory would need. Earlier in the summer, Avtostroi had simply estimated its requirements at 13,200. That figure then jumped to almost
16,000, fell to 14,000 by the start of the new year, and finally settled
at 12,700. In fact, VATO was willing to cannibalize the cadres of its
other plants; along with Avtostroi, it simply assumed that the automobile
plant's priority status would allow it to steal from other organizations when
the need arose. In early January 1931, VATO announced that it 'hoped' to
satisfy Avtostroi's current needs by transferring 600 skilled workers from
its AMO plant in Moscow. The news astonished that factory's director,
who knew that only 280 workers at his plant had the skills that VATO
required. Once VATO began to search beyond its own confines, it had
to contend with hundreds of other bureaus and enterprises that also
needed workers and often were willing to defy Moscow's orders to release
personnel to Avtostroi.

As part of its response to the STO's decree of late February 1931,
Vesenkha ordered twelve of its subordinate organizations to transfer 1080
workers and engineers to the automotive complex. More than a month
passed before even one organization complied with the decree. The others
stonewalled, sending Avtostroi's emissaries out to the provinces to talk to
the directors of their subordinate plants, who usually claimed that only
their superiors in Moscow could release workers. Some plant directors
were frank. One declared that 'without a formal reprimand' for not
complying with the decree, he 'would not even talk about it'. Another
proclaimed that 'there are no people and we will not release any' and then
invited his guest to 'write a report to Vesenkha'. Only a few directors were
willing to hand over the requisite personnel: the boss at Metallist, for

example, demanded 3710 rubles for each worker; the one at Dvigatel' Revoliutsii generously limited his price to 600 rubles.

Avtostroi demurred, and wisely so, because these costly workers surely would not have stayed long at Nizhnii-Novgorod, where the dreadful living conditions led to a fantastic labour turnover. In early January 1931, Agapov reported that more than half of the skilled workers thus far acquired had 'disappeared from the field of view' or 'dispersed to other enterprises'. Although Avtostroi was scheduled to receive fifty additional specialists that month, it had 'absolutely no idea where to put them'. Indeed, the plans so far drawn up would provide housing for no more than two-thirds of the projected work force. Making matters worse, the units constructed fell far short of the number originally targeted and were in such 'catastrophic condition' that workers 'ran from the construction site'.[9]

Despite more than two years of mishaps, delays and obstruction, Avtostroi somehow achieved enough at Nizhnii-Novgorod to begin operations on 1 January 1932 and wheel out the first complement of Soviet-produced trucks. Within a few months, however, the main assembly line had to be shut down because of a lack of parts from other shops within the complex and a dearth of supplies from ancillary industries, problems that would continue to plague production well after the plant came fully back on line. Thereafter output steadily increased, but the facility at Nizhnii-Novgorod never lived up to Osinskii's dreams. By the end of the First Five-Year Plan the Soviet Union was producing only 23,900 vehicles, some 15,000 *less* than the defeated advocates of the 'handicraft' approach had envisioned. Not until 1937 would the entire Soviet automotive industry produce the 130,000 units that had earlier been expected from Nizhnii-Novgorod alone.

The failure to achieve planned results was a direct consequence of the political decision to demand progress on every economic front at once, which in turn created an environment deadly to the rational pursuit of plans. By setting an overly ambitious industrial agenda, Moscow threw the national economy into turmoil as administrators at the centre and managers in the field fought strenuously to secure the resources needed to meet their individual responsibilities. Waste, inefficiency and bureaucratic arbitrariness rapidly overtook the economy, forcing top policymakers to intervene constantly in the administrative process to ensure that certain priorities would be observed.

The ordeal at Nizhnii-Novgorod, however, reveals the limits of such intervention and the lack of Moscow's control over the execution of its policies. Even after Vesenkha squelched the attempt to block automobilization and gave Avtostroi priority status, it could not force such subsidiary bodies as Metallostroi and Stal' to obey directives that conflicted with other tasks. Nor could Vesenkha, the STO or even the Central Committee bring individual managers to heel when their directives threatened the interests of enterprises enjoying the protection of powerful agencies in Moscow. Only through constant intervention and the reallocation of resources directly under its control was Vesenkha able to guarantee that Avtostroi would achieve the minimum desirable results.

At Nizhnii-Novgorod, as throughout the national economy, improvisation replaced planning. Although acknowledging the suzerainty of Moscow, bureaucracies at the centre and in the field, not to mention the enterprises they controlled, took on all of the characteristics of sovereign, independent states. Under conditions of extreme scarcity and severe competition for resources, they alternately negotiated or warred over the men, money and matériel necessary to complete their tasks and increase their power. Such was the reality of the First Five-Year Plan in the field of automobilization.

NOTES

[Reorganized and renumbered from the original.]

I would like to thank the Ohio State University graduate school and the Society for Historians of American Foreign Relations for fellowships that assisted my research; the history department at Ohio State for awarding an earlier version of this essay the Eugene Roseboom Prize for best graduate seminar paper of 1987; and the *Slavic Review*'s anonymous referees for valuable criticisms. Mary C. Brennan and William K. Wolf merit a special note of gratitude for their advice and patience.

1. The literature is too large to cite comprehensively, but for convenient summaries see Sheila Fitzpatrick, 'New Perspectives on Stalinism', and the responses to it in *Russian Review*, 45 (October 1986): 357–413; and the ensuing debate in ibid. 46 (October 1987): 375–431.

2. Here, too, the literature is vast. The works most useful for this study include Alexander Erlich, *The Soviet Industrialization Debate, 1924–1928* (Cambridge: Harvard University Press, 1960); E. H. Carr and R. W. Davies, *Foundations of a Planned Economy, 1926–1929* (New York: Macmillan, 1971) vol. 1; Moshe Lewin, *Political Undercurrents in Soviet Economic Debates: From Bukharin to the Modern Reformers* (Princeton, NJ: Princeton University Press, 1974); and Kendall E. Bailes, *Technology and Society under Lenin and Stalin: Origins of the Soviet Technical Intelligentsia, 1917–1941* (Princeton, NJ: Princeton University Press, 1978).

3. Maurice Dobb, *Soviet Economic Development since 1917*, 2nd rev. edn (New York: International Publishers, 1966) 230–41; Carr and Davies, *Foundations of a Planned Economy* 1: 843–74, 982.

4. E. A. Rees, *State Control in Soviet Russia: The Rise and Fall of the Workers' and Peasants' Inspectorate, 1920–34* (London: Macmillan 1987) 138.

5. Ibid. See also S. G. Wheatcroft and R. W. Davies eds., *Materials for a Balance of the Soviet National Economy, 1918–1930* (Cambridge: Cambridge University Press, 1985) chapter 3.

6. Allan Nevins and Frank E. Hill, *Ford: Expansion and Challenge, 1915–1933* (New York: Scribner, 1957) appendix 1.

7. Both Gosplan and Vesenkha had been purged of their 'more cautious planners' in October 1928 (see Rees, *State Control in Soviet Russia*, 174).

8. Nevins and Hill, *Ford: Expansion and Challenge*, appendix 1.

9. Americans who worked in the USSR during the First Five-Year Plan agreed that the tremendous turnover in labour was prompted by the search for food and better living conditions.

# THE ASSAULT ON THE PEASANTRY

Lenin, in his last testament to the party, had stressed the alliance (*smychka*) between the workers and peasants. It was imperative, in Lenin's opinion, that the workers – meaning of course the party and state – should not antagonize the peasantry as had been the case during war communism. Lenin had learned the lesson that the peasants still had the power to frustrate the long-term aims of the party. However, in 1929 Stalin unleashed an all-out assault on the peasantry. Like industrialization, the policy was built on central government agencies, enforcement squads and central exhortation. Volunteer groups of young party activists and sympathisers were recruited and sent into the countryside to build a collectivist co-operative agriculture. In the guise of a mass movement of peasants, within months vast tracts of the country were reported to have been successfully collectivized. As with industry, the targets were stepped up and, in autumn, the slogan 'Liquidate the kulaks as a class' was proclaimed. Officially, a great class struggle was sweeping the rural areas, aided and abetted by the volunteers but supposedly led by poor peasants. However, the idea of collectivization as a class struggle between peasants was a complete fiction. The communal peasantry stood together, by and large, in defence of their villages and communes. Rather, in the name of 'total collectivization' (*sploshnaia kollektivizatsiia*), a veritable war was unleashed on the peasants. Long before Soviet archives were opened we had extraordinary direct testimony to the events from documents captured by the Germans as they invaded Smolensk. In turn, Germany, too, was invaded and the documents found their way to the United States. In a remarkable compilation Merle Fainsod, in *Smolensk under Soviet Rule*, portrayed collectivization from original records. The collectivization squads often got out of control. Fainsod quoted reports of confiscation of the clothes people were actually  wearing, and of food being 'confiscated' straight from the oven (with leftovers being used to smear icons). Not surprisingly, the peasants resisted the crudely enacted policy. Many of them slaughtered livestock rather than hand it over to the new collective farms. In many places peasants resorted to as much force as they could muster.

While it was not enough to challenge the Red Army in a military sense it did precipitate a political crisis. Army chiefs warned Stalin that they would not be responsible for the actions of their troops if they were called upon to engage in bloody repression of the peasants. Like most policies of the period collectivization was pursued to the point of chaos. In any case, the winter months had, cunningly, been chosen for the assault so that actual agrarian production would be least affected. Continual deepening of the crisis into early 1930 threatened the spring sowing which was crucial to the harvest. Some sort of order had to be restored.

In a move of colossal cynicism, Stalin, having exhorted the collectivization squads to work full out, now cut the ground from under their feet. In a short sharp article entitled 'Dizzy with Success', published in the party newspaper *Pravda* on 2 March 1930, the excesses of the process were blamed on the grass roots activists themselves. In so doing, Stalin diverted blame from the central authorities. Within weeks the supposed 50 per cent of farms which had been collectivized fell to a quarter. A calmer pace of collectivization ensued and it was only in 1936 that virtually every farm had been collectivized. The costs of the process had been enormous. A figure of a million 'kulak' families driven out has become generally accepted. Many of this number were killed defending their property or died en route to their places of exile and imprisonment. Livestock numbers appear to have fallen catastrophically. Only in 1938 were the production levels of 1928 once more attained. Soviet agriculture appeared to have lost a decade of growth.

However, the largest single cost was the loss of life in the famine of 1932–3 which was engendered by the disruption of the countryside. The famine has always been one of the most controversial episodes in Soviet history. While it was happening, the authorities tried to hide it from Soviet citizens, the foreign press and, perhaps most important, from foreign, especially Japanese, intelligence which would welcome such clear signs of Russian weakness and possibly seek to take advantage of it. A number of western journalists, including Malcolm Muggeridge, succeeded in getting news of the famine out into the world's press. However, radical papers denied the existence of mass famine. In more recent times, two issues have dominated discussion – the numbers involved and the reasons for it. On the former question, a number of around five million deaths – mostly of the weakest groups of the very old and the very young – is the current best guess, making the famine the most costly episode in the 1930s in terms of loss of life, more so even than the purges. On the second issue, motivation, an attempt was made in 1986 by Robert Conquest to argue that it was deliberately inflicted, primarily to quell the rising fires of Ukrainian nationalism. Pointing largely to circumstantial evidence, notably the closing of the Ukrainian border at the height of the famine supposedly to prevent relief supplies from getting through, the argument was put forward. It succeeded in reaching a wide audience with extracts from Conquest's book being serialized in broadsheet newspapers.

The scholarly community was less impressed. For many who studied the question carefully Conquest's thesis fell at the first hurdle. The famine spread far beyond the Ukraine, having severe effects in South Russia and other parts of the Caucasus. The article by Davies, Tauger and Wheatcroft poses a much more direct challenge. Using newly-released figures for grain stocks and grain production, many of them from papers which the leadership themselves saw, the authors show that the Soviet Union was not withholding vast reserve stocks which might have alleviated the famine. Given the need for a strategic reserve in case of war – a possibility heightened by the Japanese invasion of Manchuria in 1931 – there was not enough to feed the peasants. Rather than a deliberate terror-famine the authors uncover a more plausible but almost equally chilling story of incompetence and bungling. Believing, as they had done in 1918 and 1919, that peasants were holding back hidden reserves ('hoarding' in Soviet terminology), grain squads were encouraged to fulfil very high quotas of appropriation. When the truth dawned on the authorities, in mid-winter 1932/3, much of the requisitioned grain had been disposed of, including sale abroad for machinery needed for the plan. As a result there was insufficient grain to save the peasants who, far from hoarding reserves, had lost practically everything down to the last grain. Never again were such inflated requisition targets imposed.

Overall, the verdict on collectivization has been universally damning. It led to famine, shortages and the 'crippling' of Soviet agriculture, this last, in Cold War times especially, tending to mean that Soviet agricultural production remained much lower than American. This was true but the geographical and climatic conditions were vastly different making it difficult to engage in crude, direct comparison. Nonetheless, Soviet agriculture remained a major weakness and, whatever meaning one may wish to attribute to it, the process was not imposed on the East European satellites even at the height of Sovietization in the late 1940s. Even so, while it is no justification either of the policy or, even more markedly, of the methods by which it was implemented, collectivization did mark a historic turning point. For the first time in its history, the centre of gravity of Russian society was no longer to be found in the countryside. While it was only around 1962 that the majority of the Soviet population was declared to be urban-dwelling, from 1929 onwards the peasantry, until then not only the majority of all Russians from the beginning of their history but also the bedrock of all previous Russian societies, was broken. Its traditional institutions, notably the commune which had enjoyed a golden age in the 1917–28 period, were broken up.

Also, it should not be overlooked that collectivization freed the city from the threat of famine. In 1919, Petrograd and other cities had seen mass starvation. After collectivization a stable and growing level of state grain procurement was secured. Only with this security could urbanization proceed. Similarly, the secure grain appropriation system enabled the USSR to fight more successfully in the 1941–5 period than its tsarist predecessor. Finally, the mass expulsion of peasants from land created a large, drifting, labour force which was quickly sucked into new industrial projects like the Dnepr dam, the Nizhnii Novgorod automobile plant and the massive Soviet Pittsburgh, Magnitogorsk, under construction in the Urals.

As well as being a disaster, collectivization was also a historic turning point in Russia's evolution, perhaps more so even than the revolution of 1917 itself. Stalin had made a decisive turn towards industry and modernization. In so doing, he had well and truly shredded the *smychka*. What would Lenin have said? Since Lenin's assumption was that the peasants could not be defeated he would have had to go along with the fact that, despite disregarding Lenin's solemn advice, Stalin had succeeded. Lenin's defeat by the peasants had become Stalin's victory over them.

### 4   R. W. Davies, M. B. Tauger and S. G. Wheatcroft: 'Stalin, Grain Stocks and the Famine of 1932–3'

Most western and all Soviet studies of the Stalinist economy have ignored the role played by the stockpiling of grain in the agricultural crisis of the early 1930s. Thus in his major work on Stalinist agriculture published in 1949, Naum Jasny frankly admitted that data were insufficient to reach a conclusion, merely noting that 'stocks from former years probably declined during 1932'.[1] Baykov, Dobb, Volin and Nove said nothing about grain stocks.[2] At the time, western commentators did pay some attention to the possibility that the stockpiling of grain exacerbated the famine. In autumn 1931 Japan invaded Manchuria, and in spring 1932 British diplomats reported that Karl Radek had told them that, owing to the threat of war in the far east, enough grain had been stored to supply the army for one year.[3] In February 1933 the notorious but shrewd journalist Walter Duranty wrote in *The New York Times* of 'the unexpected additional demand for grain necessitated by the Far Eastern war danger last winter'.[4] Since the food and fodder grain consumed by the Red Army in one year amounted to about 800,000 tons,[5] this would have been enough to provide a rather modest annual bread ration for several million people. A stockpile of this size was, of course, less important than the 4.79 million tons exported from the 1931 harvest or even than the 1.61 million tons exported from the 1932 harvest (see Table 4, below). But was such a military stock accumulated in those years?

Enlightenment had to await the opening of the Russian archives. The impact of the first revelations about grain stocks has been dramatic. On the basis of a preliminary, unpublished typescript by the eminent Russian historian V. P. Danilov, Robert Conquest has announced that the archives have revealed that in the famine year of 1932–3 Stalin was holding immense grain stocks, the existence of which was previously completely unknown. He wrote in *Slavic Review* 'there were 4.53 million tons of grain in various reserves – the *Neprikosvennyi Fond* and the special *Gosudarstvennyi Fond*, neither (he [Danilov] points out) justified by any danger to the country, and readily available to prevent the real danger – mass death by famine.'[6] Addressing a wider public in *The Times Literary Supplement* Conquest further explained: 'even apart from the fact that the 1.8 million tons of grain exported would have been enough to have prevented the famine, there were in addition two secret grain reserves between them holding 4.53 million tons more, which were not released to the starving peasantry'.[7] Grain stocks of 4.53 million tons would certainly have been enough to feed millions of peasants in 1932–3. One ton of grain provided a good bread ration for three persons for a year, so 4.53 million tons would have provided bread for some 13–14 million persons for a year.

In view of the importance of grain stocks to understanding the famine, we have searched Russian archives for evidence of Soviet planned and actual grain stocks in the early 1930s. Our main sources were the Politburo protocols, including the *osobye papki* ('special files', the highest secrecy level), and the papers of the agricultural collections committee Komzag, of the committee on commodity funds and of Sovnarkom. The Sovnarkom records include telegrams and correspondence of V. Kuibyshev, who was head of Gosplan, head of Komzag and the committee on reserves, and one of the deputy chairs of Sovnarkom at that time. We have not obtained access to the Politburo working papers in the Presidential Archive, to the files of the committee on reserves or to the relevant files in military archives. But we have found enough information to be confident that this very high figure for grain stocks is wrong and that Stalin did not have under his control huge amounts of grain which could easily have been used to eliminate the famine.

The definition of 'grain stocks' is a complicated business. The literature divides them into two main categories: 'invisible stocks' (*nevidimye zapasy*) and 'visible stocks' (*vidimye zapasy*). The former are those held by peasants (and in the 1930s by collective and state farms) for food, seed, fodder and emergencies. Peasant carry-over is very difficult to assess; the official estimate for 1 July 1926 was 7.21 million tons, while a careful independent estimate amounted to only 4.19 million tons.[8] These calculations were of some politico-economic importance: the central political authorities believed and sought to demonstrate that peasants and collective farms were concealing substantial stocks; peasants and collective farms sought to minimize knowledge of their stocks. During the grim winter of 1932–3, the authorities seized the seed stocks of collective farms on the pretext or belief that concealed grain stocks were available to them. In the archives widely varying estimates of invisible stocks for the early 1930s may be found; not surprisingly, they show a general decline in the course of 1931–3 and an increase in following years. The 'visible stocks' rather than the invisible stocks will be our main concern in this article. These were those which had passed from producers to traders, to state and other collection agencies and to subsequent grain-consuming organizations, plus stocks in transit.

Soviet statistical agencies estimated the total of all visible stocks on 1 July 1929 at 1.76 million tons, of which there were:

| | |
|---|---|
| held by state and cooperative collection agencies | 0.912 |
| held by consuming organizations (including industry) | 0.331 |
| miscellaneous | 0.141 |
| in transport system | 0.376 |

The figure in Table 1 for 1 July 1929, 781,000 tons, is a revised official estimate by Komzag of the figure given above for state and cooperative collection agencies, 912,000 tons. It thus excludes grain held by consuming organizations and in the transport system. This was that part of the visible stocks which the state had more or less readily at its   disposal for distribution to the population, for export and for other uses. These stocks were generally known in the statistics as 'availability with the planning organizations'; we shall refer to them here as 'planners' stocks'. Planners' stocks were further divided into 'commercially available' and 'various funds' (see Table 2). The 'funds' were those parts of the planners' stocks which were set aside for special purposes, sometimes in special stores, sometimes merely notionally. As we shall show, the funds included both the 'untouchable fund' (*Neprikosnovennyi fond*' or '*Nepfond*') and the 'mobilization fund', also known as the 'state fund' ('*Mobfond*', '*gosudarstvennyi fond*' or '*gosfond*'). 'Commercially available' was something of a misnomer: it referred to stocks held by grain-collection and related agencies which could be passed on to consumers in accordance with an approved plan of utilization.

Grain stocks naturally varied considerably during the course of the agricultural year, reaching a peak immediately after a harvest and falling to their lowest levels just before the next harvest. Harvesting and the grain

**Table 1** Published figures for grain stocks, 1928–33 (thousand tons of 'planners' stocks' in grain equivalent)

|  |  | Of this 'various funds' |
| --- | --- | --- |
| 1 July 1928 | 486 |  |
| 1 August 1928 | 367 |  |
| 1 December 1928 | 1745 |  |
| 1 January 1929 | 1531 |  |
| 1 July 1929 | 781 |  |
| 1 August 1929 | 724 |  |
| 1 January 1930 | 7838 |  |
| 1 July 1930 | 2084 | 1379 |
| 1 August 1930 | 1462 |  |
| 1 December 1930 | 9791 |  |
| 1 January 1931 | 8278 |  |
| 1 July 1931 | 2332 | 1114 |
| 1 August 1931 | 2026 |  |
| 1 December 1931 | 9264 |  |
| 1 January 1932 | 9095 | 2033 |
| 1 July 1932 | 1360 | 635 |
| 1 August 1932 | 1012 |  |
| 1 January 1933 | 8499 | 3034 |
| 1 July 1933 | 1997 | 1141 |
| 10 July 1933 | 1654 | 944 |

These figures do not include grain in transit in the transport system (*v puti*) or the grain held by grain-consuming organizations.

collections began in the south in early July but in many other areas not until August. Normally the 1 July figure was given as the minimum level of stocks; but this was not quite accurate. During July grain available from the new harvest in the month as a whole is less than grain consumed and stocks continue to fall until the last days of the month. 1 August would be a better date for assessing minimum stocks but data for that date are not always available. Thus, quite apart from the need for a permanent grain reserve, a major problem for the central authorities was the need for 'transitional stocks' (usually known as *perekhodiashchie ostatki*) to enable continuous supply at the end of one agricultural year and the beginning of the next. Ever larger transitional stocks were needed from 1928 onwards, with the attenuation of the grain market and the dependence of larger numbers of people on state supplies (including many peasants in grain-deficit areas). From 1930 onwards state allocations of grain for internal purposes only (food rations, army, industry, etc. but excluding exports) amounted to

**Table 2** Published figures for grain stocks, by type of grain, 1 July 1932 and 1 July 1933 (thousand tons of planners' stocks in grain equivalent)

| | 1 July 1932 | | | 1 July 1933 | | |
|---|---|---|---|---|---|---|
| | Commercial stocks | Various funds | Total | Commercial stocks | Various funds | Total |
| Rye and rye flour | 193 | 351 | 544 | 273 | 507 | 780 |
| Wheat and wheat flour | 246 | 125 | 371 | 248 | 369 | 617 |
| Total main food grains | 439 | 476 | 915 | 521 | 876 | 1397 |
| Fodder and minor grains | 286 | 159 | 445 | 335 | 265 | 600 |
| Total | 725 | 635 | 1360 | 856 | 1141 | 1997 |

some 1.35–1.5 million tons a month. Moreover, areas requiring supplies were often thousands of kilometers from the main grain-producing areas; and once available, the grain had to be processed and delivered.

In the course of establishing a state grain monopoly in the mid-1920s, the Soviet authorities did not succeed in building up a state grain reserve. In December 1927 the directives for the Five-Year Plan approved by the XV Party Congress stressed the importance of the accumulation of stocks in kind and foreign currency reserves during the course of the plan. The accumulation of stocks of all kinds would achieve 'the necessary insurance against large vacillations in the conjuncture of the international market, and against a potential partial or general economic and financial blockade, against a bad harvest within the country, and against a direct armed attack'. But a Soviet grain handbook published in 1932 noted that 'all attempts to create a large grain reserve did not have positive results', even though 'the difficulties experienced in 1927/28 and 1928/29 revealed the categorical necessity of creating such a reserve'. According to Soviet data, on 1 July 1929 the total amount held in the state grain fund (*gosfond*), including the remnants of the centralized milling levy from the previous harvest amounted to only 69,000 tons.

### The 1929 harvest and the 1929/30 agricultural year

On 27 June 1929 the Politburo adopted a much-increased plan for grain collection from the 1929 harvest, resolving:

In accordance with the resolution of the XV Congress on the formation of a grain fund, it is considered necessary to create an untouchable stock amounting to 100 million *poods* [1.638 million tons] of food grains ... It is considered that the untouchable stock may not be expended by anyone in any circumstances without special permission from the Politburo and Sovnarkom of the USSR.[9]

Two months later, on 29 August 1929, Stalin wrote to Molotov, praising the success of the first stage of grain collection from the 1929 harvest and emphasizing the importance of reserve stocks, that 'we must and can accumulate 100 mln *poods* [1.638 million tons] of *untouchable stocks* [*neprikosnovennye zapasy*], if we are really Bolsheviks and not empty chatterers.' By the beginning of December, 13.5 million tons of grain had been collected, well over twice as much as on that date in any previous year; and the first drive for the collectivization of agriculture was rapidly accelerating. Stalin, jubilant and jovial, again wrote to Molotov: *Greetings to Molotshtein!* ... The grain collections progress. Today we decided

**Table 3**  Reserve grain funds by fund, type of grain and organization: archival data, 1 July 1932 (thousand tons in grain equivalent)

| | Gosfond | Nepfond | Gossortfond[d] | Fond MK[e] | Total |
|---|---|---|---|---|---|
| *Zagotzerno*[a] | 138 | 159 | – | 13 | 310 |
| *Soyuzmuka*[b] | 124 | 141 | – | – | 266 |
| *Soyuzkrupa*[c] | 78 | – | – | – | 78 |
| Total | 340 | 301 | 2.6 | 13 | 656 |
| Of which, | | | | | |
| Rye and rye flour | 137 | 214 | 1.6 | 13 | 366 |
| Wheat and wheat flour | 40 | 87 | 0.5 | 0 | 128 |
| Fodder and minor grains | 163 | – | 0.5 | – | 163 |

*Source*: these figures, dated 1 September 1932, are given in RGAE, f. 8040, op. 3, d. 40 on both II. 129–30 and 148–50. Here total planners' stocks are given as 1.386 million tons. This is somewhat larger than the revised figure published in 1934 of 1.360 million tons, of which 635 thousand tons was 'various funds' (see Tables 1 and 2 above). It should be noted that *Nepfond* and *Gosfond* both unambiguously appear as component elements in the total grain stocks of 1.386 million tons.

*Notes*: Discrepancies in the total are due to rounding.
[a] State corporation responsible for grain collections.
[b] State corporation responsible for converting grain into flour.
[c] State corporation responsible for groats.
[d] State fund of high-quality seeds.
[e] Special fund of Moscow party committee.

to increase the untouchable fund of food grains to 120 million *poods* [1.966 million tons]. We will raise the rations in industrial towns such as Ivanovo-Voznesensk, Kharkov, etc.'

The grain handbook of 1932 noted that the establishment of a grain reserve 'was posed as a central and top-priority task for the grain campaign of 1929/30'. The main statistical journal, reporting record grain stocks accumulated by 1 January 1930, noted that 'a fundamental difference between the stocks of the current year and the stocks of the previous year is the formation of a special fund, not used for current needs, while in past years grain was used entirely for meeting current requirements.' The journal described this 'untouchable fund' as 'having an insurance function in case of a bad harvest or any other extraordinary needs'.[10]

Although grain collections from the 1929 harvest were extremely large, they had both to supply grain to many consumers who had previously obtained it on the peasant market and to provide for increase export. Planners' stocks increased by 1.3 million tons between 1 July 1929 and 1 July 1930, reaching 2.084 million tons. The Politburo deemed it possible to allocate only 786,000 tons of this to the Nepfond on 1 July 1930; but explained that this amount was to be 'absolutely untouchable'.[11]

## The 1930 harvest and the 1930/31 agricultural year

The harvest of 1930 was surprisingly good: collections were 38 per cent higher than in the previous year and more than twice as much as in 1928/29 (see Table 4). Planners' stocks on the peak date of 1 January 1931 were even higher than on 1 January 1930 (see Table 1); on that basis the Politburo concluded on 7 January that *Nepfond* could amount to 150 million

**Table 4** State grain collections, 1928/29–1932/33 (including milling levy; in thousand tons)

|  |  | of which, used for export |
| --- | --- | --- |
| 1 July 1928–30 June 1929 | 10790[1] | −184[2] |
| 1 July 1929–30 June 1930 | 16081[1] | 1343[2] |
| 1 July 1930–30 June 1931 | 22139[1] | 5832[2] |
| 1 July 1931–30 June 1932 | 22839 | 4786 |
| 1 July 1932–30 June 1933 | 18513 | 1607 |

[1] See Robert W. Davies, *The Socialist Offensive: the Collectivisation of Soviet Agriculture, 1929–1930* (Cambridge, 1980) 429.
[2] Ibid., 432.

*poods* (2.457 million tons) and that, in addition, the 'mobilization fund' (*Mobfond*) could amount to 50 million *poods* (.819 million tons) – 3.276 million tons in all.[12] *Mobfond* was later described by Kuibyshev as intended to provide adequate grain (and other commodities), amounting to $1\frac{1}{2}$–2 months' supply, to cover delays in supplies during mobilization and to make some provision for the largest industrial and political centres.[13] But, although planners' stocks had increased to 2.332 million tons on 1 July 1931 and remained as high as 2.026 million tons on 1 August 1931 (see Table 1), they were far below the level of reserve stocks proposed by the Politburo on 7 January 1931.

## The 1931 harvest and the 1931/32 agricultural year

Unlike the 1930 harvest, the 1931 harvest was poor (and much worse than the Soviet political authorities believed). Nevertheless, grain collections in the agricultural year 1931/32 slightly exceeded the 1930/31 level (see Table 4) and the authorities continued their efforts to accumulate substantial reserve stocks. Their aims were now somewhat less ambitious: in October 1931 the Politburo decided that *Nepfond* and *Mobfond* together should total 150 million *poods* (2.457 million tons), as compared with the 200 million *poods* specified to the Politburo decision of 7 January 1931. But it also decided to consolidate central control over the reserves: both the 'grain *Nepfond* and the grain-fodder *Mobfond*' were to be transferred from *Narkomsnab* (the People's Commissariat for Supplies) to the committee on reserves – a powerful organization, whose chair was Kuibyshev and whose vice-chair, Iagoda, was head of the OGPU. The Politburo intended that 'warehouses and personnel' should also be transferred to the committee on reserves; but at this time they apparently remained in the grain collection and processing network. Use of grain deemed to be part of *Nepfond* or *Mobfond* required permission of the committee on reserves or even the Politburo. Sovnarkom further decreed that all 2.457 million tons were to be transferred to the committee on reserves by 1 December 1931, together with large stocks of other foodstuffs, consumer goods and metals. By 1 January 1932, the grain set aside in 'various funds', nearly all of which was *Nepfond* and *Mobfond*, amounted to 2.033 million tons (see Table 1): the plan for the reserve funds had been largely achieved.

But this apparent triumph was short-lived. The demand for grain relentlessly increased. Grain exports in the agricultural year 1931/32 were one million tons less than in 1930/31; simultaneously, however, state grain allocations within the USSR increased (see Table 4). The increase in internal utilization in 1931/32 was part of a process which had been proceeding relentlessly since 1929, resulting from a substantial increase in the number of industrial and building workers and their dependants; a growing necessity to supply grain for seed and food to collective farmers and others in areas where harvests had been low and grain collections too high; an increase in the use of grain to feed sections of the population, including cotton-growers and timber-cutters who had previously obtained their grain from the market, and to feed exiled *kulaks* and others; an increased consumption of grain by industry. The total amount of grain allocated by the state for internal use increased from 8.400 million tons in 1928/29 to 16.309 million tons in 1931/32; in 1931/32 alone the increase amounted to 2.477 million tons. The pressure on stocks was relentless.

Despite demand, the Politburo endeavoured to reduce the rate of issue of grain. In March 1932 it agreed to drastic cuts in the bread ration for consumers on the lower-priority ration Lists 2 and 3.[14] Many requests for additional rations, even from high-priority industries, were refused. These reductions and the irregular delivery of bread and other food supplies led to famine in the towns in spring 1932. Among the urban population of the lower Volga region the death rate more than doubled between January and July 1932; among the urban population of the Kiev region it increased by 70 per cent; and even in Moscow the death rate rose by one-third.

But the severe measures of March 1932 failed to reduce to the level of the available grain food allocations to which the state was committed. On 23 May 1932, an alarmed Kuibyshev prepared a memorandum concerning the grain situation for the Politburo in which he outlined the additional measures needed if an uninterrupted grain supply to the main industrial centres was to be maintained until the new harvest; his proposals even included the reduction of the bread ration for workers on the Special List and List 1. The draft memorandum preserved in the Kuibyshev papers includes his handwritten note in blue crayon:

> With  a full sense of responsibility I want to emphasize that last year we had 88.8 million *poods* [1.45 million tons] [of food grains] on 1 July, and that in the current year there will be only 57.7 million *poods* [0.945 million tons].
>
> What does this mean?
>
> It means that we can cope with the supply of bread only by an exceptional level of extremely thorough organization.

Another handwritten sentence, crossed out, reads, 'I ask you to give to the committee on reserves dictatorial powers until the new harvest'.

The Politburo did not accept Kuibyshev's proposal to reduce rations for the Special List and List 1; but on 25 May it decided that it was necessary before 1 July to collect the outstanding 14 million *poods* (229,000 tons) of grain from the remains of the 1931 harvest, to add more barley to the food grains and to transfer various grain stocks from one part of the country to another. It also reduced the allocation to the military by about 16 per cent, and called for the acceleration of the import of grain from Persia and its immediate transfer to the far east. In spite of all these measures, it was estimated that planners' stocks of food grains (excluding fodder) would decline from 2.01 million tons on 10 May to 0.886 million tons on 1 July. For the difficult months of July and August 1932 when the new harvest was beginning to come in, the Politburo also resolved that all grain collected from the new harvest would be used solely to supply industrial centres and the army.

In the outcome, planners' stocks on 1 July 1932 were as low as the Politburo had anticipated in May: food grains amounted to 915 thousand tons and all grains to 1.36 million tons – 1 million tons less than on 1 July 1931 and even less than on 1 July 1930. *Nepfond* and *Mobfond*, intended to total 2.457 million tons and reaching about 2 million tons on January 1932, amounted to only 0.641 million tons on 1 July (see Tables 2 and 3). The demand for grain had impelled the Politburo to use up most of its 'untouchable' fund. On 1 July total stocks of food grain amounted to about one month's supply: in Ukraine, the lower Volga and north Caucasus less than a month's supply was available. Following the Japanese invasion of Manchuria, the authorities had utterly failed to build up grain stocks in east Siberia and the far east: total stocks of food and fodder grains in these two regions amounted to at most 190,000 tons on 1 July;[15] the 1 million tons of military stocks that Radek reported to the British was apparently sheer bluff.

## The 1932 harvest and the 1932/33 agricultural year

In May 1932, in preparing its plans for the forthcoming harvest, the Politburo somewhat reduced the grain collection plan below the previous year's level and sought to fill the gap by permitting trade in grain at market prices once collection quotas had been met. But the sharp decrease in grain stocks below the 1931 level had greatly alarmed the authorities. In spite of the reduced collection planned in May, on 16 July 1932 the Politburo again sought to set aside substantial stocks in *Nepfond* and *Mobfond* from the new harvest. It resolved that in 1932/33 *Gosfond* (state fund, another name for *Mobfond*) would amount to 55 million *poods* (0.901 million tons) and *Nepfond* to 120 million *poods* (1.966 million tons), 2.867 million tons in total. On 9 December 1932 the Politburo approved a reduced plan for grain utilization in 1932/33 by which *Gosfond* and *Nepfond* would still total 2.867 million tons on 1 July 1933; together with transitional stocks, all planners' stocks would amount to 3.699 million tons on 1 July, as compared with 1.36 million tons on the same date of 1932 (see note 5). Thus the authorities certainly *planned* to hold very substantial stocks at the end of the 1932/33 agricultural year (if not the 4.53 million tons claimed by Robert Conquest). And on 1 January 1933, with total stocks at their seasonal peak, as much as 3.034 million tons were attributed to 'various funds' (the main components of which were *Gosfond* and *Nepfond*) (see Table 1).

The grain utilization plan for 1932/33 was built on illusion. While grain exports were again reduced, this time by 3 million tons below the previous year's level, grain collections declined by over 4 million tons (see Table 4). The net decline in grain available for internal use amounted to more than 1 million tons (see Table 4, collections minus export in 1932/33 versus 1931/32), and this placed an immense strain on resources, quite incompatible with the decision to allocate 2.339 million additional tons to planners' stocks on 1 July 1933 as compared with 1 July 1932. Moreover, the grain balance of 9 December 1932 had assumed that *no* grain should be allocated to the countryside for seed and food, apart from earmarked allocations to cotton growing and other specialized areas. In the course of the first six month of 1933, the Politburo reluctantly, little by little, released between 1.99 million and 2.2 million tons in seed, food and fodder, primarily as allocations or 'loans' to areas which had been stripped of grain by the state collectors earlier in the year. While neither large enough nor timely enough to prevent the devastating famine, these allocations did use up most of *Nepfond* and *Gosfond* which had been set aside at the beginning the year.

In spring 1933, as in the previous year, leading grain officials addressed a series of urgent memoranda to the Politburo warning of shortages. In March a memorandum from Chernov to Stalin, Kaganovich, Molotov and Kuibyshev pointed out that receipts of food grain might be 0.5–0.6 million tons less than in the grain utilization plan of 9 December 1932, while expenditure might be 0.5 million tons more; the shortfall in oats and barley might amount to a further half million tons.[16] A memorandum from Kleiner to Kuibyshev, prepared in February or March, concluded that on 1 July 1933 *Nepfond* would be 0.256 million tons less than planned on December 9. Two or three months later, on 17 May, a telegram from Kleiner to Stalin and Kuibyshev makes it clear that the situation had drastically deteriorated: 'surpluses in the *Nepfond* are almost exhausted'. To provide seed, food and fodder the Politburo had agreed to release 69 million *poods* (1.13 million tons) from the committee on reserves, so that only 100 million *poods* (1.638 million  tons)  remained in all its reserves; Kleiner asked for conditional permission to use a further 15 million *poods* (0.246 million tons) from funds of the committee on reserves.[17]

Within a few weeks the situation had apparently deteriorated still further. On 4 June 1933, Chernov sent a memorandum to Stalin, Kaganovich, Molotov and Kuibyshev, setting out the results of the 1 May inventory of the remaining grain (*ostatki*) in the USSR. Chernov estimated that, as a result of commitments made in May and June, all planners' stocks would total 84.7 million *poods* (1.392 million tons) on 1 July 1933, including food grains amounting to 63.8 million *poods* (1.045 million tons), a slightly larger amount than on 1 July 1932. In several places the memorandum referred to this estimate as the 'transitional remainder including funds' (*perekhodiashchii ostatok vkliuchaia fondy*).[18]

In practice, the level of grain stocks was apparently somewhat greater than Chernov and the other officials anticipated. When Chernov submitted the grain plans for the following year, 1933/34, to Stalin Kaganovich and Molotov on 4 July 1933, he stated, as he had a month previously, that the total transitional stock, including *fondy*, on 1 July 1933 was 1.392 million tons (including 1.045 million tons of food grains). But the grain utilization plan for 1933/34 approved a month later by the Politburo recorded the 'availability' of all grains on 1 July, including *fondy*, as 1.825 million tons (including 1.386 million tons of food grains). The final official figure published in the grain yearbook was 1.997 million tons (including 1.397 million tons of food grains) (see Tables 1 and 2). We have not yet found any satisfactory explanation of the discrepancy between these three sets of figures.

The planners' stocks available on 1 July 1933 certainly included enough grain to save the lives of many peasants. But they amounted not to 4.53 million tons but to less than 2 million tons, smaller than the stocks available on the same date three years previously. The alternative figures for 1 July 1933, including the published figure (1.997 million tons), certainly include both *Gosfond* and *Nepfond*. Robert Conquest's confusion about the level of stocks may be due to a somewhat ambiguous passage in Chernov's memorandum dated 4 July 1933, submitting the draft grain plans for 1933/34 to the Politburo. He proposed that in 1933/34 *Nepfond* should be '120 million *poods* [1.966 million tons], the same level as last year', while *Gosfond* should be 'significantly increased to 72 million *poods* [1.179 million tons] instead of the 55 million *poods* [0.901 million tons] of last year'. According to this draft, then, both *fondy* together would amount to 3.145 million tons. But Chernov's tables and the figures approved by the Politburo make it clear that 'the same level as last year' did not mean the *actual* reserve stock in July 1933 but instead the stock *planned* in July 1932.[19] In 1933/34 *Nepfond* and *Gosfond* had to be built up from existing planners' stocks. Thus the plan approved by the Politburo on 7 August 1933 fixed total grain stocks on 1 July 1934 at 3.941 million tons, including a total *Gosfond* and *Nepfond* of

2.776 million tons; the Politburo compared this with the *total* stocks on
1 July 1933 of only 1.825 million tons.[20]

The failure to establish reserve stocks at planned levels also meant that
the efforts to build up grain stocks in the far east had again been
unsuccessful. According to the published data, total planners' stocks in east
Siberia and the far east amounted to only 0.147 million tons on 1 July
1932, increasing to 0.269 million tons on 1 July 1933; some additional
stocks, not included in these figures, were held by the army itself. But the
serious effort to build up grain stocks in the far east began not after
the 1931 harvest, as Radek and Duranty claimed at the time, or even
after the 1932 harvest, but only during and after the 1933 harvest. It was
not until July 1933 that Chernov received an urgent commission from
Stalin to create a 'special defence fund' of 70 million *poods* (1.147 million
tons) in east Siberia an the far east. This grain stock would require
extensive new grain stores, since those of *Mobfond* in the far east and east
Siberia had a capacity of only 0.143 million tons.

How reliable were these data on grain stocks? After the civil war, during
which local authorities underestimated the level of stocks, the Soviet
authorities were anxious to obtain accurate and timely figures. In the early
1920s a comprehensive system was established, by which monthly estimates
of grain stocks by local statistical departments were supplemented by
quarterly on-site inventories. Statistical departments telegraphed regular
'short summaries' to the centre two weeks after each survey, followed by
more detailed (and more accurate) reports sent through the mail. The same
system was used in 1930–4. In 1928 A. Mikhailovskii, at that time the
principal authority on grain statistics, claimed that the figures for the USSR
which were assembled centrally from these data were 'quite reliable'. The
data on grain stocks for 1932–3 were also, in our opinion, 'quite reliable'.
This is not to say that they should be accepted uncritically. The discrepancy
between the lowest and highest figures for all planners' stocks on 1 July
1933 – 1.397 million and 1.997 million tons – dramatically illustrates
this point. If the later and higher figure is correct, the additional 0.6 million
tons of grain could have saved many lives. But this figure does not appear
in any of the records we have used until some weeks after the end of
the agricultural year and it was evidently not known to the Politburo
before July 1933.

There were no private inventories of grain stocks kept for Stalin and
his immediate entourage, separate from those regularly assembled by
the normal state agencies; the figures in the top-secret files of Sovnarkom,
of Kuibyshev's secretariat and in the special files (*osobye papki*) of the
Politburo all coincide. These figures also agree – somewhat to our
surprise – with the figures for grain stocks published in the unclassified
small-circulation *Ezhegodnik khlebooborota* (*Grain Collection Annual*).[21]

But the relationship between public and secret statistics in the USSR was complicated. While they were identical for grain stocks, the exaggeration in the published figures for the grain harvests is well known. And our research shows that those responsible for planning and recording grain allocations did not contradict – even in private – the distorted official harvest figures; they therefore included in the grain balances a large residual item so that consumption could be brought in line with the alleged harvests.[22] And in the extreme case of the defence budget for 1931–4, the large increases in these years were concealed by the deliberate decision of the Politburo to publish falsified figures. The true figures appeared only in documents classified as top-secret and were more than treble the size of the published figures.[23] The complicated relations between archival and published data can only be established by investigating each case on its merits.

We therefore conclude:

1. All planners' stocks – the two secret grain reserves, *Nepfond* and *Mobfond* or *Gosfond*, together with 'transitional stocks' held by grain organizations – amounted on 1 July 1933 to less than 2 million tons (1.997 million tons, according to the highest official figure). Persistent efforts of Stalin and the Politburo to establish firm and inviolable grain reserves (in addition to 'transitional stocks') amounting to 2 or 3 million tons or more were almost completely unsuccessful. In both January–June 1932 and January–June 1933 the Politburo had to allow 'untouchable' grain stocks set aside at the beginning of each year to be used to meet food and fodder crises. On 1 July 1933 the total amount of grain set aside in reserve grain stocks (*fondy*) amounted not to 4.53 million tons as Conquest claimed but to only 1.141 million. It is not surprising that after several years during which the Politburo had failed to establish inviolable grain stocks, Kuibyshev in early 1933 recommended a 'flexible approach' to *Nepfond* and *Mobfond*, denied that they were separate reserves and even claimed that the flexible use of the two *fondy* had enabled uninterrupted grain supply in spring and summer 1932.

2. We do not know the amount of grain which was held by grain-consuming organizations, notably the Red Army, but we suspect that these 'consumers' stocks' would not change the picture substantially.

3. These findings do not, of course, free Stalin from responsibility for the famine. It is difficult, perhaps impossible, to assess the extent to which it would have been possible for Stalin to use part of the grain stocks available in spring 1933 to feed starving peasants. The state was a monopoly supplier of grain to urban areas and the army; if the reserves of this monopoly supply system – which amounted to four–six weeks' supply – were to have been drained, mass starvation, epidemics and unrest in the towns could have resulted. Nevertheless, it seems certain that if

Stalin had risked lower levels of these reserves in spring and summer 1933, hundreds of thousands – perhaps millions – of lives could have been saved. In the slightly longer term, if he had been open about the famine, some international help would certainly have alleviated the disaster. And if he had been more far-sighted, the agricultural crisis of 1932–3 could have been mitigated and perhaps even avoided altogether. But Stalin was not hoarding immense grain reserves in these years. On the contrary, he had failed to reach the levels he had been imperatively demanding since 1929.

NOTES

[Reorganized and renumbered from the original.]

The authors are most grateful to Oleg Khlevnyuk for his assistance in research for this article.

1. Naum Jasny, *The Socialized Agriculture of the USSR: Plans and Performance* (Stanford, 1949) 757.

2. See Alexander Baykov, *The Development of the Soviet Economic System* (New York, 1947); Maurice Dobb, *Soviet Economic Development since 1917* (London, 1948); Lazar Volin, *A Century of Russian Agriculture: From Alexander II to Khrushchev* (Cambridge, 1970); Alec Nove, *An Economic History of the USSR* (Harmondsworth, 1969).

3. Jonatham Haslam, *Soviet Foreign Policy, 1930–33: The Impact of the Depression* (New York, 1983) 84.

4. Walter Duranty, *Duranty Reports Russia* (New York, 1934) 342.

5. This figure, for the agricultural year 1932/33, includes the OGPU (secret police) armies. In this paper our discussion takes place in terms of the agricultural year, which ran from harvest to harvest, 1 July–30 June.

6. *Slavic Review* 53, no. 1 (Spring 1994): 318.

7. TLS, 11 February 1994. In *The New York Review of Books*, 23 September 1993, he drew attention more briefly to 'the figures on the millions of tons of available grain reserves' which demonstrated that 'the famine of 1933 was deliberately carried out by terror'.

8. See S. G. Wheatcroft, 'Grain Production and Utilisation in Russia and the USSR before Collectivisation', PhD. thesis (CREES, University of Birmingham, 1980) 561–65.

9. The resolution added that the Council of Labour and Defence should report to the Politburo on the size of additional *mobfond* (mobilization fund) of food grains.

10. Total visible stocks amounted to 11.756 million tons on 1 January 1930, as compared with only 3.780 million on 1 January 1929. Of these, 'planners' stocks' amounted to 7.838 million tons (see Table 1).

11. Note that by 1 August 1930 planners' stocks had fallen to 1.462 million tons (see Table 1).

12. These figures apparently included fodder grains as well as food grains.

13. We have been unable to ascertain whether *mobfond* is the same as the 'military stocks' (*voennyi zapas*) of 25 million *poods* (0.410 million tons) referred to in the protocols of the Politburo for 13 April 1930.

14. In these years the part of the population which received rations was divided into four main groups or lists (*spiski*), depending on state priorities. In order of priority these were the special list (*osobyi spisok*), and Lists 1, 2 and 3.

15. The later published figure was 147,000 tons.

16. Chernov was the principal person concerned with the practical details of grain collection and allocation.

17. The memorandum referred to food grains only. I. M. Kleiner was appointed deputy chair of the committee for agricultural collections (*Komzag*) on 5 March 1933.

18. Chernov complained that the situation was made more difficult by the plan to supply before 1 July an additional 6.1 million *poods* (100,000 tons) of food and fodder grain to the military and 4 million *poods* (66,000 tons) to the far east; he insisted that it was impossible to supply the additional fodder to the far east.

19. The mythical 4.53 million toms was evidently obtained by adding together the *planned* (and non-existent) *Nepfond* and *Gosfond* (1.966 + 1.179 million tons) and the expected *total* stocks on 1 July 1933 (1.392 million tons)! In view of the importance of this memorandum, all three of us have independently checked it and all the other documents in the file in which it appears; nowhere is there any evidence of the existence of a stock of 4.53 million tons on 1 July 1933.

20. Chernov's proposal to increase *Gosfond* to 72 million *poods* was not taken up by the Politburo.

21. These published figures are in some respects more detailed and regular than those in the archives and we have therefore used them in our tables.

22. The grain balances for these years will be discussed in R. W. Davies and S. G. Wheatcroft, *The Years of Hunger: Soviet Agriculture, 1931–1933* (forthcoming).

23. See R. W. Davies, 'Soviet Military Expenditure, 1929–33: A Reconsideration', *Europe-Asia Studies* 45 (1993): 577–608.

# IV  The Great Terror

## WHY DID THE TERROR TAKE PLACE?

The Great Terror of 1936–8 is the greatest mystery of the Stalin years. Many theories have been put forward. Isaac Deutscher saw it as a massive settling of accounts within the party. For Tucker it was a preparation for a pact with Nazi Germany. Conquest interpreted it as a conscious attempt to break Soviet society down into compliant and powerless individuals cowed by terror, to atomize it. Some saw it as a process designed to contain the conflicting pressures which had arisen from the second revolution of 1928–32. Many theories abounded among those who were its victims. Many saw it as a falling out among the great with themselves simply as debris from the conflict. Some, in complete confusion, attributed it to sunspots. Extraordinarily, many, including intelligent and relatively well-placed people like the writer Boris Pasternak, thought it was being conducted by subordinates without Stalin's knowledge. Time and again the victims thought it would all come to an end if Stalin were to be told about it. The first impulse of the arrested was often 'Why me? I'm innocent'. Once in the Gulag they realized everyone else was innocent of the charges laid against them of being 'enemies of the people'. In the outside world, and among camp guards, the belief that the convicts were guilty was very strong though no one had much idea of the actual scale of arrests and executions.

The mystery of the terror deepens when one bears in mind that in 1934 there was a brief 'thaw'. The worst of the cultural and political assaults of 1928–32 were over. Some excesses were being reversed. As we have seen collectivization was slowed down. Some arrested people, the historian Tarlé, for example, were released. Those who had attacked them, such as Leopold Averbakh, the most vociferous of the 'proletarians', replaced them in the camps. Some have even talked of a 'great retreat' though it was hardly that. Nonetheless, the assault and even the famine were over by the end of 1933. The Party Congress of 1934 was called the 'Congress of Victors'. Kamenev and Zinoviev were allowed to speak, though only to rend homage to Stalin. No one would have predicted that of the 1961 'victors' present, 1108 would be arrested by 1939.

Are we any better placed than contemporaries to assess why this devastating policy was implemented? Since the first serious stirrings of *glasnost'* (openness) in 1987 a number of avenues have opened up. Figures for the number of victims are better grounded today than some of the wilder estimates of the Cold War years. Around 900,000 executions are thought to have taken place between the mid thirties and 1953. The number of camp and other detainees seems to have peaked at around 4 million around 1939/40. The death rate in camps was about 7 per cent per year, giving deaths of about 55,000–75,000 in the purge years to 250,000 at the peak in 1942 when the whole country was under stress because of the Nazi invasion. These figures include criminals as well as political prisoners. They are bad enough even though they are much below earlier assumptions.

The second area which is now better established is that the purges were directed at a succession of groups – the party, economic ministries, the military, the Communist International – and minority nationalities, especially those like Poles, Germans, Turks and Koreans with national states outside the USSR who, it was feared, might harbour dual loyalties. This, plus the fact that certain nationals among foreign communists (notably British and Americans) were never arrested, indicates clearly that the process was not entirely arbitrary and was under some form of central control. Thirdly, in a remarkable set of interviews conducted in the 1970s and 1980s, Stalin's closest lieutenant, Molotov, constantly repeated that the purges were both necessary and directed against enemies of the people. Above all, the Nazi threat and the danger of an internal fifth column stretching from fascists to Trotskyites was still, in Molotov's mind, strong justification for the purges even though some innocents would be caught up in them by mistake.

Together, all these approaches help us to understand the purges much better. The emerging picture is one in which 'totalitarian' assumptions of central control and intent have to be taken on board but also modified, especially by the consideration that the Soviet state was bungling and inefficient. The revisionist view that the dynamism of the process built up in part from below, creating a ghastly rolling snowball effect which magnified central initiatives, also has to be incorporated. Finally, we also have to accept that the impact of the purges was very variable. The elites of the metropolises suffered more directly than the workers of Magnitogorsk. The rural collective farm peasantry was little affected.

Putting these together the picture is one of fear, even paranoia, among the leadership, especially after the rise of Hitler in 1933 and the assassination of Kirov in December 1934, that there were real enemies at large in the country and that the security services had lost their grip on them. Promoting the search for them from the centre led to local escalation, based on local 'little Stalins' settling local scores and fearing that not showing enough enthusiasm for the uprooting of enemies might raise suspicion against oneself. The outcome was chaos and disruption characteristic of all major previous Stalinist initiatives like collectivization and the First Five-Year Plan. Like them, the terror had to be reined in abruptly and the blame for chaos turned against its leading perpetrators, notably the head of the security police Ezhov who was one of the terror's last victims.

However, even the purges did not create a universal atmosphere of fear and obedience. In many ways Soviet Russia remained a fluid and mobile society filtering through the fingers of those trying to control it. One thing which all the previous contributions have shown is that there was intense debate in Soviet Russia and open conflict between varying tendencies about the direction in which the revolution was to go. While the country as a whole retained much of this atmosphere, at the centre, while conflict of opinion was not wholly eliminated, a new discipline and tendency to obey rather than to argue was building up which, under the impact of war and the grossly inflating cult of Stalin, was to be further heightened.

Among those whose work has done most to make the breakthroughs which have helped us to understand the terror better is Oleg Khlevnyuk, part of a younger generation of post-Soviet Russian scholars, and it is to his work that we now turn.

## 5   Oleg Khlevnyuk: 'The Objectives of the Great Terror, 1937–8'

The mass repression in the Soviet Union in 1937–8, variously referred to as the Great Terror or the 'Ezhovshchina', has produced a volume of monographs, articles and memoirs, which have examined the phenomena from a diversity of viewpoints.[1] However, many of the circumstances surrounding this tragedy remain obscure. In particular there is little information concerning the mechanism whereby the repression was organized and carried out. Most of the NKVD's documents for this period remain in the KGB's archives and are not available for researchers. In the still closed Presidential archives there is a large volume of material concerning the activities of the Politburo and Stalin in 1937–8. In republican, provincial and local archives there is a wealth of material on how central directives were implemented in the localities.

The detailed study of these problems will require much time and effort by historians. That work has only just started. The lack of information and insufficient research mean that many questions cannot yet be fully answered. Some of the most intriguing questions concern the relationship between centralism and 'local initiative' in the events of 1937–8. More work is needed to determine the system whereby the victims of repression were selected, the objectives of the purgers, as well as the question of the actual number of the victims who were repressed.

In the present article, which draws an new documents including those from the Politburo's special files (*osobye papki*), an attempt is made to present in general outline the mechanism of repression in 1937–8, and on this basis to determine what were the objectives of the organizers of the terror.

Almost all historians are agreed in fixing the commencement of the new stage of Stalinist repression at the end of the summer and the beginning of autumn 1936. In June Stalin instructed the NKVD to organize a new political trial of Trotskyists and Zinovievists. On 29 June the Central Committee of the CPSU dispatched to the localities a secret letter concerning 'the terrorist activities of the Trotskyist-Zinovievist counter-revolutionary bloc', on the basis of which many former oppositionists were repressed. In August in Moscow there took place the trial of the so-called 'anti-Soviet joint Trotskyist–Zinovievist centre'. All 16 of the accused, including L. B. Kamenev and G. E. Zinoviev, were shot. In the country there followed a wave of new arrests.

On 26 September on Stalin's insistence the Politburo removed G. G. Yagoda from the post of People's Commissar of Internal Affairs (NKVD USSR) and appointed in his place N. I. Ezhov, who for several years, at Stalin's behest, had exercised a supervisory role over the NKVD. On 29 September Stalin signed the Politburo decree, 'Concerning the counterrevolutionary Trotskyist–Zinovievist elements'. The decree in effect demanded the fatal destruction of former oppositionists.

In the following few months mass arrests were carried out in the economic, state and party institutions. In January 1937 there took place the second great Moscow trial of the so-called 'Parallel AntiSoviet Trotskyist Centre'.

The first results of the purge were reviewed by the Central Committee plenum of February–March 1937. On the eve of the plenum the Sector of Leading Party Organs of the Central Committee, headed by G. M. Malenkov, compiled inventories (*spravki*) of nomenklatura officials of various departments. The *spravki* comprised several lists. In the first were listed the names of leading officials, who had already been dismissed from their posts, expelled from the party and arrested. In the remaining lists were given the names of other officials who had not yet been arrested but who had committed various 'sins': who had participated in the different oppositions, who 'had deviated', who had in the past been members of other parties, etc. The majority of those named in these lists were soon to be repressed.

The *spravka* which Malenkov prepared for Stalin and dated 15 February 1937 noted the great number of former party members in the USSR. (Many of the facts and theses from the *spravka* were noted by Stalin in his speeches to the February–March plenum.) Malenkov wrote:

It should be noted in particular that at the present time in the country there number over 1,500,000 former members and candidate members of the party, who have been expelled and mechanically dismissed at various times from 1922 onwards. In many enterprises there are concentrated a significant number of former communists, with the result that sometimes they exceed the numerical composition of the party organizations which work in these enterprises'.

For example at the Kolomenskyi locomotive building works, the *spravka* noted, compared to 1408 communists there were 2000 former party members; at the Krasnoe Sormovo works there were 2200 members and 550 former members, at the Moscow Ball Bearing Works 1084 members and 452 former members, etc.

Many of the participants at the February–March plenum spoke of the presence in the country of a great number of 'anti-Soviet elements', and 'offenders'. The secretary of the West Siberia kraikom, R. I. Eikhe, reported that in 11 years from 1926 to 1937 in the krai 93,000 individuals were expelled from the party whilst in the krai party organization at the beginning of 1937 there were 44,000 communists. 'Amongst those expelled,' Eikhe declared, 'there are no small number of direct enemies of the party. They were in the party, they acquire certain political habits and will attempt to utilize this against us.' In the krai, Eikhe continued, there lived also a great number of exiles, former kulaks. Amongst these there remained 'a not insignificant group of inveterate enemies, who will attempt by all means to continue the struggle'. The secretary of the party organization of Turkmeniya, Popok, also spoke of the evident danger which was posed by former kulaks who had returned from imprisonment and exile: 'The great number of kulaks who passed through Solovki and other camps and now as "honourable" toilers return home, demand allotment of their land, making all kinds of demands, going to the kolkhoz and demanding admission to the kolkhoz.' At the plenum others emphasized the fact of the existence of millions of believers in the country with many priests who retained no small influence. The necessity of continuing the struggle with enemies was indicated by the main reports to the plenum from Stalin, Molotov and Ezhov.

In the months following the February–March plenum the policy of unmasking and arresting former oppositionists continued. On 23 May 1937 the Politburo sanctioned the expulsion from Moscow, Leningrad and Kiev to the 'non-industrial regions of the Union' of all those expelled from the party for membership of the various oppositions together with those accused of 'anti-Soviet manifestations (the dissemination of hostile views in lectures and in the press)'. Those expelled also included the families of those sentenced to be shot for political crimes, and those sentenced to imprisonment for five years and upwards. On 8 June the Politburo sanctioned the expulsion from the Azov–Black Sea krai to Kazakhstan of the families of 'arrested Trotskyists and rightists'. In March–June 1937 there continued the arrest of party and state leaders at various levels. Mass arrests now began in earnest in the leadership of the Red Army.

Up until the middle of 1937, therefore, the main blow of repression was directed against members of the party, mainly those who had in their time participated in the oppositions or who had shown some kind of dissent with Stalinist policies. Repression began also in the organs of power inside the NKVD many of Yagoda's people were arrested, in the army cases were fabricated against a number of senior military officers. The new stage in the purge was heralded by the decision of the Politburo of 28 June 1937, 'Concerning the uncovering in West Siberia of a counterrevolutionary insurrectionary organization amongst exiled kulaks'. The resolution ordered the shooting of all 'activists of the insurrectionary organization'. To speed up the investigation of their cases a troika was established comprising the head of the NKVD of Western Siberia (Mironov), the procurator of the krai (Barkav) and the party secretary of the krai (Eikhe).

Within a few days the practice of establishing troiki was extended to the whole country. On 2 July 1937 a Politburo resolution 'Concerning anti-Soviet elements' sanctioned the carrying out of operations which became a pivot of the mass repression of 1937–8. By a resolution of the Politburo the following telegram was sent to the secretaries of the oblast committees, krai committees and the Central Committees of national communist parties:

It is noted that the majority of former kulaks and criminals, who were exiled, at one time from various oblasts to the northern and Siberian regions and then with the completion of the sentences of exile have returned to their oblast – are the main instigators of all kinds of anti-Soviet and diversionary crimes.

The Central Committee ordered the secretaries of oblast and krai organizations and all oblast, krai and republican representatives of the NKVD to take account of all kulaks and criminals who returned to their areas of domicile so that the most hostile of them should be immediately arrested and shot. These cases were to be handled administratively through the troiki, whilst the remainder, the less active but still hostile elements, were to be resettled and sent to the regions designated by the NKVD.

The Central Committee required the local authorities within five days to present to the Central Committee the composition of the troiki, and the number to be shot as well as the number to be exiled.

In the following weeks lists of the troiki and information concerning the number of 'anti-Soviet elements' were received from the localities, and on this basis orders were prepared within the NKVD for the implementation of the operation. On 30 July Ezhov's deputy in the NKVD, M. P. Frinov-skii, who had been assigned responsibility for implementing this action, sent to the Politburo for its approval the NKVD's operational order: N00447, 'Concerning the operation for repressing former kulaks, criminals and other anti-Soviet elements'. The order fixed the beginning of the operation, depending on region; from 5–15 August; it was to be completed in four months' time.

Above all the order laid down 'the contingents to be subject to repression'. In reality it included all who in whatever degree had struggled against Soviet power or had been victims of former repressions: kulaks, those released from or who had fled from exile, former members of disbanded parties (SRs, Georgian Mensheviks, Mussavats, Dashnaks etc.), former White Guards, surviving tsarist officials, those arrested, charged with terror and spying-diversionary activities, political prisoners, those held in labour camps etc. On one of the later places in this list were included criminals.

All those to be repressed, in accordance with this order, were divided into two categories: first those subject to immediate arrest and shooting; second those subject to imprisonment in labour camps or prison for periods from 8 to 10 years. All oblasti, krais and republics in the order were assigned quotas (*limity*) for those to be repressed for each of the two categories (on the basis of information concerning the number of 'anti-Soviet elements', which the local authorities had sent to Moscow). A total of 259,450 individuals were to be arrested, of these 72,950 were to be shot (including 10,000 in the camps). These figures were deliberately incomplete since the quotas omitted a number of regions of the country. The order gave local leaders the right to request from Moscow additional quotas for repression. Moreover, to those imprisoned in camps or in exile might be added the families of the repressed.

Troiki were established in the republics, krais and oblasts to decide the fate of those arrested. As a rule they included the narkom or administrative head of the NKVD, the secretary of the corresponding party organization and the procurator of the republic, krai or oblast. The troiki were accorded extraordinary powers, to pass sentences (including shootings) and issue orders for their implementation without any check. On 31 July this order of the NKVD was approved by the Politburo.

From the end of August the Central Committee received from local leaders requests to increase the quotas for repression. From 27 August to 15 December the Politburo sanctioned increasing the quotas for various regions for the first category by almost 22,500 and for the second category by 16,800 individuals.

Besides the general operation to liquidate 'anti-Soviet elements' there were organized several special actions. On 20 July 1937 the Politburo ordered the NKVD to arrest all Germans who were working in defence factories and to deport some of them abroad. On 9 August the Politburo confirmed the order of the NKVD USSR 'Concerning the liquidation of the Polish diversionist group and organization POV' (Polish Organization of Military Personnel). On 19 September the Politburo approved the NKVD order 'Concerning measures in connection with the terrorist diversionary and spying activities of Japanese agents of the so-called Harbintsy' (former workers of the Chinese Eastern Railway, who had been resettled in the USSR following the sale of the Chinese Eastern Railway to Japan in 1935).

In the second half of 1937 there was carried out also the mass expulsion from frontier regions of 'unreliable elements'. The largest expulsion was the deportation from the Far Eastern krai of the entire Korean population to Kazakhstan and Uzbekistan which was implemented on the basis of the Central Committee–Sovnarkom resolution of 21 August 1937 with the stated aim of 'suppressing penetration by Japanese espionage in the Far Eastern krai'.

An important component part of the mechanism of mass repression was the conducting of numerous trials both in the capital and in the localities. As distinct from the secret courts and the absolutely secret sessions of the troiki open trials fulfilled an important propaganda role. Therefore sanction for the conducting of the main trials was given directly by the Politburo. It also as a rule determined in advance the sentence, most commonly shooting. The Politburo was a officially active in the second half of 1937 in sanctioning the organizaton of these trials. From 8 August to 17 December 1937 the Politburo approved conducting of about 40 trials in various regions of the country.[2]

At the beginning of 1938 signals were issued from Moscow which it seemed indicated a cessation of the purge. On 9 January the Politburo ruled as incorrect the dismissal from work of relatives of individuals, arrested for counterrevolutionary crimes, only on the grounds of their being relatives, and charged the USSR's Procurator, A. Ya. Vyshinskii to give corresponding instructions to the organs of the procuracy. On 19 January the press published the resolution of the Central Committee, 'Concerning the mistakes of party organizations in the expulsion of communists from the party, of the formal-bureaucratic attitude to appeals of those expelled from the CPSU and of measures for correcting these deficiencies', which demanded greater attention to the fate of party members. Certain token measures in connection will these resolutions was undertaken by the leadership of the USSR's Procuracy and by Narkomyust.[3]

The true meaning of these political manoeuvres still remains obscure. Certain indications concerning the preparation of the campaign allow us to assert that the operation against the 'anti-Soviet elements', as noted above, was to be completed in four months, i.e. by November–December 1937 (depending on region). It is possible, that having this circumstance in mind Stalin was prepared at the beginning of 1938 to terminate the purge and that he wished to give a clear signal to this effect to the January plenum of the Central Committee. In support of such a proposition might be cited the fact that the announcement of the 'relaxation' at the beginning of 1939 at the XVIII party congress was also carried through on the basis of the slogan for a more attentive attitude to the fate of communists. The report on this question at the January plenum and at the XVIII party congress were both made by G. M. Malenkov.

Whatever the truth of this argument the resolution of the January plenum of 1938 remained no more than a political declaration. The purge could not be completed in four months. On 31 January 1938 the Politburo adopted the proposal of the NKVD USSR 'Concerning the confirmation of additional numbers of those subject to repression of former kulaks, criminals and active anti-Soviet elements'. By 15 March (in the Far East by 1st April) it was prescribed, within the operation for eliminating 'anti-Soviet elements', to repress an additional 57,200 individuals, of whom 48,000 were to be shot. Correspondingly the powers of the troiki, who were to carry out this work, were extended. Also on 31 January the Politburo authorized the NKVD to extend until 15 April the operation for destroying the so-called 'counterrevolutionary nationalist contingent-Poles, Letts, Germans, Estonians, Finns, Greeks, Iranians, Harbintsy, Chinese and Romanians'. Furthermore, the Politburo charged the NKVD that it should complete by 15 April analogous operations and destroy (*pogromit'*) the cadres of Bulgarians and Macedonians, both those of foreign origin and those who were citizens of the USSR.

After confirming these new quotas for repression the history of the previous year was repeated: local leaders began to request increasing the quotas and extending the duration of the operation. From 1 February to 29 August 1939 the Politburo approved additions to the January quotas for those to be repressed by about 90,000 people.[4] And this meant also in fact approving the breaching of the April deadline on the duration of the operation.

In 1938 the campaign of political trials was continued. For the year as a whole the Politburo sanctioned the conducting of about 30 trials, of which seven were in January 1938.

Only in the autumn of 1938 was the terror reined in. The examination of cases by the troiki was forbidden by the directive of Sovnarkom–Central Committee of 15 November 1938. The joint Sovnarkom–Central Committee resolution of 17 November 1938 forbade the carrying out of 'mass operations for arrest and exile'. On 24 November Ezhov was released from his post as narkom of the NKVD. The great terror was brought to an end.

This brief enumeration, which does not cover all the actions, that comprised what is known as the great terror, allows us to make some observations.

The mass repression of 1937–8 was unquestionably an action directed from the centre, which was planned and administered from Moscow. The Politburo gave orders for the carrying out of the various operations, it approved the operational orders of the NKVD, it sanctioned the organization of the most important trials. The question of the activities and reorganizations of the NKVD, and the appointment of the responsible officials of this commissariat, occupied in 1937–8, to judge from the protocols, the leading place in the Politburo's work.

The activity of the troiki, as already noted, was regulated by means of quotas on the numbers to be incarcerated in camps and those to be shot. Sentences imposed on a significant proportion of those tried by the Military Collegium of the USSR's Supreme Court, the military tribunals and other 'judicial bodies' were in fact determined in advance by the Politburo's Commission for Legal Matters and confirmed by the Politburo. In this period the Commission for Legal Matters presented its protocols for the approval of the Politburo once a month on average. The texts of these protocols remain unavailable. But evidently they include the 383 lists 'of many thousands of party, soviet, Komsomol, military and economic workers' which, as N. S. Khrushchev revealed at the XX party congress, Ezhov sent to Stalin to be approved. (Ezhov was included in the composition of the Politburo Commission on Legal Matters on 23 January 1937 and evidently during the repression played a leading part in it). An example of one of these lists was given in the speech by the deputy chairman of the Committee of Party Control Z. T. Serdyuk at the XXII party congress in October 1961:

Comrade Stalin,
   I send for your approval four lists of individuals which are to be sent to the Court of the Military Collegium.
   1.  List 1 (general)
   2.  List 2 (former military officials)
   3.  List 3 (former workers of the NKVD)
   4.  List 4 (wives of enemies of the people)
I request that you sanction that they all be sentenced to the first category.
*Ezhov*

In spite of the fact that the majority of directives concerning the terror were formulated as decisions of the Politburo their true author, judging from the existing documents, was Stalin. The Politburo itself in the years of the terror evidently met irregularly. On 14 April 1937 there was adopted the resolution 'with the aim of preparing for the Politburo and in case of especial urgency – also for the resolution of questions of a secret character … to create attached to the Politburo of the CC CPSU a permanent commission comprising comrades Stalin, Molotov, Voroshilov, Kaganovich, L., and Ezhov'. The inclusion in this group of Ezhov (who, incidentally, became only a candidate member of the Politburo several months later) testifies to the fact that this simplified procedure was designed primarily to examine questions relating to the NKVD's activity. This was so in practice. Several resolutions, judging by all the evidence, Stalin adopted in fact on his own. The directives of the Central Committee to the localities about the arrests and organization of trials bore Stalin's signature. In a number of cases Stalin dispatched telegrams with instructions from himself in person. For example on 27 August 1937 in reply to a request from the secretary of the Western obkom of the party, Korotchenko, concerning a trial of 'wreckers active in agriculture in Andreevskii raion' Stalin telegraphed: 'I advise you to sentence the wreckers of Andreevskii raion to be shot, and the shootings to be publicized in the local press.' A similar telegram from Stalin personally the same day was sent to Krasnoyarsk obkom. With a great measure of confidence it is possible to assert that when the documents from the Presidential archive are available, much more evidence will be revealed concerning Stalin's leading role in the organization of the terror.

The centralized initiation and direction of the terror as a whole does not mean that there were no elements of a spontaneous character. Indeed they existed in all such actions – during the course of collectivization and forcible grain requisitioning in 1932–3, in the so-called struggle against 'terrorism' following the murder of Kirov, etc. In official language these phenomena were referred to as 'excesses' (*peregib*) or as breaches of socialist legality. To the 'excesses' of the mass repression of 1937–8 it is possible to adduce the high number of deaths during interrogation or the exceeding by local organs of the quotas for arrests and shootings established by Moscow, etc. For example, according to incomplete information, the troika of the NKVD of Turkmeniya from August 1937 to September 1938 tried 13,259 individuals although they had a limit of only 6277. This fact of exceeding the quota by more than double, and also the murder of prisoners under investigation, which was concealed by the local organs and not given in accounts, must be taken into consideration in assessing the total number of those repressed.

However, as a whole such spontaneity or initiative by local authorities was planned, deriving from the nature of the orders which were issued by the centre, from the constant demands of Moscow to 'strengthen the struggle with the enemy', from the assignment to the NKVD of the primary task of ruthlessly implementing and breaking all minor attempts to oppose the terror. Up to a certain point the leadership of the country in fact encouraged breaches of their own directives, untying the NKVD's hand, although it was fully cognisant of the fact that the terror went beyond the limits established by the 'control figures'.

As the mass terror of 1937–8 was an action which was directed from the centre, it is logical to ask what aims did it serve for the organizers of the repression and in particular for Stalin. This problem has been repeatedly examined in the literature. Historians have directed attention to such facts as the elimination of a significant proportion of those communists with pre-revolutionary party service, the growing threat of a new war, the replacement of the ruling elite, the unstable state of Stalin's own psychology, etc. What we know today regarding the mechanisms of the 'Great Terror' allows us to assert that the main aim of the mass repression of 1937–8 was the removal of all strata of the population which in the opinion of the country's leaders were hostile or potentially hostile.

The purge at the end of the 1930s was carried out in accordance with the policy of repression implemented in earlier years. The actions that followed one another – expulsions from the party and the arrest of oppositionists, collectivization and 'dekulakization', the struggle with 'sabotage of grain requisitioning' and 'theft of socialist property', arrests and exile after the murder of Kirov, mass expulsions from the party and arrests in the course of the exchange of party documents etc. – affected many millions of people. By the middle of the 1930s in the country, as already noted, there were 1.5 million former party members, millions of prisoners in the labour camps and in the so-called labour settlements. There were also millions of people who were free but who at various times had been brought to legal account, etc. A great-problem for the government was the return from exile of 'kulaks' who by the middle of the 1930s were being released and under the new Constitution had their rights restored. Thus the number of those with a grudge (*obizhennyi*) and thus under suspicion (together with their families) included a significant proportion of the country's population. In the conditions of a threat of a new war many of them were considered as a potential 'fifth column'. Amongst those who fell under the constant suspicion of the Kremlin leadership were the immigrants, representatives of national minorities, many of whom had certain contacts with their co-nationals who lived abroad.

With certain of the formerly repressed individuals the government attempted reconciliation. The resolution of TsIK and Sovnarkom USSR of 16 January 1936 for example foresaw lighter punishments or early release of some of those sentenced by the notorious law of 7 August 1932 concerning the safeguarding of socialist property.[5] The narkom of Justice Krylenko and chairman of the Supreme Court of the RSFSR Bulat, informed M. I.. Kalinin, chairman of TsIK USSR, that in implementing this resolution by July 1936 (the resolution foresaw the work would be completed in six months) more than 115,000 cases were to be reexamined. Almost 49,000 of those imprisoned had their sentences cut and about 38,000 were released. This aroused amongst several hundred of prisoners the expectation of being granted a full amnesty.

A still larger action of a similar kind occurred when the mass repression was in full swing. On 23 October 1937 the Politburo charged the USSR's Procuracy and Narkomyust to carry out for the whole union and autonomous republics, krais and oblasts a check on criminal cases, which involved those who had held positions in the village soviets, kolkhozy, MTS, as well as village and kolkhoz activists. They were to check all cases beginning from 1934. At the same time the Politburo, undertook to drop cases and free from punishment those kolkhozniki accused of minor offences (property, administrative infringements, etc.). This action continued for more than two years.[6] The examination of criminal cases moved 1.5 million people. By 10 March 1940 were delivered *spravki* concerning the quashing of convictions on almost 450,000 people and releasing from prison almost 30,000. The cases against 128,000 people were closed, whilst 25,000 had their punishments reduced.

On 22 October 1938 Sovnarkom USSR adopted a resolution which authorized the granting of passports to the children of those in special labour settlements and in exile on attaining 16 years of age 'on the general basis and not to place in their way obstacles to go to education or to work', although it preserved restrictions on departure to so-called 'regime localities'. Before the war about 100,000 people were released from exile by this resolution.

However, the Stalinist leadership always considered terror as its main method of struggle with a potential 'fifth column'. The cruel repression of 1937–8 was above all determined by biographical particulars. The basis for shooting or dispatch to the camps might be an unsuitable pre-revolutionary past, participation in the civil war on the side of the Bolsheviks' enemies, membership of other political parties or oppositionist groups within the CPSU, previous convictions, membership of 'suspect' nationalities (Germans, Poles, Koreans etc.), finally family connections and association with representatives of the enumerated categories. Corresponding accounting of all these contingents of the population through the years was done by the NKVD and the party organs. Following orders from Moscow to the localities the lists were compiled and on this basis arrests were carried out.

Already in the order of the NKVD N00447 'Concerning the operation for the repression of former kulaks, criminals and active anti-Soviet elements' the organs of the NKVD were instructed to investigate 'all criminal contacts of those arrested'. As revealed by numerous memoirs and documents the fulfilment of this task was one of the main objectives of the NKVD's staff. Adopting torture, they fabricated numerous cases of 'counterrevolutionary organizations', in which were numbered the friends, co-workers and relatives of those arrested. On this basis new arrests were carried out. The repression was thus extended to those strata of the population which formally were not subject to the purge. Some of those judged in the purge by biographical data were rehabilitated at the end of 1938–9.

It was by these crude means that the repression was carried out amongst members of the party and leading workers both in the centre and in the localities. At first those arrested were those who in their time had participated in oppositions or had some 'political deviation' (the lists of such workers, compiled on the basis of the study of archival material, was in the hands of the NKVD). Then on the basis of their testimony, obtained in many cases by torture and duress, new arrests were carried out. For 1936 alone 134,000 people were expelled from the party, in 1937 more than 117,000 and in 1938 more than 90,000. Some of them were reinstated. However, many were arrested after their expulsion. As a result of the purge of the party the composition of the ruling elite changed substantially. At the beginning of 1939 the Sector of Leading Party Organs accounted for 32,899 leading workers, which were included in the nomenklatura of the Central Committee (narkoms of the USSR and RSFSR, their deputies, heads of chief administrations and obedinenie – administrative units – of the commissariats and their deputies, administrators of trusts and their deputies, directors and 'chief engineers of many industrial enterprises, directors of MTS and sovkhozy, heads of the political departments of the sovkhozy, directors of higher educational institutions and scientific-research institutes, chairmen of oblast and krai heads and deputy heads of departments of executive committees, heads of railway lines and construction projects, etc.). Of these, 43 per cent were promoted in 1937–8. Still more significant was the replacement of the leading party workers. Of 333 secretaries of obkoms, kraikoms and Central Committees of national communist parties who were working at the beginning of 1939, 194 were promoted in 1937–8; of 10,902 secretaries of raikoms, gorkoms and okrugkoms of the party 6909 were appointed to their posts in 1937–8. The changes in the apparat took place through the advancement of young officials and workers.

Not all by any means of the leaders who were repressed suffered for 'political unreliability' (past political sins or close contact with former oppositionists). As with other strata of the population there were amongst the leading workers who suffered many who had an unblemished biography. Researchers have repeatedly noted that with the help of the terror the Stalinist leadership resolved a real existing problem of replacing the older cadres with younger and more educated people.[7] For Stalin such a cadres revolution also had political significance. On the one hand, the promotees, younger cadres advanced as a consequence of the repression, were more amenable to the *vozhd'* (boss) than the old guard. On the other hand it was possible to place all responsibility for former lawlessness, economic errors, the difficulties of life of ordinary Soviet people on the repressed leaders.

Those leaders who were repressed did indeed bear their share of responsibility for what had taken place in the country. The dictatorship created the conditions which allowed incredible abuses of power to occur, and many officials took full advantage of this. Having previously encouraged the tyranny of local leaders, the Moscow *vozhd'* in the years of terror turned against these leaders and actively demonstrated his resolution to 'defend' the people from bureaucrats and enemies. For example, on 14 May 1937 the Politburo examined the question of the cases of assaults on kolkhozniki in various raions of Kursk oblast, and adopted a proposal submitted by Vyshinskii.

> on the adoption by the courts in cases of assaults on kolkhozniki and their public humiliation, of deprivation of freedom as a means of punishment, reviewing sentences that imposed insufficiently harsh punishments in these cases. To publish in the local press sentences for the most important cases, connected with assaults on kolkhozniki and their public humiliation.

On 10 June 1937 the Politburo examined the cases of a number of officials of Shiryaevskii raion in Odessa oblast who were accused of humiliating kolkhozniki. The Procurator of the USSR was charged to send investigators to Shiryaevskii raion to examine the most important cases and to complete the investigation in ten days' time. The matter was heard by the Ukrainian Supreme Court in open session in the locality. The sentences were published in the press, both local and central. A specially secret point of this resolution envisaged the sentencing of all the guilty in the case to loss of liberty from 3 to 10 years' imprisonment. This policy appears to have been applied widely. In numerous open trials which were carried out in all regions of the country, those judged – mainly local leaders – were most often accused of abuse of power and coercion. The victims of their oppression – ordinary citizens – often gave evidence in the courts. The reports of such 'show-trials' were carried in the press.[8]

This policy it seems bore fruit. In the memoirs of a peasant woman from Novosibirsk oblast, M. D. Mal'tseva, who herself was subject to 'dekulakization' and exile, she recounts the period of mass repression of the 1930s:

> People suffered so much in that time, but one never heard people criticizing Stalin; only the local leaders were blamed; only they were criticized. Because of them we all suffered, and how many people died because of them is unknown.

I don't know, perhaps I am wrong, but I say that in 1938 many were taken, perhaps because they heeded our tears, since there were good reasons to take them, that's what I think.

Similar opinions, it seems, were widespread.

With the aim of discovering the reasons for the instigation of the mass repression of 1937–8 it is necessary to take into account the following circumstance. Terror and force were two of the basic methods for creating the Stalinist system. In this or that measure with their help were resolved practically all social-economic and political problems – the securing of social stability, raising industrial production, ensuring Stalin's personal power etc. These and other factors at each stage underwrote the existence of state terror and mass repression. However each of the terror campaigns in turn raised the level of coercion higher, since so to speak the 'usual level' had its concrete reason. For example, the mass exile of peasants at the beginning of the 1930s served the purpose of collectivizing the countryside. The terror at the end of 1932–3 was a means of escaping from the sharp social-economic, and political crisis which developed between the first and second Five-Year Plans. The mass repression of 1937–8 also had its direct causes, as noted above.

In the mind of the Stalinist leadership this was precisely a purge of society, an attempt by one blow to rid themselves of all those who in this or that measure had been subject to coercion in the preceding years or had fallen under suspicion on some other count. This operation was conceived as a means of eliminating a potential 'fifth column' in a period when the threat of war was increasing, and also as a means of disposing of loyal cadres who for various reasons were no longer needed by Stalin.

This view of the purges as a means of eliminating a potential 'fifth column' is not new. The argument was forcefully advanced by the American ambassador in Moscow in the 1930s, Joseph E. Davies.[9] Trotsky, whose writings Stalin avidly read, repeatedly warned of the danger of a prolonged war (whether in the case of victory or defeat), in the absence of a revolutionary upsurge in the west, leading to a capitalist restoration, 'a bourgeois Bonapartist counterrevolution' in the USSR.[10] Isaac Deutscher in his classic biography of Stalin gives an imaginary conversation between Stalin and the ghost of Nicholas II where the relationship between war and regime stability is discussed.[11]

It might be noted further that this was indeed the whole thrust of Stalin's two reports to the Central Committee plenum in February–March 1937, as well as the reports of Molotov, Ezhov, Kaganovich and others. The revelations from the archives now strongly reinforce that view. It is supported by evidence from the directives of the highest leadership of the country concerning the implementation of the purge in 1937–8, by the way these actions were understood by contemporaries, and by the explanations given later by Stalin's own colleagues.[12]

Writing his final, agonized letter to Stalin in December 1937, appealing for his life to be spared, emphasizing his loyalty and respect for Stalin personally, Bukharin noted the 'great and courageous idea of a general purge', associated with war preparations and paradoxically the transition to democracy, heralded by the Stalin Constitution. The purge, he noted, directed at the guilty, those under suspicion and those who might waver, should ensure a 'full guarantee' for the leadership in the event of an emergency.

The most explicit statements in support of this view were uttered by Molotov in the 1970s, when he declared:

> 1937 was necessary. If you take into account that after the revolution we chopped right and left, achieved victory, but the survivals of enemies of various tendencies remained and in the face of the growing threat of fascist aggression they might unite. We were driven in 1937 by the consideration that in the time of war we would not have a fifth column ...

> And there suffered not only the clear Rightists, not to speak of the Trotskyists, but there suffered also many who vacillated, those who did not firmly follow the line and in whom there was no confidence that at a critical moment they would not desert and become, so to speak, part of the 'fifth column'.

> Stalin, in my opinion, pursued an absolutely correct line: so what if one or two extra heads were chopped off (*puskai lishnyaya golova sletit*), there would be no vacillation in the time of war and after the war.

The complex relationship between war and revolution, which had almost seen the tsarist regime toppled in 1905 and which finally brought its demise in 1917, was a relationship of which Stalin was acutely aware. The lesson of history had to be learnt lest history repeat itself.

### NOTES

1. See, for example, R. A. Medvedev, *Let History Judge: The Origins and Consequences of Stalinism* (New York, 1971); R. Conquest, *The Great Terror: A Reassessment* (New York, 1990); J. A. Getty, *The Origins of the Great Purges: The Soviet Communist Party Reconsidered, 1933–1938* (New York, 1985); G. T. Rittetsporn, *Stalinist Simplifications and Soviet Complications; Social Tension and Political Conflicts in the USSR, 1933–1953* (Philadelphia, 1991); J. A. Getty and R. T. Manning (eds), *Stalinist Terror: New Perspectives* (Cambridge, 1993).

2. It is difficult to give precise figures for the number of trials sanctioned by the Politburo since in a number of cases the resolution does not give a precise figure. For example on 14 November 1937 the Politburo instructed the Archangel obkom to conduct two or three cases of 'wreckers in the timber industry'. From the decisions

of the Politburo it is also not always clear whether they had in mind an open trial. For example on 15 November the Politburo charged the Novosibirsk obkom that 'those apprehended concerning the explosion at Prokop'evsk should be brought before the court and shot, the shooting to be publicized in the Novosibirsk press'.

3. P. H. Solomon Jnr., 'Soviet Criminal Justice and the Great Terror', *Slavic Review*, vol. 46, no. 3, 1987, pp. 405–6.

4. It is not possible to determine precisely what proportion of these were subject to be shot, since in many, cases the Politburo confirmed general figures for the fast and second category.

5. Approved by the Politburo on 15 January 1936.

6. On 27 July 1939 Sovnarkom USSR adopted a resolution 'Concerning the reexamination of cases of individuals from the kolkhozy and village aktiv, judged in 1934–1937', which recognized the unsatisfactory course of presenting evidence for gaining convictions and demanded the completion of this work in its entirety for the whole country by 1 November 1939.

7. S. Fitzpatrick, 'Stalin and the Making of a New Elite' in S. Fitzpatrick, *The Cultural Front: Power and Culture in Revolutionary Russia* (New York, 1992) pp. 149–82.

8. S. Fitzpatrick, 'How the Mice Buried the Cat: Scenes from the Great Purges of 1937 in the Russian Provinces', *The Russian Review*, vol. 52, July 1993, pp. 299–320 (included as the next item in this volume).

9. Joseph E, Davies, *Mission to Moscow* (London, 1942).

10. L. D. Trotsky, *The Revolution Betrayed* (London, 1967) p. 229. Trotsky quoted the following passage from *The Fourth International and War*, published in 1935: 'Under the influence of the critical need of the state for articles of prime necessity, the individualistic tendencies of the peasant economy will receive a considerable reinforcement, and the centrifugal forces within the collective farms will increase with every month … In the heated atmosphere of war, we may expect … the attracting of foreign allied capital, a breach in the monopoly of foreign trade, a weakening of state control of the trusts, a sharpening of competition between the trusts, conflicts between the trusts and the workers, etc. .. In other words, in the case of a long war, if the world proletariat is passive, the inner social contradictions of the Soviet Union not only might, but must lead to a bourgeois Bonapartist counterrevolution.'

11. Deutscher, *Stalin: A Political Biography* (Harmondsworth, 1968) pp. 373–4.

12. M. Sholokhov for example wrote in 16 February 1938 to Stalin: 'Cases of apprehension as part of the purge of the rear need also to be rechecked. Those apprehended include not only active Whiteguardists, émigrés, executioners, in a word those whom it is necessary to apprehend, but under this rubric have been taken away also true Soviet people'.


## THE PURGES IN THE PROVINCES

Oleg Khlevnyuk mentioned the existence of numerous local show trials. Sheila Fitzpatrick has produced the most detailed analysis of them. In an examination of 35 trials held in rural areas, almost all in Russia itself, Professor Fitzpatrick lays bare many of the raw emotions of the countryside. Since 1929 the villages of the USSR had been ravaged by a series of vicious campaigns. 'Total collectivization' had become 'Liquidate the kulaks as a class'. Disruption had given way to mass famine. Famine was followed by purges. As a result local resentments and feuds were at boiling point. But in addition to that, this contribution shows the remoteness of the ordinary rural population from the great events of the centre. Far from following a Stalinist lead from the centre, still less being cowed into obeisance to the growing cult of Stalin's personality, Stalin is barely even mentioned in the course of the local show trials. Clearly this is not true of local officials portrayed but it does reflect the experience of the masses. In particular, bitter hatred of the local authorities is clearly evident, particularly those officials who abused their power. They are the villains of the peasants' world, the ones who forced them into collectives and used the farms ever after as their personal fiefdoms – an accusation repeated time and time again in Professor Fitzpatrick's sources.

There was also little sympathy apparent for so-called kulaks who had initially been dispossessed and deported in the early stages of collectivization but were now being rehabilitated. Restoration of land and resources evoked a new round of local battles and recriminations. In some ways, this account contradicts the view that in many cases the commune peasants supported kulaks and defended them in 1929. However, it may be that the cases referred to here were those of groups the peasants had traditionally disliked – former 'separators' who had 'stolen' communal land under the pre-revolutionary Stolypin reforms and local entrepreneurs who had waxed fat on the proceeds of exploiting peasants via mills, creameries, timber yards, stores or other rural enterprises. Some returning 'kulaks' appear to have been relatives of the former local landowner. More precise research would be needed to resolve this conundrum. Similarly, the attitude of the peasants to the central authorities remains unclear. It is most likely that, as Fitzpatrick surmises, they were deeply hostile to Stalin but knew better than to proclaim their antagonism in the open. However, what is certain is that, once again, we have a picture of a very dynamic society which, while it was undoubtedly deeply affected by the central authorities, was by no means under their control. Nor was it deeply in thrall to the local police. Rather like their forefathers in tsarist times, the peasants of the 1930s knew what was happening and took what few opportunities presented themselves to pursue their own interests. Local show trials were one such opportunity. At the same time, however, they knew the authorities had all the cards in their hands and resistance at the wrong moment would be painful.

*Note on terminology*

A number of Russian-derived terms are used frequently in the following article. The main ones are: *raion* – district; *sel'sovet* – rural soviet; *sovkhoz* – state farm (in which peasants are employed by the state for wages); *kolkhoz* – a collective farm (in which peasants pool their land and resources and are paid according to the success of the farm and their contribution to it measured in 'labour days'); *kolkhoznik* – a collective farmer.

## 6 Sheila Fitzpatrick: 'How the Mice Buried the Cat: Scenes from the Great Purges of 1937 in the Russian Provinces'

The ground trembled under him, he was feared, he was hated. 'Brigand' was what the population always called him. People learned to go out of their way to avoid him, so as not to catch his eye more often than necessary. They say that even little children ran away screaming when they saw him. And when he disappeared, the whole street breathed a sigh of relief behind their gates.

He enjoyed his notoriety and was proud of it. Showing off the 'education' acquired who knows where, he often pronounced with a grim, self-satisfied smirk: 'Where I go, the grass will not grow for ten years.'

Kochetov behaved toward the citizenry exactly like a conqueror toward the conquered. He exacted tribute and called it 'fines for the state treasury.' ... And people paid up. People preferred to pay because it was safer than not paying. If anyone dared doubt that, Kochetov himself appeared with his 'activist' – and then the floors shook, dishes rattled and children cried. ... If you don't deliver, I'll dig it out of you like God scooping out a turtle.'

*Sovetskaia iustitsiia (Soviet Justice)*, no. 20 (1937): 22

The villainous Kochetov was a small time Soviet boss in a rural district (*sel'sovet*) in Russia's agricultural heartland. In 1937 he fell victim to the Great Purges that swept the Soviet bureaucracy. Along with his immediate superior, the chairman of the *raion* soviet, he was one of a group of local officials indicted for 'counterrevolutionary' crimes and put on trial in Aleshki, the administrative centre of an obscure rural *raion* in the Voronezh region.

The Aleshki trial was one of dozens held in *raion* centres in the Soviet Union in the autumn of 1937.[1] These trials were not products of the normal workings of the judicial system. They were show trials with a political message. Nineteen thirty-seven was the height of the Great Purges, in which hundreds of thousands of members of the Soviet Communist elite – party and government officials, industrial managers, military officers – as well as members of the intellectual elite were arrested and subsequently sent to labour camps or shot as 'enemies of the people'. In the notorious Moscow trials of August 1936, January 1937 and March 1938, Bukharin, Zinoviev and other former leaders of the Soviet Communist Party astonished the world by confessing that they had long been secret counterrevolutionaries, wreckers, terrorists, agents of the exiled 'Judas-Trotsky', and spies for hostile capitalist powers.

But Moscow was a long way from Aleshki, and the Aleshki version of the Great Purge was both rhetorically and substantively worlds apart from the Moscow trials that inspired Arthur Koestler's famous novel, *Darkness at Noon*. The petty bureaucratic tyrants and oppressed citizens we meet in reports of the Aleshki and other *raion* trials of 1937 could have come straight from the pages of such nineteenth-century Russian satirists as Saltykov-Shchedrin and Chekhov, who chronicled the follies and abuses of local officials and the dreariness of provincial life. These officials are corrupt, venal, illiterate and almost invariably drunk. They are often ludicrously ill-equipped for their positions, like the head of the *raion* sector of animal husbandry who had formerly been a ladies' hairdresser, or his assistant who had been manager of the local public bathhouse. They make pompous but only semiliterate speeches full of Soviet malapropisms. They invite young female tractor-drivers into their offices and tell them to strip for 'medical inspection'.

In contrast to the Moscow trials, highly stylized productions involving fantastic scenarios of conspiracy and treason, the *raion* trials were relatively down-to-earth and straightforward. The former officials on trial in the *raiony* were described as 'enemies of the people' or under the influence of 'enemies'. But only rarely were political offences like espionage or contacts with the Trotskyists or other party oppositionists suggested in the *raion* trials; and only in a few cases did the prosecution argue that the indicted officials had intentionally sabotaged agriculture (by acts like infecting animals with disease, laming horses and so on) because they were counter-revolutionaries who wanted a return to capitalism. The accused officials were encouraged to confess their guilt, as in the Moscow trials, but in fact they often recanted in court and tried to defend themselves, so that the *raion* trials had little of the sinister, mysterious atmosphere of their Moscow counterparts.

Another important difference between the Moscow show trials and their provincial counterparts was that in rural *raion* trials the core of the indictment was not treason and political conspiracy but *exploitation and abuse of the peasantry* by Communists holding official positions at the *raion* and *sel'sovet* levels. These accusations, in contrast to their Moscow counterparts, were almost always completely plausible. In many instances, what the officials were accused of doing (for example, dictating unrealistic sowing plans or extracting so much grain after the harvest that the peasants went hungry) was simply what their jobs and their superiors required them to do. In other instances, the behaviour that was condemned in court (for example, bribe-taking, bullying or forcing through appointments of kolkhoz chairmen against the objections of kolkhozniki) was standard practice for Soviet rural officials in the 1930s.

Finally, a distinctive feature of the rural *raion* trials was that the state's case usually rested largely on the evidence of peasant witnesses. Their passionate and circumstantial testimony in court against former *raion* and *sel'sovet* leaders was generally the dramatic centrepiece of the show trials, which were held in the largest auditorium of the *raion* centre before large audiences of kolkhozniki who had been brought in from all over the *raion* for the occasion. This was political theatre no doubt, but it was a participatory political theatre in which peasant witnesses and auditors appeared to revel in the humiliation of their former bosses. My title, reflecting the *Schadenfreude* (*zloradstvo*) that seems the dominant mood of the rural *raion* show trials of 1937, is that of a popular eighteenth-century Russian woodcut showing the funeral of a large cat, long believed to represent Peter the Great, whose corpse, firmly tied down, is being carried to the grave by a group of dancing and celebrating mice.[2]

## *The Master Plot*

If the show trials are to be viewed as theatre we have to ask who was writing the plays. At one level, this question has a simple answer: the texts at our disposal were almost all written by journalists of oblast daily newspapers.[3] The newspapers ran long and detailed reports of local show trials, often including allegedly verbatim reports of particularly exciting testimony and court exchanges; they generally appeared sequentially in three or four issues. These reports belong to the Soviet version of the genre of exposé journalism, generally focused on local bureaucratic abuses or court cases, whose ostensible function of political (moral) instruction was combined with an unacknowledged but unmistakable entertainment function. They tended to be written with verve and literary flair, pouring sarcasm and scorn on the delinquencies and hypocrisy of the 'bureaucrats' who were their most frequent targets. These 'exposé' stories and feuilletons were oases in the desert of the Soviet press in the 1930s, which was otherwise largely devoted to unrelenting and mendacious boosterism of Soviet economic achievements, official communiqués and the publication in full of long speeches by party leaders.

But the journalistic texts were only representations of other 'texts', namely the show trials themselves. While it is unlikely that the *raion* trials were scripted with anything like the same care as the central Moscow trials, they were still very far from spontaneous events. At a minimum, they had had the same kind of detailed advance planning in the oblast prosecutor's office and local NKVD branch that any major criminal trial in the United States would be given by the prosecuting counsel – with the important difference that, in the absence of any significant opposition from defence counsel, the prosecutors' plans were less likely to go awry.[4]

The trials' 'scripts', moreover, were drawn from two additional sources. One was the set of signals from Moscow that provided what I will call the 'master plot'[5] of the rural *raion* show trials of 1937 – that is, the generic model on which local variants were based. The other source, on whose identity I will speculate a little later, provided the detailed information on local abuses and crimes that was used in a particular *raion* trial. Despite the existence of a 'master plot', Moscow's hand in the framing and controlling of local show trials should not be exaggerated. The virtually unanimous failure of local trials to take up the hint that Stalin should be lauded for correcting local abuses, or indeed to mention Stalin at all, provides persuasive evidence of the limitations of Moscow's control.

The word 'signal' had a special meaning in Stalinist discourse. It referred primarily to information about important policy shifts that was transmitted from the centre to lower-level officials via a nonbureaucratic channel such as the central party newspaper, *Pravda*. A signal was not the same thing as a law or an administrative order, although it might coexist with an explicit instruction given privately by a superior authority to a subordinate one. It was essentially a message about political mood and current priorities, transmitted in the form of a slogan ('The Five-Year Plan in four years!'), a remark (Stalin's interjection at a conference that 'a son does not answer for his father'), an exemplary story, or – as in the cases we are concerned with – an exemplary or 'show' trial (*pokazatel' nyi sud*) that received national publicity. The reception of signals was treated as an instinctive rather than an intellectual act, and people who were not tuned into the right Communist wave length were likely to miss them.[6] In the case of the flood of rural *raion* show trials in the fall of 1937, the signals came in a series of reports and commentaries in *Pravda* highlighting the mistreatment of peasants is by local Communist officials.

The first report – perhaps more of a forerunner than one of the series – concerned a show trial of former party and soviet leaders in Lepel' *raion* in Belorussia that was held in March. The accused were charged with illegally confiscating peasant property as payment for tax arrears, despite the recent law forgiving arrears in the light of the exceptionally poor harvest of 1936. According to *Pravda*'s report, the Lepel' investigation was sparked by letters of complaint from local peasants, and the Belorussian state prosecutor took action on instructions from Andrei Vyshinsky, state prosecutor of the USSR. Peasant witnesses testified at the trial, which was held at the Lepel' municipal theatre, and the court had reportedly received dozens of letters from peasants grateful for deliverance from their former oppressors.

Three months later, *Pravda* reported a similar show trial from the Shiriaevo *raion* of Odessa oblast in the Ukraine. There, top *raion* officials had been found guilty of 'outrageous' treatment of kolkhozniki and routine violations of the 1935 Kolkhoz Charter,[7] including illegal confiscation of peasant property, extortion, night-time searches, arbitrary exaction of taxes and of subscriptions to state loans, imposition of impossibly high grain procurement quotas in 1936, and 'insulting behavior' toward kolkhozniki. These crimes had come to the attention of the party's Central Control Commission, which had instructed the Ukrainian state prosecutor to take action. The main evidence against the accused in the Shiriaevo trial came from peasant witnesses, more than thirty of whom were called to testify.

A few weeks later, *Pravda* reported similar show trials in Novominsk, a Cossack *raion* in the Black Sea oblast of Rostov, and in the Danilov *raion* of Iaroslavl oblast. The Novominsk trial featured severe economic exploitation by local officials that had provoked thousands of peasants to leave the collective farms. In the Danilov trial, the *raion* leadership was charged with illegally liquidating the 'New Life' kolkhoz and confiscating all its property when officials were unable to resolve a dispute with kolkhoz members. *Pravda*'s coverage of the Danilov affair was notable for its report that at the end of the trial, after stiff sentences had been handed down, local kolkhozniki sent thanks to Stalin for defending them against their enemies – a signal that seemed to fall on deaf ears.

Early in August, *Pravda* elaborated the message of Shiriaevo and Danilov trials in an editorial warning local officials not to mistreat the peasantry. *Raion* officials had been condoning all kinds of violations of the rights of kolkhozniki, *Pravda* stated. Officials had disposed arbitrarily of kolkhoz land and property, behaving as if it were 'their own private property, their own little kingdom'; they had even liquidated entire collective farms, as in the Danilov case. This was to forget the golden rule that 'kolkhozniki are the masters of their own kolkhoz'.

Emerging from all this was a master plot on the theme of abuse an exploitation of the collectivized peasantry by Soviet officialdom at the *raion* level that formed the basis fox the thirty-odd show trials held in rural *raion*s of the Soviet Union in September–October 1937. It may be summarized as follows:

Enemies of the people, linked in a mutual-protection and patronage network, had wormed their way into key positions in the *raion* and used their official positions to plunder the peasantry mercilessly. Because of the officials' stupidity and ignorance of agriculture, their incessant orders and interference had done great harm to the collective farms. The peasants, outraged and indignant, had done their best to resist unlawful demands. They had brought suits and written letters of complaint to higher authorities, but these had often been blocked by the mutual-protection ring. Finally, however, the news of the scandalous behaviour of local officials got out, and the guilty parties were brought to justice. The simple people – who demanded the severest punishment for their former oppressors – had triumphed over the officials who had cheated and insulted them.

While it is not possible to establish with certainty who were the 'authors' of variants of the master plot used in specific local show trials, the evidence points strongly to a natural (but perhaps, to Sovietologists, unexpected) source – the local peasantry.

Peasants were inveterate letter-writers, complaining about and denouncing those in immediate authority above them in the 1930s. They wrote to party and government leaders like Stalin and Mikhail Kalinin; they wrote to the highest organs of the Soviet and republican governments; they wrote to oblast party committees, prosecutors' offices and NKVD branches; they wrote to oblast newspapers and central newspapers, especially the mass-circulation peasant newspaper, *Krest'ianskaia gazeta*. They wrote letters and complaints with or without cause, for good reasons and bad, and they generally sent them outside their own *raion*, to the oblast centre or even to Moscow, because of their belief that the bosses in any given *raion* would back each other up.

Such peasant complaints often triggered the investigations of official wrongdoing at the *raion* level that led to the rural *raion* trials of 1937. Local complaints are mentioned as a stimulus in three out of the four 'model' trials reported in *Pravda*: in the Lepel' case, Vyshinsky's attention was alerted by 'complaints from the toilers of Lepel' *raion*'; 'complaints from kolkhozniki' are mentioned in the Shiriaevo case; and in Danilov, 'letters of *sel'koryi*' (correspondents from the village) disclosed the abuses of the *raion* leadership, which consequently did its best to suppress them. Similar references to complaints and petitions from the village abound in the *raion* show trials that took place in the autumn.[8]

Since the general tenor and substance of the grievance aired by peasant witnesses at the *raion* show trials of 1937 correspond remarkably closely to those of the peasant letters of complaint received by *Krest'ianskaia gazeta* (Peasants' Gazette) at the same period, the hypothesis that the scenarios of rural *raion* show trials were often directly based on local peasant complaints seems extremely plausible. This raises the intriguing possibility that the peasants who appeared as witnesses in the trials were not only full-fledged actors in this political theatre but were also (to pursue the theatrical metaphor) *playing themselves*.

*The Defendants*

The standard cast of characters under indictment at the rural *raion* trials consisted of the former secretary of the *raion* party committee (the top-ranking official in a *raion*), the chairman of the *raion* soviet (the second-ranking official), the heads of the *raion* agriculture depart- ment and sometimes the taxation (finance) and procurement agencies, along with other agricultural officials, and a sprinkling of *sel'sovet* and kolkhoz chairmen.

The typical defendant – and, indeed, the typical Soviet official at *raion* or *sel'sovet* level in the 1930s – was a poorly educated man of peasant origin, probably in his thirties or forties, who was a member of the Communist Party. The senior *raion* officials were likely to have spent a year or so at Soviet party school in addition to their basic primary schooling, and they had usually seen something of a broader world through service in other *raion* centres within the oblast and perhaps its immediate neighbours. *Sel'sovet* and kolkhoz chairmen, by contrast, were lucky to have completed primary education, rarely had job experience outside the *raion*, and seem usually to have been natives of the *sel'sovet* in which they served.

If accusations of participation in 'counterrevolutionary Trotskyite conspiracies' were rare in the rural *raion* trials, this surely reflected the fact that few Communists at this low level of the Soviet bureaucracy had ever had personal contact with an actual member of any Communist opposi- tion group.[9] Nevertheless, it became standard practice in these trials to charge at least the senior defendants with counterrevolutionary crimes, using Article 58 of the Criminal Code – although, interestingly enough, Article 58 does not seem to have been used in any of the 'model' trials reported in *Pravda* in the period March–July 1937.[10] The sentences, accordingly, were more severe in the autumn trials than in the spring, and became still harsher in the course of the autumn. Ten years' imprisonment with confiscation of property was the harshest sentence handed down in any of the 'model' trials, while some defendants got off with as little as six months. In the autumn trials, by contrast, it was usual for two or three of the top-ranking defendants to be sentenced to death while other defen- dants received eight- to ten-year sentencers.[11]

In two instances (the Andreevka trial in the Western oblast and the Aleshki trial in Voronezh oblast), second hearings were held in order to impose stiffer sentences.[12] The Andreevka case is of particular interest because the new Smolensk *obkom* secretary, Korotchenko, had made the mistake of sending a rather boastful message to Stalin *before* the verdict was brought in informing him of the success of the Andreevka trial in educating the peasantry and raising vigilance. Stalin responded the next day with a curt instruction that all the Andreevka 'wreckers' should be shot, but by that time the court had brought in its verdict sentencing them to various terms of imprisonment. The oblast prosecutor had to lodge a protest that resulted in an immediate rehearing of the case, which presumably resulted in death sentences for the accused.

The defendants in the rural *raion* trials were strongly encouraged to confess their guilt, as in the central Moscow trials, but they were a good deal less cooperative than their Moscow counterparts, especially where charges of counterrevolution were concerned.[13] In the Aleshki trial, none of the main defendants made a confession that was satisfactory from the prosecutors' standpoint. While the top-ranking defendant (Kolykhmatov, the *raion* party secretary) had admitted to counterrevolution under pretrial interrogation, he recanted in court and maintained that he was guilty only of failing to curb his subordinates' overzealous actions that showed poor judgement and offended the local population. Seminikhin, the former chairman of the *raion* soviet, was similarly recalcitrant, constantly attacking the credibility of the witnesses on the grounds that they were venting personal grievances: 'Every few minutes he would jump up and announce to the court that the witness was personally antagonistic towards him'. As for Kochetov, the villainous *sel'sovet* chairman, he stubbornly asserted that while he might be guilty of abuse of power, he was not guilty of counterrevolution.

In the Andreevka trial, two defendants persistently denied their guilt for any counterrevolutionary crimes, even at the retrial held as a result of Stalin's unpublicized intervention. One of the defendants (K. V. Rumiantsev, the former senior *raion* land-surveyor) was particularly obdurate when questioned about his role in the *raion*'s decision to merge collective farms against the will of their members:

> RUMIANTSEV: Not guilty. I didn't know that forced merging was a counter-revolutionary crime.
> PROSECUTOR: Did you know you were committing crimes?
> RUMIANTSEV: I knew I was carrying out the will of the head of the *raion* agriculture department and the party committee.
> PROSECUTORS: That is, consciously carrying out wrecking work.
> RUMIANTSEV: (*keeps silent*).

### The Charges

Many of the actions for which officials were indicted in the *raion* trials were not crimes in the ordinary sense. In some cases officials were clearly being made scapegoats for local economic disasters. In others they were being held to account for behaviour that was really part of their job description (as in the Rumiantsev case cited above) or for state policies that were unpopular with the local peasants. An interesting subset of offences had to do with treatment of kulaks, a subject on which opinion at village level seemed to be distinctly at odds with Moscow. Overall, the most striking common characteristic of the 'criminal' behaviours attributed to the defendants was that they were harmful to peasants, especially kolkhozniki, and offended the peasants' sense of fairness and propriety.

*Abuse of power*
The many accusations made by peasant witnesses under this heading are among the most colorful and bitter. Curses, insults, beatings, humiliation, intimidation and unjustified arrests were described as commonplace in the behaviour of rural officials towards peasants. In one trial, an eighty-year-old peasant woman related 'with tears' how the *sel'sovet* chairman beat her husband and dumped him in a wheelbarrow; he died two weeks later as a result of his injuries. Another witness described how a *raion* official once made four kolkhoz brigade-leaders climb on the stove and stay there, guarded by the local policeman, for four hours. 'When people asked the kolkhoz chairman ... why he countenanced this, he said "What could I do? After all, [he] was the boss, he could have made me get onto the stove too." '

The wild behaviour of Radchuk, a *sel'sovet* chairman, was described by many peasant witnesses in the Novgorod *raion* trial. Radchuk's speciality was physical assault and forced entry (connected with various forms of extortion) into the homes of kolkhozniki. One witness described how Radchuk began breaking down the door of her house.

> 'Now', he cried, 'I'll chop down the door with an axe, you just watch'. I took fright, jumped out the window, and ran to the post office to telephone my husband in Novgorod. But when he came home Radchuk had already gone, and the door was broken down with an axe.

Peasants frequently complained about the imposition of arbitrary fines and money levies (sometimes described as 'taxation' or 'contributions to state loans') by *sel'sovet* authorities. In Shiriaevo, for example, it was said that 'a night brigade' had been organized for the purpose, descending on peasants in dead of night to conduct house searches and take inventories of property that might be seized. From the standpoint of peasant witnesses, this was extortion regardless of whether the money went to the state or to individual officials, but they frequently implied that the latter was the case. It was alleged that in Aleshki Kochetov had imposed fines on kolkhoz members totalling sixty thousand rubles in 1935 and 1936: 'He imposed the fines on any pretext and at his own discretion – for not showing up for work, for not attending literacy classes, for "impolite language", for not having dogs tied up.'

The *raion* soviet chairman indicted in the same trial, Seminikhin, was reportedly even more creative in his fund-raising from the population:

> In 1936, two hundred kolkhozniki recruited for construction work went off from Aleshki to the Far East. They were already on the point of boarding the train when three militiamen appeared, read out a long list of names and took all those on the list off under guard to the *raion* soviet and the offices of the chairman.
>
> 'Aha, tax delinquents!' Seminikhin greeted them. 'You thought you could get away? Pay up and look lively about it. Pay up, or I won't let you out of the office and will not permit you to get on the train. And I'll take your suitcase.'
>
> He posted a militiaman at the door and gave the order to let out only those who showed a receipt for payment.
>
> In this manner, the *raion* soviet chairman 'squeezed' seven hundred rubles of their last savings from the kolkhozniki.

In many areas, kolkhozniki had extremely little money to take, so the main form of extortion was seizure of property. There were many and varied accounts of *sel'sovet* and *raion* officials behaving 'as if in their own little kingdoms' and 'exacting tribute from the population'. One country chairman took four or five kilograms of meat from each calf or pig slaughtered, plus vodka whenever he visited the village. A second 'opened unlimited "free credit" for himself on products [at the local store]. On occasion, he even roused the manager of the store from his bed at night, demanding immediate issue of vodka and snacks for himself. And when he needed potatoes, he simply sent to the nearest kolkhoz for them with an accompanying note to the person in charge of stores.' Kolkhoz chairmen were also accused of treating kolkhoz property as if it were their own private property, selling buildings and (illegally) leasing land on their own initiative and pocketing the profits.

In Aleshki, *raion* chairman Seminikhin had established a so-called 'auxiliary farm' of the *raion* soviet containing thirty sheds, ten cows, seven horses and other items commandeered from various parts of the *raion*, feeding his herd with feed taken from the kolkhozy. He was particularly successful in raising pigs, selling pork at the local peasant market as well as earning fifteen hundred rubles by selling pigs to the state procurement agency. The ironic comment going the rounds among the peasants was: 'The *raion* soviet has built up a real kulak farm!'

A more malign variant of extortion than regular, small-scale 'tribute' was to strip a kolkhoznik of *all* his possessions in one swoop. In one case cited in the Shchuche trial, a country chairman, coveting the flourishing kitchen garden of a kolkhoznik, 'abruptly dekulakized him and took away all his property'. When he discovered that the victim's wife had managed to sell some small household items before he could confiscate them, 'he took away the money and behaved so abusively that she was reduced to a state where she was sent to a psychiatric hospital.'

## Expulsions and liquidations

Complaints by peasants about their expulsion or forced departure from the kolkhoz were among the most frequent of all peasant grievances, judging both by the 1937 *raion* trials and the letters received at the same period by *Krest'ianskaia gazeta*. This may seem paradoxical, given the peasantry's hostility to collectivization less than a decade earlier. But by this time it had become clear that, as a result of heavy state taxation and other factors, peasant farming outside the kolkhoz was not a viable long-term option. Besides, when a member of a kolkhoz was expelled, he not only lost his share of the kolkhoz assets but also risked losing his private plot and even his house. Expulsion conflicts most frequently arose when members of the kolkhoz departed to work for wages elsewhere, usually leaving wives and families in the village. Departure for wage-work was a traditional cause of struggle between the Russian village commune (of which the kolkhoz was in many respects the heir) and individual peasants. It was often in the peasant's interest to depart, either temporarily or on a long-term basis, but in the village's interest to keep him (that is, retain his labour power and tax-paying capacity). After collectivization, as in the old days of serfdom and post-Emancipation redemption payments, peasants needed permission to depart, which now had to be obtained from both the kolkhoz and the *sel'sovet*. In the narratives of the 1937 *raion* trials, however, the kolkhoznik's right to depart was usually taken as a given, and conflicts over departure were thus represented as struggles between righteous peasants and power-abusing kolkhoz and *sel'sovet* chairmen.

Almost twenty witnesses testified in the Aleshki trial that they had been unjustly expelled from the '*Path to Socialism*' kolkhoz. Among them was Matrena Okuneva, who said:

> They expelled me from the kolkhoz because I married a worker on the railways, although I continued to live in Lipiagovka and work in the kolkhoz. I never complained, because I thought that's how it was supposed to be. Soon after that Kachkin and Kabanov [kolkhoz chairman and party organizer respectively] appeared in my yard and demanded that I go to weed the beets. I refused because I considered myself expelled from the kolkhoz. Then Kachkin said that the *sel'sovet* would fine me fifty rubles. ... They took a man's jacket from me, and Kabanov said: 'Be grateful to us, we could have burned [your house] down, only we took pity on the neighbours.'

Other 'expulsion' cases cited seem essentially to have been cases of unauthorized departures of kolkhozniki who were on the brink of starvation because of the harvest failure of 1936. In the Ostrov trial (Pskov oblast), for example, witnesses stated that more than one thousand households had left collective farms in the *raion* in 1935–6 because they could not survive on the meagre amount of grain the kolkhoz was giving them. In the Nerekhta trial (Iaroslavl oblast), peasants blamed the *raion* leadership for 'mass expulsions and forced departures from the collective farms' at the same period. These witnesses clearly felt that the *raion* bosses, like the old estate-owners in the time of serfdom, owed it to their peasants to help them out in time of trouble. For example, they related with indignation how

> after there was a fire in a kolkhoz and sixteen houses burned down, [the kolkhoz chairman] appealed to accused Begalov [chairman of the *raion* soviet] for help, saying that otherwise the kolkhozniki would all leave. In answer to the request, the accused Begalov said: 'To hell with them, let them go.' As a result, twenty households left the kolkhoz.

The liquidation of an entire collective farm by order of *raion* officials was an extreme (and illegal) action that can best be understood from the peasant standpoint as expulsion of all the households that constituted the kolkhoz, resulting in the total loss of all village assets including land. In the case of the 'New Life' kolkhoz in Danilov, *raion* officials followed the formal announcement of liquidation by swiftly confiscating all collective property and animals – and then, adding insult to injury, demanded that the former kolkhozniki immediately pay the heavy tax that was levied on noncollectivized peasants. When the 'Forward' kolkhoz in Kirillovo *raion* was liquidated, its land was distributed among neighbouring collective farms in what was officially described as a 'voluntary renunciation'. The *raion* authorities went on to confiscate the kolkhoz's horses, agricultural equipment, stock of seed potatoes and other collective property. From the standpoint of the kolkhozniki, who had owned this same property as individual households before collectivization, the liquidation of the kolkhoz must have seemed a second and definitive seizure of their assets. No wonder that, as witnesses related, the Kirillovo peasants wept when their kolkhoz was dissolved.

Only one of the reported instances of kolkhoz liquidation came from the fertile Black Earth region of the country, and it occurred several years earlier than the non-Black Earth liquidations. Witnesses at the 1937 trial in Ivnia *raion* (Kursk oblast), stated that in 1933 – that is, during the famine – the 'Lenin' kolkhoz was liquidated by order of the local Machine-Tractor Station (MTS) and its lands given to the neighbouring state farm, despite the fact that twenty-eight of thirty-one households voted against it. As a result of the transfer, the peasants were reduced overnight to the status of landless agricultural labourers working for a wage on the state farm.

In both the Danilov and Kirillovo cases, conflict between local officials and kolkhozniki preceded the liquidation of the kolkhoz. In Kirillovo, it was a violent confrontation over the spring sowing plan in 1936, which the kolkhoz general assembly refused to accept, to the outrage of the *sel'sovet* chairman. The Kirillovo trial narrative implies that liquidation of the kolkhoz was essentially a punitive response by local authorities to the peasants' insubordination. In the narrative of the Danilov trial, however, there are suggestions that the *raion* leadership may have had more venal motives for liquidation, perhaps wanting to get hold of kolkhoz property for their own use or that of their friends.

### Agricultural disasters

There was nothing new about blaming Soviet rural officials for harvest failures. The accusations made against officials in the *raion* trials of 1937 differed from earlier charges in one important respect, however: the officials were not being blamed for failing to meet state grain procurements targets, as had frequently happened in the early 1930s. This time, they were being blamed for failing to meet the *peasants'* needs – that is, allowing so little grain to be distributed among kolkhoz households after the harvest that the kolkhozniki were brought to the brink of starvation.

Most charges of this kind related to the exceptionally bad harvest of 1936, whose consequences had been felt most acutely in the spring and summer of 1937 before the next harvest came in.[14] In the Krasnogvardeisk trial, a kolkhoz chairman, Alekseev, admitted that he had brought the kolkhoz to economic ruin and described his reaction.

> In 1936 the kolkhozniki received zero payments per labour-day [that is, no grain was distributed after the harvest]. When I saw it all, I decided to run away from the kolkhoz. I told the chairman of the *raion* soviet, Gornov. He said: 'Get away as fast as you can.'

Alekseev took this friendly advice, but not fast enough (probably because he made the mistake of trying to take his house with him, using kolkhoz horses), and he was arrested, together with Gornov, by the NKVD.

In Ostrov *raion*, as a result of the 1936 harvest failure, average kolkhoz earnings dropped by 20 to 50 per cent, it was reported at the Ostrov trial. But because state grain procurements took precedence over peasant needs, many collective farms cut their payments in kind to members much more drastically, and this was treated as a crime in the 1937 *raion* trials. The indicted officials were held responsible for the departure of large numbers of hungry kolkhozniki who went to work for wages in the towns or the state farms in order to survive.

A number of *raion* trials featured charges from kolkhozniki about inept agricultural instructions from *raion* authorities that had caused hardship to peasants and damaged agricultural productivity. 'Unrealistic sowing plans' figured prominently in these complaints, and, despite the fact that it was part of the *raion* agriculture departments' duty to give orders to the collective farms about what crops to sow and where and when to sow them, the rhetorical conventions of the trials allowed peasant witnesses to speak of such instructions with undisguised resentment and contempt. In the Krasnogvardeisk trial, the testimony of a peasant from 'Thirteen Years of the Red Army' kolkhoz was reported to have 'left an enormous impression on all present at the court':

> [The witness] talked about how kolkhozniki tried to protest against wrecking plans and went specially to Manninen, [head of] the *raion* agriculture department. With contemptuous effrontery, that enemy of the people announced to the kolkhozniki: 'If you go to the oblast to complain about our plans, we will add more.'

Peasant witnesses cited many instances of agriculturally illiterate instructions from the *raion* authorities and MTSs. One kolkhoz, for example, was ordered to turn water-meadow and shrubbed area into plough and, leaving nowhere to pasture cattle. In another kolkhoz, the *raion*'s sowing instructions were predicated on the false assumption that its hayfields covered over two hundred hectares, which according to the peasants was double their actual extent ('Under the heading of hayfield, the wreckers included pastureland for cattle, quicksands, and the private lots of kolkhozniki').

Another kind of agricultural disaster that figured prominently in a few *raion* trials was the large-scale loss of livestock. In the trial in Shchuche *raion* (Voronezh oblast), which lost almost one thousand horses in the first half of 1937, this was attributed to lack of fodder associated with the 1936 harvest failure, compounded by an epidemic that started in a Shchuche horse-breeding state farm and spread rapidly throughout the *raion*. The defendants in Shchuche were charged with gross negligence in the livestock losses, not intentional malice.

In two other cases (the Kresttsy and Sychevka trials), however, officials in *raiony* with heavy livestock losses were accused of intentionally infecting animals with diseases. Of all the charges made in the rural *raion* show trials of 1937, these are the least plausible and most reminiscent of the fantastic accusations of conspiratorial counterrevolutionary sabotage that characterized the Moscow trials of the Great Purges. The director of the Sychevka state farm (a former member of the Social-Revolutionary Party, one of the Bolsheviks' political competitors in 1917) was charged with leading a conspiracy to destroy the farm's livestock, using the prevailing unsanitary conditions as a cover for infecting 80 per cent of the animals with diseases. Then, it was alleged, the *raion* veterinarian had done his bit to spread the epidemic throughout the country by sending animals from the infected herd to be shown at the All-Union Agricultural Exhibition in Moscow.[15]

A somewhat similar accusation was made against *raion* leaders in the Porkhov trial, although in this case the actual sabotage had been performed by aggrieved peasants. One of these was a noncollectivized peasant who allegedly poisoned kolkhoz cows and horses with arsenic at the behest of the *raion* party secretary. The other was a former kulak who, working as a kolkhoz stablehand after his return from exile, was said to have intentionally lamed the kolkhoz horses.

*Favouritism toward former kulaks*
Kulaks (prosperous peasants, regarded by Communists as exploiters of poor peasants and potential capitalists) had been 'liquidated as a class' by the Soviet regime at the beginning of the 1930s. What this meant in practice was that a good proportion of kulaks had been sent to labour camps or deported along with their families to distant areas of the Soviet Union, while others had been expropriated and evicted from their homes without arrest or deportation. Of the former group, some had returned from labour camps to the villages by the late 1930s (though the deportees were still forbidden to return). Of the latter group, many had left the countryside and gone to work in the towns, but some were still living in the area, and a few had even joined the collective farms. Official policy toward the group softened around 1936, when the Stalin Constitution restored full citizenship and voting rights to former kulaks and other old 'class enemies'. In the villages, however, the presence of former kulaks often produced conflicts because of their efforts to recover the property that had been confiscated from them and the new owners' and occupiers' efforts to hang on to it.

Peasant witnesses in the trials made many accusations that officials had done favours for former kulaks, presumably often as a result of bribes. It was said that kulaks had managed to get houses and horses back, that they had been given good jobs in the collective farms, and that, once admitted to the kolkhoz, they had taken revenge on peasants who were Soviet activists. In Borisovka *raion* (Kursk oblast) the prosecutor claimed that in 1936 and the first half of 1937, 75 houses were returned to the kulaks who were their former owners, and 134 kulaks had their voting rights restored.[16] Returning the houses meant that schools, kindergartens, kolkhoz clubs, and other communal institutions had to be evicted, but the *raion* leaders were unmoved by their plight. This was held to be the more offensive since the party secretary, Fedosov, had behaved so brutally toward ordinary peasants in the raton: 'Everything was taken from the population down to their socks, but [the *raion* party leaders] returned to the kulaks the property that had been legally confiscated from them.'

When kolkhozniki complained to the Borisovka party leaders about the concessions being made to former kulaks, it was reported that the party leaders 'oriented those present at the meeting toward reconciliation with the class enemies'. This is not surprising, since reconciliation was the party's general line at the time in connection with the promulgation of the new constitution.[17] What is more surprising is that in 1937, without any overt change in the party line and with the constitution still in force, this could be treated in Kursk as a political crime.

Kursk was not the only place where this happened. At the trial in Sychevka *raion*, the two senior *raion* officials were also charged with distorting party policy on kulaks by announcing that it was time to forget about the whole idea of class enemies and make appointments and judgements of individuals on the basis of merit. They had instructed *sel'sovet* chairmen to destroy all the existing lists of kulaks and other persons who had earlier been disenfranchised or subject to other forms of discrimination – a reasonable interpretation, on the face of it, of the spirit of the new constitution. But then they had gone further – probably further than the new party line required, and certainly further than public opinion in Sychevka would stand for – and appointed a landlord's son as director of the school and several former kulaks as kolkhoz chairmen, as well as put former merchants in charge of village co-ops. According to peasant witnesses at the trial, the former kulaks who were appointed as kolkhoz chairmen 'caused enormous damage', 'persecuted Stakhanovites and beat them up', and destroyed the horses'.

### "Suppression of Kolkhoz Democracy"

According to the Kolkhoz Charter of 1935, collective farms were self-governing bodies whose chairmen were freely elected at the kolkhoz general meeting. But this was not in practice the way chairmen were selected. The normal custom was for local authorities (the *raion* agriculture department or the local MTS) to nominate a chairman, whom the kolkhozniki then duly 'elected'. In the early 1930s the chairman was often an outsider – a Communist or worker sent out from the towns. But by the second half of the 1930s it was becoming increasingly common for locals (kolkhoz members or peasants from elsewhere in the *sel'sovet*) to be nominated as chairmen. It remains uncertain how seriously the central political leaders meant the charter to be taken with regard to democratic election of kolkhoz chairmen, but it seems clear at any rate that peasants wanted this provision taken seriously, and that newspapers were willing to endorse and publicize their complaints.

'Suppression of kolkhoz democracy' was one of the standard charges brought against *raion* officials in the rural show trials of 1937. In the Kazachkin trial in Saratov *krai*, for example, the *raion* authorities were accused of forcing a kolkhoz to accept a former *raion* official as chairman despite the protests of the kolkhozniki. This man subsequently robbed the kolkhoz of its assets, proving that the kolkhozniki had been right all along.

Sometimes it was alleged that *raion* or *sel'sovet* authorities applied extreme measures of coercion in conflicts with kolkhozniki over chairmen. The liquidation of the 'New Life' kolkhoz in Danilov *raion* was said to be the result of such a conflict. In the Aleshki trial,

> witnesses I. N. Goltsev and V A. Mishin related how, when they and other kolkhozniki got up at the general meeting in the 'First of May' kolkhoz and criticized the work of the (kolkhoz] administration, demanding that the kolkhoz chairman be fired for failure to carry out his duties, the *sel'sovet* chairman, Kochetov, disbanded the meeting. Four of the most active kolkhozniki, including the two witnesses, were arrested on the basis of his provocative and false statement.

In reporting the trials, oblast newspapers often played up the democracy theme. The Voronezh newspaper, commenting on the revelations of the Shchuche *raion* trial, added its own editorial flourish:

> Ask any kolkhoznik of the 'Red Bitiug' (Red Shire Horse) kolkhoz why they elected Zazadravnykh chairman, and they will answer: 'But we didn't elect him. Kordin [the *sel'sovet* chairman] foisted him on us. We protested and didn't want to accept him, but they made us.' And that is completely true. That was the system there.

### Various Peasants and Evil Bosses

In the narratives of the *raion* trials, evil bosses exploit and abuse, and peasants are their victims. The relationship of peasants and bosses was presented in clear antithetical terms; there was scarcely any shading of the stark black-and-white contrast between victimizers and victims. Rarely if ever did peasant witnesses mention a good boss at the *raion* level – one who, say, interceded for them or understood their problems. By the same token, in only a few instances did the gallery of defendants include a peasant who was not an office-holder of some kind, and in those instances the evil peasant was usually a kulak returned from exile.

These same conventions prevailed in peasant letters of complaint to *Krest'ianskaia gazeta*, no doubt reflecting peasants' general disinclination to look anywhere but on the dark side. In real life, however, the dichotomy between rulers and ruled in the Soviet countryside was by no means so straightforward. In the first place, there was a gulf in real life between the status and powers of the *raion* authorities and those at *sel'sovet* and kolkhoz level. In the second place, *sel'sovet* and kolkhoz chairmen were not far removed from the local peasantry. The majority were local peasants themselves by origin – natives of the *sel'sovet* or even, in the case of many kolkhoz chairmen, of the village. There was considerable turnover in these lower offices; and, as we have seen, peasants were pushing with some success for veto power over appointments of kolkhoz chairman. The kolkhoz chairmen, moreover, were not salaried: they were paid (like other kolkhozniki, albeit more generously) with a proportion of the kolkhoz's harvest and income.

The premise that an impassable divide separated evil rulers from virtuous peasants was dramatized many times in the *raion* trials, and not only by peasant witnesses. For example, in the Shchuche trial, which is unusual in the context of *raion* trials for the defendants' willingness to participate in their own indictment, two defendants gave the following answers when the prosecutor asked why they did not try to recruit peasants and workers into their anti-Soviet activities:

SEDNEV (plant director): Undoubtedly if they [the workers] had known that I was a Trotskyist wrecker, they would have torn me limb from limb.

POLIANSKII (MTS director): Well, if I had even hinted of wrecking, they [the peasants] would have beaten me up if I was lucky, but more likely would simply have killed me.

The peasant testimony at the trials presented many vivid images of the local 'masters' taunting peasants with their powerlessness.

- So you went to VTsIK [that is, laid a complaint with the Russian Republican government in Moscow]! But we are the people in power here. I do what I want.
- I am a Communist and you don't belong to the party. However much you complain about me, you won't be believed.
- You should have shot the bastard; you wouldn't have got into any trouble for it (a *raion* official's comment to a subordinate, who had beaten a peasant].
- If five people croak, that will teach you how to work, you idle bastards [a *raion* official's remark to kolkhozniki during the 1933 famine].
- Grain has to be given to the horses. The kolkhozniki can survive without grain.
- The clever ones left the collective farms long ago, and all that remain are the fools.

Reports of the trials stressed the 'deep hatred' with which peasants spoke of their former oppressors in courtroom testimony. Before and during the trials, newspapers reported, resolutions and petitions came in from neighbouring collective farms demanding the death sentence for the accused, who were referred to with such epithets as 'contemptible swine' and 'rotten bastards'. The halls where the trials were held were always described as packed, with the audience listening intently, full of indignation against the accused.

Each evening, crowds of kolkhozniki gather near the school. ... During the trial, as many as fifty statements indicating new facts of abuse and illegality performed by Seminikhin, Kolykhmatov and the others were personally handed by citizens to the oblast prosecutor, who is attending the trial.

In one of the most dramatic confrontations reported in the press, a peasant witness, Natalia Latysheva, turned on the former leaders of Novgorod *raion* as soon as she took the stand.

LATYSHEVA: Comrade judges! Are these really human beings? They are ogres, swine. (*Movement in the hall, cries of approval, confusion on the bench of the accused.*)
CHAIRMAN: Witness, it is facts that are asked of you.
LATYSHEVA: Forgive me, comrade judges, but when I saw those swine, I couldn't contain myself. And it is a fact that they are scoundrels! ... There they sit, damn them. The kolkhozniki will never forgive them for what they did.

In Latysheva's story, as in those of many other peasant witnesses in the trials, the district's interference in agriculture (for example, in the giving of sowing plans) was completely unjustified and stupid, since the officials had no idea what they were doing. On Latysheva's kolkhoz, for example, the *raion* had tried to discourage the peasants from developing a stud farm and forced them to grow unprofitable and inappropriate crops. But the kolkhozniki were not to be browbeaten.

LATYSHEVA: We did not give up. We decided to breed trotters. And we did – those enemies of the collective farms did not break our spirit. To the astonishment of all, we built up a horse farm, and now we have twenty-one horses of pure Orel stock. (*Spontaneous applause breaks out in the hall, cries of 'Good for you!' and 'Well done!' are heard.*)
CHAIRMAN: Witness, have you anything more to add?
LATYSHEVA: I have. (*The peasant woman turns to the accused, and stands face to face with the enemies of the people* ...) All the same, our side won, not yours. We were victorious!

*Our side won!* It would be tempting to end the story on this note of populist triumph. But had the peasant mice really won a significant victory over the oppressor cats? After all, the death of a cat does not change the essential relationship of cats and mice; and in Stalinist Russia the downfall of a Kochetov or even many Kochetovs in 1937 does not seem to have produced any lasting changes in an exploitative system of collectivized agriculture and a rural administrative structure that tended to generate petty local despots. To be sure, 1935–7 was a period of relatively conciliatory state policies toward the peasantry, in contrast the harsh conflicts of collectivization at the beginning of the decade, but by 1938–9 the screws were being tightened again.

In the woodcut 'The Mice Bury the Cat', as in the real world of the Soviet Union in 1937, it is not at all clear who killed the cat that the mice are so gleefully burying. It is hard to believe that the mice themselves were the killers – that is, that peasants had the political strength to take revenge on corrupt bosses without outside encouragement, or, if they had had the strength, that this would have been their chosen form of revenge. It is more plausible, certainly, that the peasant mice should have helped bigger predators locate their prey by writing letters of complaint and denunciation against particularly unpopular cat bosses. But peasant denunciations against local bosses were a constant feature of life; moreover, to say that they were probably used in constructing the show trials is not to say that the show trials could not have been constructed without them.

One thing we can be fairly sure of is that once the cat was dead, the mice danced at the funeral. The *raion* show trials of 1937, it seems, were a kind of Soviet carnival[18] – not just an outing for the local peasants, when they got a trip into the *raion* centre where vodka was probably on sale, but a real *prazdnik* (festival) in which for a few days the world was turned upside down and mice could taunt and mock cats with impunity. Of course, this was not exactly a Bakhtinian Carnival: the mockery had a sly, malicious, almost corrupt quality that is alien to Bakhtin's notion of popular revelry. But then it is likely that real-life medieval carnivals were always a bit crueller and less innocently joyful than they appear in the retrospective view of twentieth-century intellectuals.

If carnival is the appropriate metaphor for the rural *raion* trials, this throws a disconcerting light on the big show trials in Moscow, and perhaps on the Great Purges as a whole. In the familiar *Darkness at Noon* picture of the Moscow trials, victims such as Nikolai Bukharin – the Marxist theorist whom Lenin called the party's favourite – are revolutionary martyrs, tragically destroyed by the cause to which they have devoted their lives. From within this paradigm it seems inconceivable that anybody could see a similarity between the idealistic intellectual Bukharin and the crude and brutal Kochetov. From the standpoint of peasants, however, was one

Communist boss any different from another, except in degree of rank and power? If there was reason to dance at Kochetov's funeral, was there not also reason to dance at the funeral of a Kochetov-writ-large such as Bukharin?

Almost certainly the potential carnival appeal of the Great Purge trials was not lost on Soviet political leaders. We can see signs that efforts were made by Stalin and on his behalf to tap into ordinary people's envious resentment of power and privilege. One of these is *Pravda*'s early report in connection with the Danilov trial that kolkhozniki of the *raion* had sent thanks to Stalin for restoring their kolkhoz (which the *raion* leaders had liquidated) and protecting them from their enemies. Another is Stalin's toast to 'the little people' at a reception for Stakhanovite workers in October, when he said that 'leaders come and go, but the people remains. Only the people is eternal'.[19]

It should have worked. According to the conventional wisdom of historians, Russian peasants have always been 'naive monarchists' eager to believe that if the Tsar only knew of the injustices perpetrated by his nobles and officials, he would come riding to the people's rescue.[20] This 'naive monarchism' of the Russian peasant, many Russian intellectuals believe, lay at the root of the Stalin cult, which allegedly could have developed only in a peasant country.[21]

Remarkably, the 'naive monarchism' ploy failed. Ignoring *Pravda*'s hint, peasant witnesses in later trials did *not* credit Stalin with bringing corrupt lower officials to justice. They did *not* report that he had responded to their letters of complaint or attribute to him any guiding role, and they stead-fastly avoided such, 'naive monarchist' formulations as 'If Stalin had only known what was going on'. In fact, in reported testimony at the trials there are virtually no references to Stalin at all.

This reticence must surely be understood in terms of the peasants' hostile reaction to collectivization and their strong belief that Stalin personally was the man mainly responsible for their sufferings in the early 1930s. That these attitudes had not disappeared in the mid-1930s is shown by the striking reaction of peasants in the Western oblast to the murder of Sergei Kirov, the Leningrad party leader, in December 1934. Although Kirov is usually described by historians as a relatively popular leader, peasants evidently regarded his death as a fortunate event (on the general grounds that the mice had one less cat to worry about) that called for rowdy celebration. A ditty that appeared in more than one region of the oblast had as its concluding lines: 'They killed Kirov; we'll kill Stalin' (*Ubili Kirova, ub"em Stalina*).[22]

Could it be, then, that Latysheva's '*Our side won!*' was not so far from the mark after all? Were the mice at the cat's funeral really dancing to Stalin's tune? Or was that their own subversive ditty, *Ubili Kirova*, that they were singing?

NOTES

[Reorganized and renumbered from the original]

1. This account is based on reports of 35 show trials held in rural *raion* centres in the Russian Republic (32 trials), the Ukraine (two trials) and Belorussia (one trial) reported in the regional and central press from March to November 1937. The great majority of trials occurred from August to October 1937, and almost all the reports were published in oblast newspapers.

2. On the provenance of the woodcut 'The Mice Bury the Cat' see Dianne Ecklund Farrell, 'Medieval Popular Humor in Russian Eighteenth Century Lubki', *Slavic Review* 50 (Fall 1991): 560–2.

3. Virtually all my sources are newspaper reports of rural *raion* show trials, not court records or memoir accounts. If any court records of the trials have survived in Soviet oblast archives, they have yet to be discovered. The Smolensk Archive (available in the West) includes no court records, though it contains valuable related material, some of which has been analysed by Roberta Manning in her unpublished article, 'The Case of the Miffed Milkmaid'. In A. I. Solzhenitsyn, *The Gulag Archipelago*, vols 1–2 (New York, 1973), 419–31, there is an account of one show trial (held in Kady *raion*, Ivanovo oblast) which appears to be based on information from one of the indicted officials or a family member.

4. There were defence counsels in some and conceivably most of the rural *raion* trials (see, for example, the Lepel' trial, as reported in *Pravda*, 13 March 1937) but, as was usual in the Stalin period, their role was limited to asking for a more lenient sentence for their clients.

5. I have borrowed this term from Katerina Clark's discussion of the 'master plot' of Socialist Realism in *The Soviet Novel: History as Ritual* (Chicago, 1981) 5–15.

6. Note that, in accordance with this metaphor, it was also possible for signals to be sent 'from below' and received by the top party and government leadership. The peasant complaints and petitions discussed below fall into this category.

7. By 1937 the great majority of Soviet peasants were members of a collective farm (kolkhozniki). The Model Charter of the Agricultural Artel approved by the Second Congress of Kolkhoz Shockworkers, was issued as a law by the Soviet government on 17 February 1935. It was in effect the kolkhoz constitution, defining the rights and obligations of kolkhoz members and kolkhozy.

8. The term 'toilers' covered peasants as well as workers, and other honest wage-earners, but in this case it probably refers to peasants. In the 1920s the term 'sel'kor' was usually reserved for the small group of villagers that had consciously taken on the role of 'the eyes and ears of Soviet power' in the village. By the latter part of the 1930s, however, it was used more broadly to refer to any villager who wrote to a newspaper complaining about or giving information on fellow peasants.

In the Andreevsk trial, for example, peasant witnesses mentioned that they had sent a telegram of complaint to the people's commissar of agriculture. In Shchuche the complaint had been sent to the Central Executive Committee of Soviets of the Russian Republic (VTsIK). In Aleshki peasant complaints against Kochetov were forwarded to the Central Commission of Soviet Control in Moscow by a sympathetic secretary of a neighbouring *sel'sovet*.

9. My sample of thirty-two *raion* trials discloses not a single actual Oppositionist among the defendants. The closest to a serious accusation of Trotskyite conspiracy was in the Shchuche trial (which was also unusual in combining industrial and kolkhoz/agricultural themes and personnel), where one of the defendants, director of a sugar plant, admitted that he had been influenced by a Trotskyite he met after graduating from a party technical school in Moscow in 1928. In another trial the former *raion* party secretary was accused of softness on Trotskyites (but not membership of a Trotskyite conspiracy) because he let the director of the local veterinary school, a former Trotskyite, go into hiding to avoid arrest.

10. In the Lepel' trial the accused were indicted under Art. 196 of the Belorussian Criminal Code (violation of Soviet law and abuse of power), and in the Danilov trial they were accused of destruction of socialist property under the law of 7 August 1932.

11. Sentences were reported for ten of the trials and can be deduced for an eleventh.

12. In the Aleshki trial (Voronezh oblast) in September, only two death sentences were imposed, though the prosecutor asked for four. This verdict, too, was subsequently appealed by the oblast prosecutor, resulting in a retrial in November at which three additional death sentences were imposed (*Kommuna*, 6 September 1937 and 20 November 1937).

13. In his account of the Kady trial (see above, note 3) Solzhenitsyn suggests that a defendant's withdrawal of his pre-trial confession unhinged the whole proceedings and even caused the *raion* show trial as a genre to be abandoned. In my sample of *raion* trials, however, recanting in court on earlier admissions was not unusual and did not have a devastating effect on proceedings, since most *raion* cases were built more on peasant testimony than on confession by the accused.

14. In one exceptional case from the Nerekhta *raion* trial, the accusations made against a *raion* soviet chairman included his treatment of peasants during the 1933 famine.

15. Roberta Manning, 'The Case of the Miffed Milkmaid', gives a fascinating account, drawn from the Smolensk Archive, of the events in Sychevka leading up to the show trial. See note 3.

16. This is anomalous because the 1936 Constitution had in fact already restored voting rights to kulaks, priests and other former 'class enemies'.

17. For a discussion of the changing policy on class in the 1930s see Sheila Fitzpatrick, 'L'Usage Bolchévique de la "Classe": Marxisme et Construction de l'Identité Individuelle', *Actes de la Recherche en Sciences Sociales*, no. 85 (November 1990) 75–80.

18. On carnival see Natalie Zemon Davis, 'The Reasons of Misrule', in her *Society and Culture in Early Modern France* (Stanford, 1975), 99–123; Peter Burke, *Popular Culture in Early Modern Europe* (London, 1978), chapter 7; and Mikhail Bakhtin, *Rabelais and His World*, trans. Hélène Izwolsky (Bloomington, 1984).

19. I. V. Stalin, *Sochineniia*, 14 vols, ed. Robert H. McNeal (Stanford, 1967), 1:254. Although eminently quotable, Stalin's aphorism was not widely quoted and does not appear in any of the *raion* trial reports I have read (though admittedly it came too late for many of the trials).

20. For a sceptical examination of the idea of 'naive monarchism' see Daniel Field, *Rebels in the Name of the Tsar* (Boston, 1976).

21. For a rebuttal of this argument see the comments by the distinguished historian of the Russian peasantry, V. P. Danilov, in *Voprosy istorii*, 1988, no. 1211.

22. Note that the Russian verb in the first clause is ambiguous as to person: it could mean either 'They killed Kirov' or 'We killed Kirov.'

# V  The Great Fatherland War

The name which Russians give to the Second World War is 'The Great Fatherland War'. This gives us the first clue to how it appears in Russian eyes. Above all, it was a vast struggle for national survival against a dangerous and ruthless enemy. In *Mein Kampf* Hitler assigned Slavs to the tasks of being the 'hewers of wood and drawers of water' for the coming thousand-year Reich. In other words they would be its slaves. In addition, in Hitler's twisted mind, Communism was a central feature of the world Jewish conspiracy and the communist and Jew were practically synonymous in Hitlerian rhetoric. In the event, most of the victims of the Final Solution were Jews living in Polish and Soviet territory. Behind the Jewish holocaust was a holocaust of Slavs, some two million of whom are thought to have been put to death in Nazi slave labour and extermination camps. Even before the Nazis came to power a ferocious street enmity existed between them and the German communists, especially in Berlin. Once in power Hitler quickly annihilated the German Communist Party, the largest outside the USSR.

Stalin quickly adapted his internal and external policies. The line of 'class war' which had been proclaimed during the second revolution was replaced by a turn towards class conciliation at home, as recorded by Sheila Fitzpatrick in the preceding contribution. In accordance with this new line, the 1936 Constitution based the Soviet state on the alliance of workers, peasants and working intelligentsia. Internationally, Moscow encouraged the formation of Popular Fronts with other anti-fascist forces in Spain, France and elsewhere. Threatened by rampant German imperialism and the drive for *lebensraum* (living space) in the west and a resurgent Japanese assault on the Asian mainland in the east, the Soviet government tried to take refuge in collective security. While France urged closer ties with the Soviet Union, Britain and the United States kept Russia out of the international loop, though the United States, prompted by a common hostility to Japanese expansion, did recognize the Soviet Union for the first time in 1935. However, Britain, with its eye on its vast worldwide empire which was at its peak in terms of territory in the interwar years, tried to stay aloof from extensive continental entanglements. Should Germany and the Soviet Union go to war, so much the better, it was thought, because it would weaken both powers. Inactivity when Germany swallowed up Austria in 1938 and the Munich Treaty of

1938, which partitioned a hapless Czechoslovakia, seemed to indicate that Britain was pushing Germany to the East. In Soviet eyes, Britain's inexplicable and unrealizable guarantee to Poland after allowing the more defensible Czechoslovakia to be destroyed was puzzling and Moscow sensed a trap. At the last minute, to buy time for further improvement to its defences, Stalin replaced his western-oriented foreign minister, Maxim Litvinov, with the tougher Molotov and sent him to Berlin to sign a treaty of non-aggression with Germany. The ensuing agreement had secret provisions demarcating a line of separation in East Central Europe giving Germany control of most of Poland, with Eastern Poland and the Baltic States (all former parts of the Tsarist Empire) to revert to Soviet rule.

Stalin had miscalculated badly. Though it could do nothing about Poland and for some time only a 'phoney war' opened up, Britain did declare war on Germany. In 1940, France collapsed like a house of cards and the remnants of allied forces, including the British Expeditionary Force, were forced back across the channel from Dunkirk. Italy, opportunistically, joined the looting of France. Britain, through the courage of its aircrew, hung on by a thread in the Battle of Britain but, even so, Hitler's domination of the continent was supreme. In early 1941 he turned on the Balkans. Yugoslav and Greek resistance held him up longer than anticipated. This may have cost Hitler the war because it delayed by six weeks his big operation of 1941, the long-heralded attack on the Soviet Union. In the interim, frantic war preparations had taken place in Russia but they were outweighed by the gains of Hitler. The result was that the Soviet Union was in a worse position relative to Germany in 1941 than it had been in 1939. Soviet weakness was such that Stalin tried everything to deflect Hitler from attacking in that year. Stalin had it firmly in mind that Hitler would not attack until 1942 and he went to enormous lengths to prevent any action the Nazis might consider to be 'provocation'. This even extended to refusing to give the order to fight back when the Luftwaffe and the Panzer regiments opened up the blitzkrieg attack on 22 June 1941. As a result, the Soviet Army and airforce lost phenomenal quantities of men and material. In effect, after six weeks of war, there was nothing but distance between the German armies and Moscow. Stalin, according to a reasonably authoritative account, summed the situation up: 'Lenin left us a great inheritance and we, his heirs, have fucked it all up.' Moscow was saved in extremis partly by the early onset of winter, which added to the delayed start of the attack and shortened the period when German ground troops were at their most efficient. However, the main reason for survival was the transfer to the Moscow Front of Zhukov's army from Siberia, which was thereby effectively denuded in the event of a new Japanese attack. They not only held their ground but pushed the German army back some hundreds of kilometres in certain areas.

The German advance had been spectacular but two major objectives – Moscow and Leningrad – had eluded it and remained outside its grasp for the duration. In some respects, the battle of Moscow was decisive. Forced by failure of blitzkrieg into a long war of attrition, Germany's vulnerabilities and the Soviet Union's strengths, especially of men and resources plus British and American aid, began to assert themselves. However, this was not immediately evident. Drawn by the prize of endless grain fields and the oil of the Caucasus and Caspian, German eyes turned to the south for the offensive of 1942. They retook Kharkov and pushed the Soviet army aside as they drove towards the Black Sea and on to Rostov in South Russia. Soviet generals saw that the long German salient hinged on the city of Stalingrad on the Volga. In an epic campaign in early winter of 1942–3 the German Sixth Army was trapped in the city and annihilated. As a result German armies in the south had to stream back westwards to avoid being cut off.

Hitler was determined to have his revenge in the next fighting season and identified the Kursk region as the one which was most vulnerable. He threw all his crack forces into the biggest offensive of the war. Little did he know that, as a result of an efficient spy ring, the Soviets were in possession of his order of battle. Vast defensive lines, in places a hundred kilometres deep, were constructed and immense numbers of tanks thrown into battle. The German breakthrough failed and instead they were forced back with the flower of the German army in tatters. The gigantic Belorussian campaign of 1944 brought the Soviet army sweeping westwards, retaking almost all 1939 Soviet territory and reaching the gates of Warsaw where, controversially, it paused to re-group for four months before attempting the hazardous crossing of the Vistula and the assault on the heavily defended city. From then on the road to Berlin was open and, within a further four months, the Soviet army was the first to arrive, initially repaying the German population in kind for the cruel occupation visited on the Soviet Union.

Only in the latter stages of the war, after D-Day in June 1944, were large-scale forces committed by the Allies in the west. By and large, the Soviet Army and airforce had broken Germany's armed might alone. At no time was less than 80 per cent of Germany's forces committed to the east. In the west, the Allied landing force faced about 20 per cent of Germany's total strength. Stalin was particularly aggrieved that the second front in the west had not been set up earlier and this played a major role in his approach to the Cold War. Nonetheless, in 1945, far from the impending defeat of 1941, Stalin had become the arbiter of Europe and the Soviet Union had become a power on the world scale. Having said that, the price the Soviet Union had paid for its victory was enormous. Conventionally, the war is said to have brought about the death of

27 million Soviet citizens; $128 billion in damage; 1700 towns and 17,000 villages destroyed; 25 million people homeless; 31,000 industrial enterprises destroyed; 65,000 kilometres of railway track destroyed; 40 per cent of agricultural output lost. Having suffered the Stalinist depredations of the 1930s the assault from Hitler had exposed the long-suffering Soviet population to far worse horrors.

While general analyses of Soviet success identify its planning system which effectively mobilized resources as well as the almost inexhaustible reserves the USSR possessed, in recent years the enormous contribution made by ordinary people has come to be better appreciated. In the selected article, John Erickson, a leading military historian, turns his attention away from the generals and the high command, from studies of which he made his name, and focuses on the war as it was seen by those who fought in the front line, especially women, many of whom were called upon to play the same roles as men in battle. The account is doubly valuable in that it not only puts the emphasis on the war as experienced by ordinary people, it also highlights the extraordinary contribution made by women. The emergent picture is one of everyday heroism and self-sacrifice without which the war effort would have come to nought.

## 7   John Erickson: 'Soviet Women at War'

Tales of individual women soldiers abound: accounts variously mythical, anecdotal or bizarre, such as the sustained masquerade of Nadezhda Andreyevna Durova, who served with distinction throughout Russia's wars with Napoleon and rose to the rank of cavalry staff captain.[1] But nothing in the history or the mythology of any country can compare with the 800,000 young girls and women in the Soviet Union who mobilized for wartime service and frontline duties with the Red Army in the wake of the German attack in June 1941. Young women, their tresses trimmed and their plaits lopped off, were hastily stuffed into ill-fitting uniforms and forced to clump about in over-size boots – all a prelude to learning military skills and mastering combat roles beyond the wildest imaginings of Nadezhda Durova or any legendary figure.

In a situation without parallel in history, tens of thousands of women became *frontoviki* (front-line fighters) themselves, serving with the Red Army in all phases of warfare, including hand-to-hand combat. At the front, in addition to filling the more traditional female roles as cooks and laundresses, women served as field surgeons and battlefield medics. They fought as snipers, machine-gunners, gun layers, tank commanders, and bomber and fighter pilots. Women also served as radio-operators, partisans, scouts, mortar crews and parachutists.

Yet battlefield sagas, partisan operations and the horrors of slave labour for the Reich are but part of the story of Soviet women at war. Indeed, as Professor Murmantseva has pointed out, the glamour which attached to women *frontoviki* inevitably eclipsed that other dimension of the achievements of women in wartime Russia, namely, as 'fighters in overalls'. This was the huge mobilization of young girls and mature women to produce the weapons of war, which their daughters, sisters, cousins and schoolfriends, not to mention fathers, husbands and brothers, either operated, readied or repaired at the front.

Even in the prewar Soviet Union, life had shown little favour to women, inured as they were to both privation and exploitation – setting aside for the moment the fact that countless millions of women (and men and children) had been sent to the Gulag during Stalin's mass purges. Foodstuffs came off the ration in 1935, but the chronic housing shortage presented monumental problems. Just to survive, women had to work fulltime. Already by the beginning of 1940 women made up 41 per cent of the industrial workforce and on the land their share of the labour force had reached 52 per cent in 1939. But nobody could possibly have foreseen the massive and immediate call on the women of the Soviet Union in the wake of the calamitous defeats and horrendous Red Army losses in the early summer of 1941. The Wehrmacht tore into Russia's vitals with full-scale, ferocious blitzkrieg warfare. In addition to the battlefield losses, the German advance sliced away many millions from the available labour force, further disrupted and diminished by the frantic evacuation of industries deep into the eastern hinterland.

The speed and extent of the German Army's thrusts virtually split the Soviet Union into three parts. First, in the occupied territory some 80 million citizens were subjected to alien and brutal rule by the Nazi invader, who regarded all Slavs, Jews and other Soviet nationalities as the *Untermensch*. Second, in the unoccupied land, the enormous demographic distortion and displacement radically changed the composition of the Soviet labour force. In the war economies of all industrialized countries in the Second World War, 'manpower' in the factories and in the fields came to be equated with 'womanpower'. In the case of the Soviet Union this had a more extensive application than elsewhere. Third, deep in the rear, beyond the Urals, wartime evacuation involved no less than 25 million people.

Each separate area of the country exacted its own hardships from Soviet women. Mothers, daughters, sisters and aunts went to war-stations in their millions: skimpy girls, harassed housewives and stout matrons produced munitions in the industrial sweat-shops and dug anti-tank ditches. Soviet women suffered the brutalities of enemy occupation or the rigours of slave labour. In grim siege conditions they gave blood, tended orphans and battled hunger. Younger women went down mines, into the cabs of cranes, trucks and locomotives, and into heavy industry, In short, after 1941 in a country which had been stripped of manpower for the field armies, girls and women of every age not only replaced the labour of the missing men but also used themselves as motive power, substituting the strength of their own bodies to replace tractors and horses commandeered by the Red Army.

Behind the immediate front line work-loads were horrendous, as statistics clearly demonstrate. Over a period of two years the largely female staff of doctors, nurses and orderlies in evacuation hospital No. 290 on the Western Front treated 515,678 casualties, loaded or unloaded 1119 hospital trains, carried out 52,848 surgical operations, applied 88,747 plaster casts and made 131,000 X-ray examinations. Laundresses washed 154,100 kilograms of uniforms and bed-sheets; seamstresses repaired 798,000 sheets and 256,000 uniforms; cobblers mended 10,476 pairs of boots. The physical labour was demanding and exhausting. Klavdia Konovalova from the Georgian Republic, serving with the 784th Anti-Aircraft Regiment, was fortunate. In civilian life a blacksmith's striker, she joined a gun crew as a gunlayer but aspired to be a loader, which meant shifting 16-kilogram shells at high speed in intensive fire. Her particular physique stood up to the strain, but not all women could have been so fortunate.

As the German armies rolled on deep into Russia and Ukraine, thousands upon thousands of women were marooned behind the lines, only to be caught up one way or another in what became eventually a mass resistance movement. Slowly, falteringly, underground resistance and partisan warfare gathered pace, fuelled either by conviction or from revulsion at what the Nazi New Order really meant. They engulfed young girls and women in a ghastly, barbaric war. By 1944 the Central Staff of the Partisan Movement recorded some 280,000 individuals active in this brutal war behind the lines. 26,000 (or 9.3 per cent) were women undertaking operational roles. Counting those in separate detachments and units, women represented 25 per cent of the total.[2]

When we come to count those not only in partisan units but also involved in the complex and secretive underground activities such as the distribution of leaflets and the organization of underground Communist Party (CPSU) cells and committees, then the numbers of women involved jump to at least 100,000. In Ukraine no less than 30,697 women were part of the partisan movement and the underground. The partisan training schools, training radio-operators and parachutists, turned out 1262 women specifically trained to operate behind the lines. N. M. Zaitseva made nineteen parachute drops behind enemy lines. A. Soboleva also dropped behind the lines in 1942 to work as a radio-operator. She killed herself with her own grenade to evade capture. To maintain contact with the partisans V. S. Grizodubova, commanding the 101st Long-Range Air

Regiment, flew 1850 missions into occupied territory, taking in ammunition and flying out the wounded.

The risks women ran as partisans were enormous. If captured, they could expect brutal interrogation with all the ferocity of the 'Fascist manicure' to start with, followed by deportation and the concentration camp.[3] The horror of deportation hung over all women in the occupied zone. Deportations took some 2.4 million persons from Ukraine, almost half of all those deported from the Soviet Union. The majority of them were young girls and women consigned to the Third Reich as handmaidens to many a German *Hausfrau* or as slave labour on farms or factories. This was brutal human traffic which ripped families apart and ignited passionate hatred of the German occupation, whatever the early, beguiling promises of a friendlier, liberal occupation regime might have been. It was also a process which scattered Soviet women throughout the slave colonies of occupied Europe and the terrible concentration camps such as Ravensbrück, where resistance was punished in horrendous fashion or by extermination in the gas chambers of Auschwitz. German conquerors tugged at the availability of women, plunging them either into slave labour or conscripting them into industrial sweat-shops to produce arms for the front. In either circumstance, they lived under the most exhausting, exacting and rigorous regimes, the due toll of which has never been fully recorded.

Enormous wartime losses coupled with German depredations had made calamitous inroads into the Soviet labour force. To replace battlefield losses and to double the strength of the Red Army (from 5 to 10 million) required the mobilization of some 12 million young men and women. The production of war materials demanded labour mobilization, even as total 'manpower' resources fell by some 26 million.[4] Tighter labour discipline had already been imposed in the summer of 1940 and apprentice training for industry expanded. Industrial training continued to expand during the war, introducing women to a range of skilled trades in engineering, transportation and power generation. A mass voluntary movement early in the war brought in some 800,000 persons, largely the unemployed, such as housewives, students and pensioners. However, compulsory direction of labour resources was quickly instituted by the Soviet Manpower Committee, which transferred workers from light industry to heavy industry and construction.

The response from women was extraordinary. In Leningrad 500 housewives took up work places in the Kirov Factory: as early as August 1941 women made up 90 per cent of the workforce in machine-shops. In Moscow 374,000 housewives turned to factory jobs. Miners' wives volunteered for work in the mines, many taking up positions with pneumatic drills at the coal-face. By the beginning of October 1942 when most of the available reserves had been mobilized for war, women made up 52 per cent of the industrial labour force in arms industries (or connected supply industries) and 81 per cent of the labour in light industry (compared with 60 per cent in May 1941).

In the third part of the country evacuation, which shifted much of the industry of western Russia deep into the eastern hinterlands, brought unbelievable hardship. Evacuation put an impossible strain on transport and created chaos in feeding arrangements. In areas under immediate German attack, it had to be a pell-mell process. Families were bundled up, marched along railway lines, then shunted eastwards to improvized shelter and housing. The flood of evacuees, and the weight of a relocated labour force, brought about the virtual collapse of housing – another prewar problem multiplied a thousandfold by the wartime exigencies of evacuation, destruction and huge shifts in population. Families dug earth shelters or turned to derelict barracks. In one giant tank factory in the east, 8,500 workers lived in mere holes in the ground. Those more fortunate were lodged in 'worker settlements' housing 15,000 people. Yet these skeletal buildings contained only six stand-pipes for water, lacked any kind of furniture and were bereft of fuel. One factory, turning out anti-tank weapons, had 22 families with assorted individuals crammed into three commandeered rooms.

With full labour mobilization, as women and young girls were marched into the factories and into the mines, great and growing competence accrued to the Manpower Committee, responsible for registering the non-working population in town and country alike and coordinating labour mobilization. Factories duly received their contingents of young women, as did the railways – taking in no less than 165,200 young women for training in railway operations in 1942 alone. Supplying industry with skilled labour continued to be the responsibility of State Labour Reserves.

At the end of 1941 thousands of women had already been drafted into railway operations, which throughout the war continued to suffer from a lack of skilled labour. The trade schools, to which the wartime government paid great attention in order to build up labour reserves, turned out 298,800 young men and women for railway duties. This was 'on the job' training which resulted in repairs to 100,000 wagons and 11,000 locomotives. Women and young girls took on every type of work on the railways – engine-drivers, driver's mates, station staff, track gangs, electricians and mechanics. The first ever woman engine-driver in the Soviet Union, Maria Aleksandrovna Arestova, who took over the footplate in 1931 amidst much festivity, returned to the war running the special, highly dangerous 'flying column' trains right up to the front. These locomotives were targets of Luftwaffe low-level strafing attacks.

The wartime labour regime proved to be harsh in the extreme. The edict of 26 December 1941 made absence without leave from a defence industry factory punishable by imprisonment ranging from five to eight years: absence equalled desertion and those so charged faced a military tribunal. In 1943 a woman named Golubeva was mobilized for war-work but failed to appear at her assigned work-place: she was duly tried by an NKVD military tribunal and sentenced to six years' imprisonment. The construction industry had already been placed under a form of military regulation in July 1941, but the difficulty of applying military law to civilian work discipline brought some relaxation in 1942. On 15 April 1943 the railways, the telegraph system and water transportation were placed, illegally, under military disciplinary codes.[5] A woman locksmith named Chadaeva, employed in water-transportation, was absent on October 8 and over the weekend of 13 to 15 October 1945. She was duly put before a military tribunal.[6]

Nor did women, whether young or old, escape the rigours of forced labour by the Soviet regime. Thousands were mobilized to dig anti-tank ditches and build barricades in the towns and cities threatened by the German advance. The decrees which placed industry and transportation under military law proved to be a boon for Beria and the NKVD, swelling the pool of forced labour – for which there was an insatiable demand – especially in 1943 when offences against the militarized labour code brought greater numbers of young girls, charged with 'absenteeism' or similar infringements, into the hands of the Soviet secret police. In the labour camps of the Gulag male and female prisoners in Beria's private industrial empire turned out impressive quantities of ammunition and equipment.

The labour situation in agriculture became acute virtually from the outbreak of war, placing an immense strain on young girls and women. Red Army mobilization not only took men for the front, it also took the machines and motive power, the tractors and the horses. What tractors did remain had to be worked very hard. Women were rushed into training courses for driving and maintaining them. This was itself a gruelling task in the absence of replacement machines, spare parts and lubricants. New machines were forthcoming only late in the war. In 1940 only 4 per cent of tractor drivers were women: by 1944 that figure had risen to 81 per cent. Handling these tractors – creaking, groaning, rasping, geriatric machines – was 'man's work' in every sense: '... The work was hard. We slept three or four hours a day. For a long time we warmed up the engines with naked flames – against all the rules. Lubricants and fuel were rationed. You answered with your head for every drop, just as for every melted bearing.'

The war economy continued to drain off men for industry from the countryside in spite of the dire conditions prevailing there – 23 per cent of those assigned for war-work came from the countryside in 1942, a figure which rose to 59 per cent in 1943 and 62 per cent by 1944.[7] The 'battle for bread' was of critical importance. Women had to shoulder much of the brute burden of agricultural work as the labour force continued to fall. There were only 4 million men on the land in 1943, as opposed to 11 million women, though further calls would still be made on them for war-work in industry. The proportion of female labour employed at large in agriculture trebled during the war – rising from 40 per cent in 1940, to 70 per cent in 1943, 82 per cent in 1944 and 91.7 per cent in 1945.[8]

Wartime conditions and wartime demands of the Soviet regime brought great impoverishment to the countryside, which suffered the chaos of the 1941 evacuations, the imposition of German rule and the pains of 're-collectivization' once the Red Army moved back into liberated Soviet territory. In 1942 the compulsory minimum of 'labour days' or 'work days' (*trudodni*) was raised to 100–20 for adult kolkhoz (collective farm) workers. In regions producing cotton, the minimum was raised to 150. For those aged between 12 to 16 the minimum was set at 50. Wartime regulations prescribed harsh penalties for failure to meet the minimum requirement. These included docking the value of 'labour days' already earned, plus additional compulsory labour. It could also mean the punitive hand of the NKVD, assignment to forced labour squads in the case of repeated offenders or, as a dire and extreme punishment, taking away the household's vital private plot, which was all that kept most families alive.

Workers on the sovkhozes (state farms), which enjoyed a certain official favour, received quite substantial monetary wages, although there was little to buy. The peasant households received 'payment in kind', if and when it was available, though every little bit added to the vital produce of the private plots. The prices paid for compulsory deliveries to the state were derisory – three kopecks for a kilogram of potatoes. Payment for the 'labour day' could be as low as 200 grams of grain and 100 grams of potatoes (in effect, one potato and a cupful of grain). Life existed largely at the level of bare subsistence for many peasant households. Along with the populace at large, they suffered from the harvest loss in the calamitous year of 1943. Some alleviation came with the Soviet army's recovery of occupied territories, but the land was ravaged once more as the Germans retreated. Thousands of villages were destroyed. Those people who survived were forced to live in earth dug-outs. Yet, as a tribute to the peasant women and the women of the 'tractor brigades', both the army and the populace were fed, not grandly nor even sufficiently, but fed – which was not the case in the First World War.

In the unoccupied land and the deep rear, working conditions were rigorous. The working day extended to 12 to 16 hours with a mandatory three hours of overtime. The factories provided communal feeding, though what passed for 'food' – suspicious soups and unpalatable concoctions – brought mocking comments from the workers. Still, communal feeding eased some of the burden as meat, fish and sugar vanished from sight. 25 million people were dependent on this source of food by 1944.

In a country stripped for war, where the slogan 'All for the Front' was taken literally, Soviet housewives struggled desperately to eke out an existence. Food and shelter assumed paramount importance. In the cities where siege conditions prevailed, as in Leningrad for many agonising months, everything edible was used, even the scrapings of wallpaper paste. Sheep gut was used for jellies; in the absence of vegetable oils an emulsion of sunflower oil, soup stock and cornflour was used for baking.

Although all civilian populations among the combatants of the Second World War experienced rationing, the Soviet Union's women had to feed themselves and their families on the most limited, restricted quantities imaginable. Rationing was not new in the Soviet Union (bread had been rationed from 1929–35), but in 1941 a graduated wartime rationing system was introduced. 'Bread norms' ranged between 800 grams and 1.2 kilos per day. The latter figure was for workers in heavy industry; 400 grams was for the remainder, with 300 to 400 grams for children and expectant mothers. In 1942 61.8 million people depended on the state bread ration supply. In 1943 this figure had risen to 67 million, and by 1944 74 million people received their daily bread from this supply. Moscow suffered the hardships of the winter of 1941–2, when the breakdown in transportation meant less food, with only 30 per cent of the meat ration honoured. By 1944, in addition to increased supplies of fish and meat, there was also more food available on the 'free market'. The Soviet housewife might well try the kolkhoz peasant markets, but this meant paying exorbitant prices.

By the end of the war living standards, according to US intelligence sources, had fallen to a level 'comparable to the worst conditions at the close of the 1920s'. Under-nourishment was all too common. Key communal services, such as baths and laundries, were subject to breakdown and fuel shortages. Water supply and sanitation systems were liable to failure. Public transport, suffering endemic shortages, could not cope with all the loads, forcing workers to walk several miles to and from the factories. Supplies for civilians dwindled almost to vanishing point. Shoe and clothing repairs became difficult. Barter between town and country replaced money since there was little or nothing to buy. Consumer goods had a rarity all their own. The 66-hour working week for all workers and managers – with one rest day a month – took its own toll. Output did not increase with the longer hours, and much research remains to be done on the industrial accident rate.

Urban sieges, rural deprivation, mass evacuation, mass deportation, the inroads of the battlefront – all played havoc with the well-being of millions of families. Urban populations were decimated: in Stalingrad only 12.2 per cent of the prewar population was left; in Voronezh just under 20 per cent remained. As best they might under these stringent conditions, the authorities instituted welfare programmes, directed particularly towards child-care for infants and children of pre-school age. Dislocation, scarcity, the lack of facilities and primitive conditions were almost universally prevalent. 'Welfare' took on a public and a private face. Both involved women in multiple roles and responsibilities. Their duties expanded in efforts to repair the damage in the occupied areas. Pressure on schools, as well as the actual destruction of schools, brought young girls and women into makeshift schools to compensate for the loss of teachers. They also assisted in campaigns against epidemics, such as the measures instituted in 1942–3 to combat tuberculosis. Everywhere there was the tragedy of war widows coupled with commitments, private and public, to make provision for the families of servicemen.

By 1942 the problem of a growing number of orphans led to the organization of orphan welfare committees, in which the trade unions (and the Orthodox Church) played a prominent part. By 1943 more than 350,000 orphans had been placed for adoption or lodged in children's homes, but in areas recovered by the Red Army thousands of waifs had to be more or less rounded up. This wearying and exhausting work, a grinding daily round, never ceased.

Soviet historians were obliged to admit that they needed a more accurate picture of what held the 'home front' together. What is also required is a more realistic treatment of the difference between the official, heroic legend and accepted popular myths. The discrepancy is greatest in the general area of public morale. It is possible to gain some insights into what women in the Soviet Union had to endure, what plagued and pained them, from letters destined for men at the front but captured by the German Army. The letters offer a tale of hardship and tribulation, of shortages, privation and the struggle to exist. Yet they still express a sturdy, dogged, mundane determination to 'keep the home fires burning' – even if their own homes had been burned to the ground, a fate suffered by many millions.

While the hardships and dangers Soviet girls and women endured on the homefront were enormous, they often found themselves thrust at frighteningly short notice into the front line, which could be anyone's street or suburb. For example, Leningrad *was* the front line for 900 days, under prolonged artillery fire which carried off 63,000 of its citizens (apart from countless numbers who died of starvation, cold or other causes). This was, after all, a war of multiple urban sieges and urban assaults, with towns and cities twice fought over in capture and re-capture. The war came to many young girls and women with terrifying suddenness. The speed of the German advance brought the fighting literally to their doorsteps. Hastily formed, poorly armed and badly trained divisions of the 'people's militia' (*narodnoe opolchenie*) faced crack German troops. Women not yet subject to the call-up signed up with a will for these home-guard units. In the shipyards of Nikolaev 584 women joined up. Out of the town's population of 8000, 2800 young girls and women between the ages 16 and 60 volunteered. In Nikolaev Oblast (Province) by late July 1941, out of 70,464 volunteers, 18,884 were women. Women also played a large part in the work of the so-called annihilation battalions, the guard and security units organized to deal with possible enemy parachutists, spies, deserters, general malcontents and 'panic-mongers'.

The contribution of women to the Soviet war effort that has been described thus far took place for the most part in the rear, behind the front lines. What is unique in the annals of warfare is that so many girls and women also became *frontoviki* themselves, volunteering for action against the Wehrmacht in planes, tanks, and rifle brigades. Theirs is a story of courage, endurance and suffering without parallel in human history. Many of the Red Army's finest soldiers happened to be women, and they won in combat their country's highest decoration – Hero of the Soviet Union – often posthumously.

Nothing could have prepared young girls and women for the horrors of battle, but many had become acquainted with military affairs and military life quite early in the Soviet period. In 1927 Defence Commissar Voroshilov, citing the Polish example of military training for women, urged the same for Soviet women. During the 1930s officers' wives in particular took an active part in military life, acquiring basic military training and setting up programmes to instruct themselves and others in driving, nursing and industrial skills. Beyond these military confines the mass programmes for elementary military and physical training run by the Association for National Defence and for Aviation and Chemical Construction (*Osoaviakhim*) trained men and women qualified to wear the GTO badge, 'Prepared for Labour and Defence', plus a badge for military marksmanship, 'Voroshilov Shot'.[9] Women carved out a special niche for themselves in pilot training, gaining distinction in a number of long-distance flights.

With or without such previous training, women and girls figured prominently among the early volunteers for the Red Army and for the front. The figures speak for themselves. For example, in the Dnepropetrovsk Oblast 3602 of 10,175 volunteers were women, in Kirovograd Oblast 1113 out of 2398, in the Donetsk Oblast 5314 out of 20,000. In this flood of genuine volunteers, 500,000 housewives came forward for war-work (together with 300,000 senior school-children), plus women students and veterans.

Young women invaded the military registration and enlistment offices. Those with recognizable skills, particularly medical students, were immediately taken into the military: 'You have two hours to pack. You are going to the front.' As yet without proper uniforms, young women such as these headed for the front virtually in what they stood up in, plaits covered by head-scarves, causing one general to growl about a 'powder-puff division'. Others, much to their disappointment, were quite sensibly advised to sign up on specific training courses. But age and appearance were deceptive. Fourteen-year-olds lied that they were sixteen (the minimum age). Tiny Polina Nazdrecheva, addressed in a line-up by an officer as 'Thumbelina' was strongly advised to 'go back to your Mom and grow a bit'. In fact, she went on to become a highly decorated frontline veteran.

Together with the Red Army, the Communist Party (CPSU) and the Young Communist League (Komsomol) also mobilized. To stiffen morale and to repair some of the massive damage inflicted on the Red Army, Party members and Young Communists, many of them young women, were despatched to the field armies. In August 1941 10,000 were drafted and sent at once to the front to join the signals troops. In the Odessa Oblast 73,200 Young Communists volunteered for the front, among them 10,000 young women. They were among the first of many thousands to follow. There would be no less than seventy five mobilizations ordered for Komsomol members, accompanied by five mobilizations of women who were full Party members.

There are countless accounts of women's courage and self-sacrifice in the early defeats of Soviet forces. In the fighting for the Ukrainian capital Kiev, the women machine-gunners of the Communist Party companies fought for their city and their lives in desperate battles. One of the Soviet Union's ace women pilots, made a Hero of the Soviet Union in 1938 for her record flight from Moscow to the Far East, flew into a very heavy battle to deliver radio equipment for partisan groups preparing to operate in the German rear. In Odessa, besieged and assaulted, the 900-strong women's militia battalion fought alongside such women Komsomol Red Army soldiers as Nina Onilova. Brought up in an orphanage, she was now an army nurse turned machine-gunner with the 54th Regiment of the 25th Rifle Division and a cool and deadly gunner. She continued her war in Sevastopol, only to die of wounds in the spring of 1942. At the approaches to Sevastopol itself, in an improvised armoured train 'Anatoly Zheleznyakov' that was directing fire on advancing German troops, army nurse K. Karenina tended the wounded, hoisted shells and helped to repair damaged track. N. Ostroukhova acted as stoker, taking the train out of danger during a night bombardment. On the front line, operating with the reconnaissance parties of the 514th Naval Infantry Regiment on frequent raids in the German rear, Senior Sergeant Maria Baida used her machine-pistol – and its butt – to kill enemy soldiers at close quarters. These exploits made her a Hero of the Soviet Union.

Together with the Komsomol, the trade union organizations, working in turn with the Red Cross, set up a crash programme to train young women as frontline medics and medical orderlies. This also involved enlisting trainees to act as orderlies on hospital trains or in military hospitals. At the front itself 41 per cent of all doctors were women, as were 43 per cent of the field surgeons, 43 per cent of the medical assistants and 100 per cent of all nurses. Little of the traditional image of the 'nurse' survived amidst the carnage of hand-to-hand fighting or modern mechanized warfare. Losses among the girl and women medics serving with the rifle battalions were second only to the fighting troops themselves.

Olga Omelchenko, a 16-year-old frontline medic, served with a rifle company and along with it was flung into hand-to-hand fighting: '... That was awful ... It isn't for human beings ... Men strike, thrust their bayonets into stomachs, eyes, strangle one another ... Howling, shouts, groans. It's just terrible, even for war.' In one incident, because of cowardice in the ranks, wounded men Olga Omelchenko had dragged into a crater were captured. 'Her' men were mutilated and killed. Later she grabbed a sub-machine gun and personally took up a position in the firing squad which carried out the death sentence on those who broke and ran. Forty thousand of these embattled, battle-tested women medics were decorated, fifteen of them with the highest award available, Hero of the Soviet Union.

In 1942, the year of Stalingrad, the gigantic demands of total war swept aside the legal qualification which quite unrealistically had limited women in military service to medical, 'ancillary' and 'specialist' roles. The battle-front, the bombed cities and the enemy-occupied territory told a different story. Mass mobilization was coupled with mass military training in reserve training centres and through the *Vsevobuch* (universal military training) and *Osoaviakhim* programmes. The Komsomol sections of *Vsevobuch* provided elementary instruction for 222,000 mortar crews, machine-gunners, radio operators, signallers and military traffic controllers.

At the beginning of 1942 the CPSU Central Committee formally considered admitting women volunteers to the field forces.[10] In the spring the Komsomol drafted 100,000 young women between 19 and 25 years of age to the Air Defence Command (PVO), followed by a second draft in October. In January 1943 70,029 women were serving with the PVO, 10 per cent of the total strength, with 41,011 manning anti-aircraft batteries. By the end of the war no less than 200,000 women were serving in the air defence forces, 121,281 with the guns, while others operated searchlights, observer posts or flew air defence fighters. On 24 September 1942 Lieutenant Khomyakova, serving with the 586th Fighter Regiment, was the first woman fighter pilot to shoot down an enemy bomber during a night raid on Saratov.

Grudgingly, but increasingly, the military drew on women with special skills as the critical shortages of manpower, brought on by calamitous losses, pushed more women into frontline support roles. In their thousands women soldiers (*zhenshchiny-voiny*), girl machine-gunners (*devushki-pulemyotchitsy*), girl snipers (*devushki-snaipery*) and women driver-mechanics in tank units now made up a distinctive and unique segment of the Soviet order of battle. The Red Army included the 1st Independent Volunteer Women's Rifle Brigade and the 1st Independent Women's Reserve Rifle Regiment: The latter was formed in November 1942 in the Moscow Military District. It trained 3892 privates, 986 NCOs and 2987 officers, and a further 514 women officers and 1504 women NCOs in 1943, 500 of whom became frontline veterans. The Ryazan Infantry School, which maintained three women's battalions, trained women platoon commanders, sending 1388 into the field in 1943, 704 of whom took over rifle sections, 382 machine-gun sections and 302 mortar crew.

Soviet women fighter and bomber pilots, together with women snipers, established a unique reputation for themselves. Even before the war Major Marina Raskova, who learned to fly with *Osoaviakhim*'s Central Flying Club, was made a Hero of the Soviet Union in 1938, having distinguished herself in long-distance flights.[11] At her prompting and prodding the Soviet Air Force, fiercely battered by the Luftwaffe throughout the summer and autumn of 1941, agreed to form not one but three women's air regiments, drawing on women instructors from *Osoaviakhim*, pilots and navigators from the civil air fleet, plus a handful of women already serving with the Air Force. The regiments entered in the aviation order of battle were the 588th (46th Guards) Women's Night Light Bomber Regiment, the 587th (125th Guards) Women's Day Bomber Regiment and the 586th Women's Air Defence (PVO) Fighter Regiment. Women pilots also flew in predominantly male air regiments.

The 46th Guards Regiment, with its battle honour 'Taman', flew no less than 23,672 sorties, and 23 women of the regiment received the award of Hero of the Soviet Union. Young women made up the entire regiment – pilots, navigators, armourers, mechanics, political officers. Formed and trained at Engels, the regiment took delivery of its U-2s, slender biplanes nicknamed 'swallows' (*lastochki*). At first unarmed, the planes offered no protection to the pilot and navigator. It was not until 1944 that the women crews were given a machine-gun.

In May 1942 the 588th Regiment went to war with the 218th Night Bomber Air Division of the 4th Air Army, launching night raids over the German lines in slow-moving open cockpit biplanes. Searchlights and German night fighters were their most formidable enemies. The regiment specialized in attacking the flak batteries themselves, one biplane deliberately drawing fire while another flew in unseen to bomb the guns and searchlights. These were nerve-racking and dangerous missions which inevitably brought losses. On the ground young women armourers struggled to load 400 kilos of bombs into the bomb racks, often when time was desperately short in order to re-arm the aircraft for five or six sorties each night before dawn broke.

Women pilots flew Pe-2 bombers with the 125th Guards Day Bomber Regiment commanded initially by Marina Raskova, while Colonel Valentina Grizodubova – prewar pilot also decorated for long-distance flights – commanded the 101st (31st Guards) Long-Range Bomber Regiment. She completed 200 sorties on bombing raids or flying into Ukrainian partisan airfields, taking in ammunition and medicine, bringing out the sick, wounded, women and children. In September 1942 aircraft from this same special regiment picked up Kovpak, Saburov and Kozlov, partisan commanders operating deep in the German rear, when they were summoned by Stalin to a conference in the Kremlin.

Operating with the Baltic Fleet, Guards Senior Lieutenant L. I. Shulaikina flew an Il-2 *Shturmovik* heavy assault aircraft. This low-flying plane dropped bombs and fired rockets or cannon aimed at German transports and escort vessels at sea. By 1944 1749 women were serving with the 13th Air Army in the Trans-Baikal Military District, with a further 3000 attached to the 10th Air Army of the Far Eastern Front. They were soon to be fully activated in operations in the 'lightning campaign' of 1945 against Japan.

The award of Hero of the Soviet Union went to thirty women aircrew. An appreciable number were posthumous decorations. Senior Lieutenant Anna Yegorova-Timofeyeva, navigator with the 305th Air Regiment, had to wait for her decoration. In August 1944, flying her 277th sortie, she led a group of sixteen Il-2 ground-attack *Shturmovik* aircraft on a raid, only to receive a direct hit in the engine which set her aircraft on fire. Badly burned in the crash, and with spinal injuries and a dislocated arm, she was taken prisoner and put in solitary confinement in Kustrin POW camp. She was eventually liberated by Soviet troops. She received her award in May 1965.

A deadly battlefield skill at which girls and young woman excelled was that of sniper. One woman, Lyudmila Mikhailovna Pavlichenko, 'No. 1 sniper', became a wartime celebrity, visiting the United States where she sang with Paul Robeson and met President Roosevelt. Born in 1916, she worked as a lathe operator in a Kiev factory but studied the rifle together with N. Kovshova and M. Polivanova at *Osoaviakhim* courses for snipers. The war found her in Odessa where she reported to the *voenkomat* and was assigned to the 25th 'Chapaev' Rifle Division. She took part in the defence of Odessa and the siege of Sevastopol, from which she was evacuated after being badly wounded. Her toll of German soldiers reached 309, 78 of whom were snipers like herself. In 1942 she graduated to the rank of *snaiper-nastavnik*, master instructor for the rifle and the sniper's art.[12]

Snipers for the Red Army came from the Central School of Sniper Instructors, which in 1943 was re-designated the Central Women's School for Sniper Training. It was then placed under the command of a regular Red Army woman officer, N. P. Chegodaeva, a graduate of the Frunze Military Academy. A veteran of the Spanish Civil War and more recently of the Volkhov Front, Chegodaeva was closely involved in setting up the women's air regiments. As the war rolled on, the school turned out 1061 snipers and 407 instructors. The graduates of this sniper school accounted for some 12,000 enemy soldiers. The platoon of women snipers commanded by Nina Lobkovskaya, attached to the 3rd Shock Army, reportedly accounted for no less than 3112 enemy soldiers. The cost, however, was heavy. Among the casualties was junior sergeant Tamara Kostyrina, who shot 120 enemy soldiers and was twice wounded, before being killed herself in a hand-to-hand engagement in 1944. She was among those twenty five women serving with Red Army rifle troops decorated as Hero of the Soviet Union.

For all their deadly skill the fate of women snipers was as pitiful as it was inevitable, especially in sniper duels. One captured German officer expressed his astonishment at the loss of so many of his men through head wounds only, asking to see such a skilled marksman. The Soviet commander could not oblige him since the particular 'marksman', a young woman sniper named Sasha Shlyakova, had herself just been killed in a sniper duel. Less dramatic but equally doleful was the fate of Nina Pavlovna Petrova. She was 48 years of age when she went to the front, an excellent sniper who claimed 122 enemy soldiers. She was assigned as instructor to Red Army men for sniper training and sniper tactics, and became known as the 'snipers' Mom'. She was killed herself in a road crash in February 1945.

Red Army tank troops expressed early reservations about young girls and women being involved in tank battles, but women persisted in seeking to play their part. They went on to be not only medics but also driver-mechanics, tank commanders[13] and even platoon commanders. They operated with medium tanks (T-34s), save for one notable exception. Junior Lieutenant Alexandra Boiko, together with her husband, volunteered for the front. It took a letter from the Boikos to Stalin himself, offering a donation of 50,000 rubles to build a tank and requesting a frontline posting, to facilitate both being sent to the Chelyabinsk Tank Technical School in 1943. Husband and wife took over a monster, the 45-ton Stalin tank, the IS-122, which mounted a 122mm dual purpose gun. Alexandra Boiko commanded the crew of four, including her husband, who acted as driver-mechanic. They fought their way through the Baltic states, Poland, Czechoslovakia and into Germany.

Maria Oktyabrskaya, a posthumous Hero of the Soviet Union, also 'purchased' her entry into tank warfare. After her husband was killed in action with a rifle division, she approached the authorities with her savings, offering to pay for a tank in return for training on it and fighting with its crew. In October 1943, fully trained, she joined 26th Guards Tank Brigade with her tank, 'Amazon' (*Boevaya podruga*). She was killed in it in action in 1944.

There are many other incidents of girls and young women forcing their way to become tankers. Irina Levchenko volunteered as a 17-year-old in 1941, serving first as a medic in a frontline dressing station and later with a tank battalion in the Crimea. When she was badly wounded, a medical commission recommended her removal from the military register. Not to be beaten, she enrolled in the Stalingrad Tank School, joining the tank troops. She ended the war as Lieutenant-Colonel Levchenko, Hero of the Soviet Union, a 'medic-tanker'. Yekaterina Petlyuk fought in a tank, nicknamed 'The Kid' (*Malyutka*), paid for by an Omsk schoolgirl, her family and public donations. Petlyuk's 'Kid' fought at Stalingrad, in the massive tank battle at the Kursk salient and during the recapture of Kiev at the end of 1943. Marina Lagunova volunteered for the front and was at first refused training on tanks, whereupon she approached M. Kalinin, President of the Supreme Soviet. She was admitted to a tank-training brigade, graduating as a driver-mechanic. She fought at Kursk and took part in the drive to the Dnepr River. In September 1943 German guns destroyed her tank, wounding her so severely that both her legs had to be amputated. Once out of hospital she learned to drive again, and returned to a tank training brigade as an instructor. One 'tank family' went to a common wartime grave. On the death of Colonel Kodenets, his daughter Yelizaveta volunteered for the tank troops, serving as a gunner/wireless operator, only to be killed in action in Berlin in April 1945 at the very end of the war.

The almost one million young girls and women within the Red Army's ranks made an invaluable contribution to the Soviet cause, but at the same time they presented wholly unfamiliar problems in training, psychology, medicine and material. The Red Army command was unprepared (and often unwilling) to make particular provision for women, either in accommodation, sanitary arrangements or medical care. Officers were dismissive or indifferent: the women soldiers were an encumbrance. Even uniforms were a problem at the outset: 'We were issued with greatcoats; they were thick and too large. We moved about, looking like hayricks. We didn't walk, we waddled. ... There were boots but they were all men's sizes.' Skirts were 'manufactured' by cutting the bottom out of kitbags.

Many women had to struggle to get the jobs for which they were qualified. Red Army soldiers reacted like soldiers everywhere. If generals harrumphed about 'powder-puff' divisions, soldiers hooted or just spat. Some Red Army men also looked on female snipers with a certain reservation, if not outright dislike:

> When two women crawl out to kill someone in no-man's-land with a sniper's rifle, it looks like 'hunting', I should say. ... I was a sniper myself and I took part in shooting. But after all I'm a man. Perhaps I would take a woman like that along on a scouting mission but not for a wife.

There seems to have been considerable reluctance to commit women to action, partly out of masculine reservation (or shame) and partly out of concern that women were 'not up to the job'. Women veterans said of their male commanding officers: 'They tried not to send us. You had to request to be sent out or to earn the right, to distinguish yourself in some way.' But the business of proving themselves was arduous: 'You are women, why should you go to the front line?' was one comment. 'You have chosen to fight, girls: very well, but don't do anything else. Don't lower yourselves', was another. 'Why have you brought these girls here?' was a typical reaction. Women showed that they could handle weapons, even some of the heaviest, but in many instances they had to earn the right to fight, or else it was 'the kitchens'. However, once they showed reliability and competence, having passed their 'initiation tests', they were put to work with a will. Nina Osipova joined the 326th Rifle Division in 1941, to shouts of 'Who's this babe?' 'She's small, tender-hearted, where will she hold her machine-gun? First shot and she'll ask for a transfer to the rear.' But she did not run away and ended the war as Lieutenant Osipova.

A subtle discrimination showed up, however, at the higher echelons of command. Apart from the three air regiments, women fought largely at the sub-unit, battery and weapon crew level. They exercised command only up to platoon level; their officer rank ranged from senior lieutenant to lieutenant-colonel, or in rare instances, colonel. For all the massive role played by girls and women in the partisan movement, only one woman – Alexandra Zakharova – rose to occupy the key post of commissar to a unit, the 207th Gomel Region Partisan Unit. For all the glamour surrounding women fighter pilots, snipers and tank commanders, women were valued most by fellow male soldiers as medics and signallers. One senior commander uttered a reproof to young women aching for action and seeking a transfer to the front: men could replace women in most tasks, but women were irreplaceable in those two categories.

In fact, thousands of women served as sappers and signallers, but they saw just as much action and danger as women in other frontline jobs. Women signallers in the fearful maelstrom of the Battle of Stalingrad stuck at their posts even under a literal rain of fire. Women radio operators were also assigned to establish communications with partisan groups, working with forward Red Army reconnaissance groups and setting up radio stations in enemy-occupied territory. Women also took charge of the military mail and field post offices, running considerable risks to bring up the 'long-range shells' (i.e., mail) to frontline units. The award of Hero of the Soviet Union went to four women serving with Red Army signals.

Women sappers were actively discouraged in view of the dangers of the work, but they persisted and operated as commanders of field engineering platoons, having graduated from the Moscow Military Engineers School.

Hardship, danger and discouragement notwithstanding, after the mass mobilizations of 1942, the presence of women in all branches and operational formations of the Red Army, Navy and Air Force continued to grow. 'Soviet women' embraced a wide range of nationalities. In 1942, 43,662 young women of the Komsomol were in the Red Army, 8863 of them in frontline service. In 1943, 265,616 had been mobilized, with more than half (61.5 per cent) of these, 163,172, already at the front. In 1945 the figure for women *frontoviki* rose to 246,530. This represented over 76.5 per cent of all those mobilized. In the field armies themselves between 1943 and 1945 the average complement of women soldiers varied between 2000 and 3500, plying various military trades. In each army of the 1st Belorussian Front in 1944 there were some 3000 to 3500 women. On the Leningrad Front in January 1944 there were 22,000 women soldiers. In January 1945 on the 2nd Belorussian Front more than 20,000 women were in action, including 3636 officers and 5081 NCOs.

Adding to the women's difficulties, many commanders remained not only unsympathetic but positively hostile towards the physical and medical requirements of female soldiers. These ranged from the need for separate sleeping quarters and lavatories to rooms for personal hygiene. The Chief Gynaecologist of the 1st Belorussian Front, Medical Lieutenant-Colonel Ye. M. Kaplun, reported that the unsatisfactory state of affairs in the field was not due solely to the conditions. In some units an 'unhealthy atmosphere' surrounded the women. There were cases of 'irregular conduct' towards pregnant women soldiers. Some commanders viewed pregnancy as a breach of military discipline, believing it debased and insulted the woman, hindering her ability to carry out duties.

'Hygiene rooms' should have been set up for women soldiers, with hot water, washing facilities, cotton wool, soap, stools and disinfectant solutions. Few of these necessities were available in military units, leading to urino-genital inflammation and infection. Medical Major A. L. Kaplan reported from the 2nd Belorussian Front that setting up adequate facilities for women soldiers meant a huge effort. It meant overcoming the objections and even the direct opposition of some commanders, but such attitudes had to change to reduce the incidence of sickness among women soldiers. In small units a 'hygiene room' or corner could be set up, in or near the medical post. In the Moscow Air Defence Front 3060 'hygiene rooms' or corners were set up to accommodate 15,020 women; and 13,162 kilograms of cotton wool were distributed, with each woman receiving an extra ration of 100 grams of soap per month. A woman medic was posted in these rooms to supervise the issue of cotton wool and soap. At the same time they dispensed advice recommended by military doctors.

For all the wartime hyperbole of the heroic legend and the postwar style of what has been derided as 'World War II writing', war and the involvement of women. at the front meant mud, blood, lice, discomfort, disease and not infrequently death. Heroic legends play their indispensable part in all countries at war in maintaining and boosting morale, but in the Soviet Union the result was only too often a series of stereotypes which, if anything, obscured true heroines, true heroism and the real martyrs. The plain unvarnished facts, though never part of any wartime bill of fare, more often than not suffice in themselves to convey the scale of sacrifice and the degree of patriotic commitment, without even a hint of the vainglorious. In the words of one woman veteran:

> We didn't shoot. I cooked porridge for the soldiers and I was given a medal for that. I cooked porridge and the soldiers' soup and dragged cauldrons and mess-tins about. Heaven knows, they were heavy. I remember our commander saying, 'I'll shoot holes through those mess-tins. ... How are you going to give birth after the war?'[14]

Her commander did eventually blaze away and his men 'liberated' smaller mess tins in some village.

The contribution of women and young girls of all ages in the Soviet Union to their country's great, possibly unsurpassed feat of survival was immense, yet even now it remains without its proper chronicle. The bulk of the material is either anecdotal, valuable in its own way, or else statistical, great clusters of numbers and figures which are not without significance but which are bereft of social meaning. To do full justice to this monumental subject and to the relevance of this singular phenomenon requires not merely access to the archives but the services of historians, economists, psychologists, sociologists, demographers and the medical profession at large.

The response and reaction of these women to conditions of maximum stress have yet to be explained. While it goes part way, the heroic myth does not tell the whole story. Much of the glorification of the role of the Party, a standard propagandistic theme in days now passing, tended to obscure the major role played by voluntarism and to ignore the importance of improvization. This, after all, was a 'people's war' not a

'Party war' (although under Brezhnev the Party tried to make it just that). The early passions of patriotism were genuine enough, even preceding the official government line and the evocation of all that Mother Russia represented. Voluntary collective action on the part of women more often than not compensated for administrative shortcomings and blunders and acted as a shock-absorber where the population was either 'rudely coerced or callously abandoned'. Hatred of the enemy for all the spoliation and calamity he visited on them was also an important factor. This was not 'hurrah-patriotism' but a deeper, more profound reaction, one to justify and generate sacrifice:

> This was her one and only daughter, but she did not spare her and could not forgive her for the shame she had brought by returning home ... She didn't even try to keep her daughter back? No, she kissed her and said: 'Your father is fighting, you go and fight too.'

Group cohesion and group pressure governmental enactment and decree, the psychology of mass mobilization, individual family fate and fortune, the primitivism of vengeful feelings, and not least the self-discovery of talents and capabilities hitherto unexplored or unexploited, even the exhilaration of danger and the stimulus of action, all combined to produce this remarkable, sustained response. But the cost, as yet without accurate tabulation, even assuming that this could be possible was horrendous, not merely in the dead but also in the survivors.[15] As many of those women who would rightly and proudly wear their war medals, there were those who hid them from sight, psychologically scarred and physically maimed. In the totality of the tragedy, there were even more who silently, continually mourned the children they would never have and lamented that the 'mother role' which they had fulfilled in wartime could never be one they might enjoy in the peace they had done so much to secure.

## NOTES

[Reorganized and renumbered from the original.]

1. In 1806 at the age of 23 Nadezhda Andreyevna Durova ran away from home disguised as a man, enlisted in the light cavalry and fought against the French in 1807. Joining first the Mariupol Hussars and later the Lithuanian Lancers under the name of Alexander Andreyevich Aleksandrov she was decorated and advanced to officer rank. Durova fought in the Battle of Borodino in 1812 and in the final campaigns against Napoleon, serving also as orderly to Field Marshal Kutuzov, commander-in-chief of all Russian forces. In 1816 she retired from the army with the rank of cavalry staff captain (*shtabs-rotmistr*). She then devoted herself to writing and to her memoirs, which were published in 1836 in the new journal *The Contemporary* (*Sovremmenik*), with a foreword by none other than Alexander

Pushkin, the journal's editor and founder. *The Cavalry Maiden. Journals of a Female Russian Officer in the Napoleonic Wars*, trans. Mary Fleeting Zirin (London, 1988).

2. Statistics give some notion of the numbers involved in certain specific areas. For example, 7000 women were in the partisan units of Belorussia, and 2000 in units in the Leningrad Oblast.

3. The 'Fascist manicure' involved the pulling of finger nails out of the fingers. Such tortures were often followed by public execution.

4. For data, see Mark Harrison, *Soviet Planning in Peace and War 1938–1945* (Cambridge, 1985) – see table on the Soviet labour force 1940–45, p. 138.

5. In addition to being only semi-legal at best, this was not a wholly successful measure, for in cases where the NKVD turned up, the young workers were too frightened to carry out their tasks.

6. Cited as examples of wartime labour discipline in Harold J. Berman and Miroslav Kerner, *Soviet Military Law and Administration* (Cambridge, MA, 1955), pp. 153–5.

7. Mark Harrison, *Soviet Planning in Peace and War 1938–45*, p. 146.

8. See Alec Nove's excellent essay, 'The Soviet Peasantry in World War II', in *The Impact of World War II on the Soviet Union*, ed. Susan J. Linz (New Jersey, 1985), pp. 77–90.

9. On *Osoaviakhim*, see the monograph by William E. Odom, *The Soviet Volunteers: Modernization and Bureaucracy in a Public Mass Organization* (Princeton, NJ, 1973).

10. These included 25,000 young women to the Soviet Navy, 21,92 assigned to naval bases and installations as electricians, lab assistants, drivers, mechanics. In addition, 30,000 women were assigned to river transportation; for example, Captain Sanchenko and First Mate Grishina, and the all-female crew of a steamer on the Amur River.

11. See Von Hardersty, *Red Phoenix. The Rise of Soviet Air Power, 1941–1945* (Washington, DC, 1982), pp. 48–9 on Grizodubova, Osipenko and Raskova, and their 1938 record-breaking flight in an ANT-37 across the entire Soviet Union, a distance of 3672 miles, in 26 hours, 29 minutes.

12. After the war Lyudmila Pavlichenko went on to become a 'scientific associate' with the Main Naval Staff of the Soviet Navy and continued to lecture at several military academies on the role and tactics of the sniper.

13. One such woman tank commander was Ye. S. Kostrikova, the daughter of Sergei Kirov, the prominent Bolshevik assassinated in 1934.

14. S. Aleksievich, *War's Unwomanly Face* (Moscow, 1988), p. 105.

15. There is, however, a most illuminating essay by Barbara A. Anderson and Brian D. Silver, 'Demographic Consequences of World War II on the Non-Russian Nationalities of the USSR', in *The Impact of World War II on the Soviet Union*, ed., Susan J. Linz, op. cit., pp. 207–40, with graphs, appendices and an invaluable bibliography.

# VI  The Final Years

## THE COLD WAR

At the end of the war the paradox of Soviet international power was already evident. Although it was greatly weakened by its incredible war losses referred to above, the Soviet Union, nonetheless, had become a military force to be reckoned with. Dismissed as marginal by strategic experts in the 1920s and 1930s, in 1945 the USSR was the globe's second military power. That being said, however, there are a number of points to bear in mind. First, Soviet influence came about by default. The war had left rival powers in tatters. Germany was destroyed; France's military reputation had collapsed; Britain had lost its empire and its two-hundred year naval supremacy. In the east, China was racked by civil war and Japan was on the verge of annihilation. That left only the USSR and the USA as still-powerful fighting forces. However, the United States was far stronger. Economically it benefited from the collapse of its commercial rivals and swept the globe economically, politically and culturally to replace them with its own, almost limitless, informal empire. Europe and Japan became utterly dependent on the USA for any potential capitalist recovery. Second, there was no real equality of power between the USA and USSR. The United States reach became global. Massive investments and a string of worldwide military bases underscored its vast supremacy. By comparison, the USSR was, and arguably remained, a regional power. Admittedly its 'region' was the Eurasian land mass but it had no significant influence in Africa, the Americas or the wider Pacific. Essentially, it threatened its immediate neighbours but no one beyond that. It had no global bases, infrastructure or navy, all of which would be essential to global reach.

The asymmetry of the two powers was, for a while, heightened by American acquisition of nuclear weapons. It took some years for the nuclear age to really dawn in international and strategic terms but by 1948 the US had an expanding nuclear arsenal with forward-based delivery systems in the form of nuclear bombers in Britain. By 1949 the USSR produced its first nuclear bomb but it was not until the 1960s that it developed delivery systems capable of reaching the United States, other than no-return bombing runs.

Such was the framework of international relations in the last years of Stalin. It soon congealed into the Cold War. Perhaps more ink has been spilled over arguments about the origins and evolution of the Cold War than any other historical issue. This is hardly surprising since it was the basic reality of global life for a half century and its impact is still far from dead. It influenced culture, economics, politics as well as international relations. Whether traditional (i.e. blaming the Soviets and seeing the Cold War as a crusade for liberty) or revisionist (i.e. seeing the United States as at least partly to blame for its origins and suggesting America used Cold War anti-communism as a cover for establishing global economic, cultural and political hegemony) most of the scholarship on this issue tended to be based on American and other western sources for obvious reasons. Access to confidential Soviet material was practically non-existent. Even now, access to Soviet diplomatic sources is difficult. However, since Gorbachev came to office more source materials have become available and there has been greater open discussion of the issue in Russia, including franker contributions from key figures in the framing of Soviet policy like foreign ministers Molotov and Gromyko.

The whole debate, of course, remains too vast to be dealt with here but certain points are worth commenting on. First, there is no sign of any Soviet plan for 'world domination'. The concept of the 'Soviet threat' was fundamental to western Cold War ideology. Revisionists argued that Soviet interests, including the establishment of Soviet-dominated regimes in Eastern Europe, were to be understood as primarily defensive. In Moscow's eyes, it was the United States that threatened. After all, it had the global reach, spouted virulent anti-communist ideology (returned in kind, of course, by the USSR in the form of communist anti-capitalist rhetoric) and, above all, made military dispositions which were unequivocally directed at the USSR including extensive nuclear targeting. Knowing the extent of its own internal economic weakness, the Soviet leadership was aware of its own limitations. Second, there appeared to be some hope, in Moscow, that the wartime Grand Alliance might give way to a joint world condominium.

Clearly, the Marshall Plan of 1947 was a crucial moment. Was it ever intended by the United States that the Soviet Union might be included? Did Stalin seriously believe that he might join it? In the event, the dramatic Soviet walkout on the negotiations, ordered personally by Stalin, was a monumental rupture in East–West relations. Synthesizing a wide array of sources, many of which have only recently become available and published in post-Soviet Russia (for instance, the confidential telegrams of Novikov, the Soviet Ambassador to Washington), Geoffrey Roberts shows these crucial events in a better-informed and more balanced light.

## 8   Geoffrey Roberts: 'Moscow and the Marshall Plan: Politics, Ideology and the Onset of the Cold War, 1947'

Moscow's decision to reject Soviet and East European participation in the Marshall Plan is seen by many historians as a key moment in the origins and development of the Cold War. For it was in the aftermath of this decision in summer 1947 that the Cold War on the Soviet side began in earnest.

According to Wilfried Loth's account,[1] for example, Moscow initially welcomed the Marshall Plan and the possibility of Soviet participation in a US-funded European reconstruction programme. Participation in the Marshall Plan meshed with Moscow's then foreign policy aims of (a) continued cooperation with the Western powers, (b) the prevention of the emergence of a West European bloc led by the United States, and (c) the political and economic stabilization of Europe as a whole. Moscow was opposed, however, to the idea of a coordinated multilateral aid programme, which was seen to threaten the Soviet political and economic position in Eastern Europe. It was over this issue that the Anglo-Soviet-French Marshall Plan negotiations broke down in early July 1947. The USSR then withdrew from the Marshall Plan project, insisted that its East European allies do likewise, and subsequently embarked on a new foreign policy strategy: a strategy of isolation, and of the consolidation of Soviet and communist power in Eastern Europe as a counter to the emerging West European bloc signalled by the Marshall Plan. Moscow's rejection of the Marshall Plan was followed by the founding of the Cominform (Communist Information Bureau) and Zhdanov's proclamation of the two-camps doctrine in September 1947, by the ending of West European communist support for reconstruction and postwar national unity, and, most notably, by the Stalinist *Gleichschaltung* (co-ordination) of Eastern Europe.

In his analysis of the immediate sources of this great turn in Soviet foreign policy Loth, like many others,[2] emphasizes Moscow's fear of the consequences for its strategic position of independent East European participation in the Marshall Plan – a danger which the Soviet leaders averted by exerting massive pressure on their communist-dominated allies to reject American aid.

As a broad description and analysis of Moscow's initial response and subsequent reaction to the inception of the Marshall Plan a summary along these lines seems reasonable enough. However, a more detailed examination of Moscow's decisions regarding the Marshall Plan reveals a rather more complex scenario than that presented by Loth and others.

First, despite its general predisposition to seek cooperation with the West, Moscow was uncertain and hesitant in its approach to the proposed European discussions about the Marshall Plan. The meaning of the plan was unclear to Moscow. Only in the context of negotiations with the British and French in Paris in June–July 1947 did the Soviet leaders arrive at their final conclusion about its purpose and act accordingly. Second, the usual story about Soviet blocking of East European participation in the Marshall Plan requires some amendment, for it seems that Moscow's exercise of its undoubted veto was as much a response to pressures from communist leaders in Eastern Europe as its own initiative. Third, Moscow's rejection of the Marshall Plan was far from being the only source and inspiration for the radical turn in Soviet policy in autumn 1947. Internal political and ideological shifts also need to be brought into the picture. Finally, the form of this radical shift in policy – the adoption of a dogmatic, militant leftist stance in both foreign and domestic affairs – was very much related to the peculiar character of Soviet ideology as a discourse of communicative action. The Cold War took the extreme ideological form that it did because it had to within the terms of Soviet political discourse.

More generally, there is a need to construct a narrative that more adequately conveys and explains how it was that in a few weeks over the summer of 1947 the USSR came dramatically to change its policy from one of coexistence, detente and cooperation with the West to a stance of isolation, conflict and confrontation.[3]

This article is presented as no more than a preliminary contribution to this task, using the few pertinent sources available to me at this time.[4]

*Moscow and participation in the Marshall Plan*

The Marshall Plan was publicly launched in a speech by the American Secretary of State at Harvard University on 5 June 1947. Marshall put forward the idea of a US programme to aid European recovery, reconstruction and stabilization – a coordinated programme that would be developed on the initiative of Europe itself (not excluding the USSR and Eastern Europe). Marshall's proposal was then taken up by Britain and France.[5] Bevin and Bidault met in Paris on 17–18 June and on 19 June issued a statement welcoming Marshall's speech and inviting the USSR to an Anglo-Soviet-French conference that would discuss the elaboration of a common European recovery programme backed by US aid.[6]

The initial Soviet response to these developments, as expressed in press articles, was negative in tone. *Pravda Ukrainy*, *Pravda* itself and *Soviet News* all published articles linking Marshall's proposal with the Truman Doctrine and depicting US financial aid to Europe as the crude deployment of economic power for the purpose of political interference in European affairs.[7] However, another straw in the wind was the publication by *Pravda*, without comment, of the Anglo-French communique on the Marshall Plan. On 21 June the Politburo met and endorsed a positive reply to the Anglo-French proposal for a meeting of foreign ministers to discuss the Marshall Plan.[8] In their reply the next day the Soviet leaders welcomed the idea of an American aid programme and accepted the invitation to a joint conference to discuss its terms and conditions.[9] Moscow's suggestion that Paris should be the conference venue and that it should begin on

27 June was subsequently agreed by the British and French. At the same time Moscow telegraphed its East European embassies with instructions that the people's democracies should ensure their own participation in forthcoming Marshall Plan discussions.

It seems clear that the initial Soviet response to the Marshall Plan constituted a decision by Moscow to participate on a serious basis in discussions about the terms and organization of a US aid programme for Europe. In adopting such a stance Moscow was far from committing itself to eventual participation in any Marshall Plan, but the decision to negotiate with the British and French did signal that Moscow was seriously contemplating the possibility of US financial aid to both itself and its East European allies.

To many contemporary observers this turn of events was somewhat surprising, for Moscow's constructive response to the Marshall Plan came in the wake of two major setbacks for the prospect of an East–West detente: the proclamation of the Truman Doctrine in March 1947 and the effective breakdown of allied negotiations on the future of Germany at the Council of Foreign Ministers conference in Moscow in April.[10] In spite of these ill omens, in June 1947 Moscow evidently decided on a positive response to the Marshall Plan idea.

Behind this apparently contrary policy stance lay in the first instance a set of general conditions. At the moment of the Marshall Plan's announcement the USSR was still, despite all the postwar conflicts and difficulties in Soviet–American relations, committed to a policy of peaceful coexistence, detente and collaboration with the West. Detailed studies demonstrate that in the period 1945–7 the Soviet outlook on foreign relations was dominated by the conviction that the postwar continuation in some form of the wartime grand alliance was both necessary and possible. This international outlook was rooted in a diversity of political and ideological sources: the priority attached to domestic reconstruction; confidence in the postwar international strength of the USSR and in its new-found position in Eastern Europe; a belief that inter-imperialist contradictions were stronger than inter-systemic ones between capitalism and socialism; a perception that the USSR and the major capitalist powers had a common interest in peace and commerce; a calculation that co-operation with the West was necessary to contain the long-term threat of a resurgent Germany; and an analysis of changes in the nature of capitalism that emphasized the political role of the working class and progressive forces in shaping its character and direction.[11]

Perhaps the most notable expression of what might be called the anti-Cold War policy of the USSR was a series of statements and interviews by Stalin in 1946–7 in which the Soviet leader reaffirmed his commitment to postwar international cooperation.[12] Just a few weeks before the announcement of the Marshall Plan Stalin gave two important positive pointers to his attitude towards East–West relations. In April 1947 he described a session of the Council of Foreign Ministers on the German question as:

> something like combat reconnaissance. When the partners have exhausted one another, the moment for a possible compromise arrives. The result may be attained at the next session rather than the current one, but on all important issues, such as democratization, political organization, economic unity and reparations, compromise is within reach.[13]

In May 1947 Stalin gave an interview to the Republican Senator Harold Stassen:

> In answer to Stassen's question whether he – Stalin – thought that the Soviet economy and the free enterprise economy of the USA could coexist, Stalin replied: 'Not only can they coexist, but they can also co-operate; if they did so during the war, why not now? Lenin said that the co-operation of the two systems was possible, and Lenin is our teacher.'[14]

So, the initial Soviet embrace of the Marshall Plan was commensurate with the pro-detente policy the USSR was still clinging to in mid-1947. However, it also arose from a more specific set of political calculations. To see what these were it is necessary to examine further the Marshall Plan's reception in Moscow in June 1947.

The announcement of the Marshall Plan was, it seems, interpreted in a threefold light in Moscow. Firstly, as already noted, as quite simply an extension of the Truman Doctrine in which financial aid would be used as an additional means of applying political pressure on European states, particularly those in Eastern Europe. Secondly, as a project for extending France's Monnet Plan for modernization and re-equipment to other countries, with the aim of using this as the basis for the creation of a US-led West European bloc. This was the view expressed by Novikov, the Soviet Ambassador to the United States, in a telegram to Moscow on 9 June, which concluded: 'in this American proposal are the perfectly clear outlines for a West European bloc redirected against us.' Novikov reaffirmed this view in a further despatch on 24 June:

> A careful analysis of the Marshall Plan shows that in the end it amounts to the creation of a West European bloc as an instrument of US policy ... instead of the previous uncoordinated actions directed towards the economic and political subjection of European countries to American capital and the formation of an anti-Soviet grouping, the Marshall Plan envisages more extensive action aimed at resolving the problem in a more effective way.

Thirdly, the Marshall Plan was seen as a means of staving off a postwar depression in the United States. Marshall aid would help close the 'dollar gap', boost US exports to Europe, and ameliorate the growing problem of overproduction in the American economy. This was the view expounded by Varga in a confidential memorandum to the Soviet leadership dated 24 June.[15] This was the line, too, of an article published in *Soviet News* on 26 June, which noted that

> there can be no doubt that Mr Marshall's proposal is conditioned by the present position of the economy of the USA. It is an almost universal opinion that the postwar boom in the USA is drawing to a close and that the threat of an economic crisis draws daily nearer ... The Marshall plan, it would appear, represents a programme for the solution of the American export problem, providing for the overcoming of the ever-sharpening dollar crisis in many European countries.

The implication of this kind of view was that there might be a mutual economic basis for an American aid programme to Europe (i.e. a boost to the US economy in exchange for reconstruction funds for Europe, including the USSR). But was this the consensus in Moscow? The answer to this question is far from clear, but it seems that the Soviet leadership reserved its final judgement on the nature of the Marshall Plan. As the *Soviet News* article pointed out, only when the real content of the Marshall Plan is unfolded and the conditions of aid are ascertained will it be possible to answer with certainty ... the question of the relationship between the Marshall Plan and the Truman Doctrine.' At the same time Moscow proceeded on the basis that it represented a genuine opportunity to secure US financial aid on an acceptable political basis. As Erofeev, Molotov's secretary, later recalled about the government's position: 'It was necessary to agree to this proposal and to seek the maximum reduction of all negative aspects.'[16] However, Moscow was also mindful of the dangers of being drawn into a project with ulterior political motives, such as US interference in East European affairs and the formation of an anti-Soviet bloc – dangers which had been noted by Varga[17] as well as Novikov.[18] This concern found expression in the guidelines drawn up for the Soviet delegation to the Paris conference with Britain and France. These specified that the main Soviet aims in the talks were (a) to ascertain the kind and extent of American aid that was on offer; (b) to ensure that 'the question of American economic aid for European countries must be considered not from the point of view of drawing up an economic programme for European countries but from the point of view of ascertaining their economic needs for American aid (credits, delivery of goods), on the basis of demands drawn up by the European countries themselves'; and (c) to object to aid terms which threatened interference in the internal affairs of recipients. The delegation was also instructed that there should be no discussion of the German question in Paris, which was a matter for the Council of Foreign Ministers.[19]

Molotov arrived in Paris at the end of June accompanied by nearly 100 advisers – a definite sign of the seriousness of Moscow's approach to the talks. Molotov immediately found himself confronted, however, with Anglo-French proposals which had the appearance of a Monnet Plan writ large, i.e. a proposal for a US-financed European economic plan under which states would agree modernization programmes supervised by a central European organization which would dole out American money.[20]

Whatever their actual intent, the Anglo-French proposals raised for the Soviet Union the twin spectre of a US-controlled West European bloc and Western incursions into its sphere of political influence in Eastern Europe. Not surprisingly, in his first speech to the conference on 28 June Molotov strongly objected to the kind of coordinated economic aid programme being proposed. 'The task of the conference', he argued, 'is that of bringing about collaboration between the European nations with a view to drawing up a list of these countries' requests for American aid, of clearly defining the possibility of such economic assistance from the United States, and of facilitating the acceptance of this aid by the countries of Europe.' To this end Molotov proposed the establishment of a series of committees that would ascertain needs and deal with requests for American aid.[21] Molotov's position was also reflected in his draft agenda for the conference and in a formal Soviet resolution submitted to the conference on 30 June.[22]

Up to this point the Soviet negotiating stance in the conference was firm but businesslike and constructive – which was in line with the delegation's brief and was also reflected in a telegram from Molotov to Stalin on 29 June.[23] However, this position changed rapidly as the British and French stuck to their original position of a coordinated economic programme or nothing. On the night of 30 June Molotov telegraphed to Stalin:

> Both England and France are in a highly difficult position and they do not have in their hands any serious means of overcoming their economic difficulties. The only hope is the United States, which demands from England and France the creation of some kind of all-European body for the purpose of United States interference in both the economic and political affairs of European countries. The utilization of this body for their own interests constitutes the calculation of Britain and, in part, France.

On 1 July Molotov reported to Stalin: 'In view of the fact that our position is fundamentally different from the Anglo-French position, we are not counting on the possibility of any joint decisions on the substance of the issue in question.'

With the negotiations deadlocked, the conference moved towards collapse. On 2 July Molotov made his final statement to the conference, and it was a resounding rejection of the Marshall Plan:

> The question of American economic aid ... has ... served as a pretext for the British and French governments to insist on the creation of a new organisation, standing above the European countries and intervening in the internal affairs of the countries of Europe, even to the extent of determining the direction in which the main branches of industry in these countries are to develop ... There are two roads of international cooperation. One road is based on the development of political and economic relations between states with equal rights ... There is another road of international cooperation which is based on the dominating position of one or several strong Powers in relation to other countries, which thereby fall into the position of some kind of subordinated states, deprived of independence ... What will the fulfilment of the Franco-British proposal ... lead to? It will lead to nothing. It will lead to Britain, France and the group of countries that follow them separating from the rest of Europe, which will split Europe into two groups of states.[24]

As stated by Molotov, the main reason for Soviet rejection of the Marshall Plan was the Anglo-French insistence on a centrally coordinated programme of American assistance. However, it may be that Soviet fears concerning Germany's role in the projected reconstruction of Europe were also a central motivation. The Soviet delegation's instructions for the conference included a directive that German economic resources could not be used as part of the reconstruction programme. At the conference Molotov badgered the French on whether or not their plans involved using German resources for European recovery rather than the payment of reparations.[25] Of crucial importance may be the fact that in the midst of the Paris conference Molotov received secret information from Moscow that the British and Americans had agreed that Germany would be central to any European reconstruction plan and that they would oppose the payment of reparations to the Soviet Union from German current production.[26] The receipt of this telegram coincided with the beginning of a hardening of the Soviet position at the conference. Finally, we should note that in his closing speech Molotov raised the German question strongly, linking the Anglo-French position on the Marshall Plan to the spectre of a Western-inspired division of Germany.[27]

*Moscow and East European participation in the Marshall Plan*

Following the collapse of the Paris talks the British and French governments issued an invitation to 22 states in Europe to participate in a conference that would establish an all-European organization to supervise a Marshall aid assistance and reconstruction programme. All the countries of Eastern Europe were invited to attend.[28]

The Soviet Union's withdrawal from the Marshall Plan discussions meant that East European participation in any American aid programme to Europe was very unlikely. Such indeed turned out to be the case. No East European state attended the Anglo-French conference and none took part in the European Recovery Programme that eventually emerged from the Marshall aid discussions. The agency of this outcome, we are told in numerous books and articles, was Moscow's exercise of its veto on East European foreign policy – the most famous case being the Czechoslovak reversal of a decision to attend the Anglo-French Marshall Plan conference. However, the recent evidence published from Soviet archives suggests that there is much more to the picture than just a simple case of a Moscow veto of East European participation in the Marshall Plan.

As we have seen, before the Paris Conference Moscow had encouraged its East European allies to get involved in Marshall aid discussions. For their part, the Polish and Czechoslovak governments responded to Moscow's advice with enthusiasm.[29] But what would be Moscow's attitude following the collapse of the Paris talks? On 5 July 1947 Moscow sent two messages to all its ambassadors in Eastern Europe. The first message was an instruction to deliver to the local foreign ministry an explanation of the Soviet stance at the Paris Conference. This explanation consisted of a straightforward summary of the already known position of the USSR on the Marshall Plan. It contained no policy directives other than the implication that the East European states should take up the Soviet critique of the British and French proposals on an American aid programme for Europe. The second message was for delivery to the leaders of the communist parties. This message concerned the British and French conference invitation to European countries. This message did have a policy directive. Surprisingly, it urged that the East European countries *should accept* the Anglo-French invitation and attend the conference that was scheduled to open on 12 July:

> Some countries friendly to the Soviet Union, it seems, are considering refusing participation in the conference, on the grounds that the USSR has decided not to participate. We think it would be better not to refuse participation in this conference but to send delegations to it, in order to show at the conference itself the unacceptability of the Anglo-French plan, not allow the unanimous adoption of this plan and then withdraw from the meeting, taking with them as many delegates from other countries as possible.

The fact that Moscow was prepared to countenance any East European participation in Marshall Plan discussions is of some significance, and not only because of what it reveals about Soviet tactical thinking at this time. East European participation in the forthcoming Anglo-French conference carried with it the possibility that East European countries would apply for and receive Marshall aid, providing that certain political conditions were met – most notably no undermining of Soviet and communist influence in the region.

This might seem a somewhat strained interpretation of the quoted Soviet position but bear in mind that Poland was to become a *de facto* participant in the European Recovery Programme in the period 1947–9. As Anderson has convincingly argued, during this period 'the Soviet Union allowed Poland considerable freedom of movement in the economic sphere and ... Poland made an important contribution to the success of ERP, especially through the export of coal to Western Europe'. As Anderson points out, despite the East European boycott of the Marshall Plan Poland continued both to seek IBRD loans and to increase its trade with Western Europe.[30] There is also some evidence that the Hungarian government remained interested in developing connections with the proposed ERP even after its official rejection of the Marshall Plan. In a memoir-history of the period Kertesz, who was Hungarian ambassador in Italy at this time, cites a telegram from Budapest on 13 July 1947 which indicates that the government there was still thinking of some kind of participation in the Marshall Plan despite its earlier announcement of its rejection of the Anglo-French conference invitation.[31]

The second point of interest in this message to communist leaders is, of course, the reference to the fact that some East European countries did not want to attend the Anglo-French conference. One of these countries was Tito's Yugoslavia. Moscow's telegram to its Belgrade embassy on 5 July noted Tito's opposition to participation and urged the Yugoslav leader to change his mind. On 6 July Molotov sent another telegram, this time to Warsaw as well as Belgrade, suggesting the sending of envoys to Moscow from Poland and Yugoslavia in order to achieve a united stand on the conference. However, on 7 July Moscow sent another message to all communist leaders in Eastern Europe. This urged that any answer to the Anglo-French invitation should be delayed until 10 July because 'in some countries the friends declare against participating in the conference'. The next day yet another message was sent to communist leaders, and this one revoked the 5 July proposal that East European states should participate in the conference and proposed that no delegations should be sent. In line with this new Soviet position all the countries of Eastern Europe (and Finland, too) announced their rejection of the British and French invitation.

There was only one hitch in the implementation of the Soviet-led boycott of the conference. Czechoslovakia had already, on 7 July, accepted the invitation to attend the conference[32] – a decision that appears to have been heavily influenced by Moscow's earlier pro-attendance stance. This Czech decision was only reversed following discussions in Moscow between the Soviet leadership and a Czechoslovak government delegation headed by the Prime Minister and Communist Party leader, Gottwald.[33]

Of particular interest from what we know of these Soviet–Czech discussions in Moscow are the indications from Stalin's statements to the Czechs on 9 July that there were two main reasons for the boycott line: (a) anti-participation representations from Yugoslavia and Romania (and possibly Poland), and (b) Soviet fears that the main aim of the forthcoming conference and of the Marshall Plan was the further political isolation of the USSR. Stalin also made it quite clear that there could be no question of Czechoslovakia breaking the anti-Marshall Plan united front of Slav states.[34] No such question arose. The Czechs submitted without protest and on 10 July announced their withdrawal from Marshall aid discussions.

In summary, this review of Soviet–East European relations in the aftermath of the failure of the Paris conference suggests that communist leaders in the people's democracies played an important role in precipitating a hardening of Moscow's rejection of the Marshall Plan. Such a scenario should come as no surprise. The more archive material that is released the more evident it becomes that Soviet relations with its communist allies were not a one-way street. The latter were often as much the voluntary agents of hardline Soviet policies as passive conduits of implementation.[35]

### The Marshall Plan and the turn in Soviet foreign policy

The announcement of the Soviet and East European boycott of the Marshall Plan was followed in summer 1947 by the launch of a Soviet propaganda campaign against the plan. The main points of the Soviet critique of the plan were (a) that it was a plan for the formation of a US-led Western bloc, (b) that it aimed at developing Western Germany into a mainstay of the 'imperialist camp' in Europe, and (c) that it was directed against Soviet influence in Eastern Europe and the anti-capitalist road that was being taken in those countries. In September 1947 the Deputy Foreign Minister, Vyshinsky, proclaimed the Soviet position on the Marshall Plan at the United Nations:

> The Marshall Plan constitutes in essence merely a variant of the Truman Doctrine ... the implementation of the Marshall Plan will mean placing European countries under the economic and political control of the United States and direct interference in the internal affairs of those countries ... this

plan is an attempt to split Europe into two camps ... to complete the formation of a bloc of several European countries hostile to the interests of the
democratic countries of Eastern Europe and most particularly to the interests of
the Soviet Union.[36]

Vyshinsky's speech was followed by Zhdanov's denunciation of the Marshall Plan at the founding meeting of the Cominform[37] and Molotov's
speech on the thirtieth anniversary of the October Revolution which
depicted US foreign policy in Europe as being one of imperialist expansion
and encirclement of the USSR.[38]

The battlelines had been drawn and the ensuing story of Cold War crisis
and the tightening of Soviet control in Eastern Europe is well known.
Clearly, the Marshall Plan episode was a major precipitating factor in the
Soviet declaration of the Cold War and the radical turn in Moscow's
ideological and political policy in autumn 1947. But the Marshall Plan was
not the only catalyst for the change in Soviet foreign policy. There were, it
appears, other influences and forces at work in Moscow and Soviet fears
concerning the Marshall Plan provided an opening for their policy
expression.

First, and most obvious, the analysis of American foreign policy in terms
of anti-Sovietism, international supremacism, the military threat to the
USSR, and the construction of a European bloc came to fruition over a
long period of time. The internal details of this process remain obscure and
will remain so in the absence of Soviet archival material. But we do have
one piece of evidence and that is the so-called 'Novikov telegram'.[39] This
'telegram' is a long despatch from the Soviet ambassador in Washington
dated 27 September 1946. It consists of an analysis and critique of
American foreign policy that was to become publicly familiar in the Cold
War years that followed.

The idea of a summary document on the postwar foreign policy of the
United States originated at the Paris Peace Conference of summer 1946.
Novikov was ordered to compose such a document, which he did, and
which Molotov read with obvious interest.[40]

So, the kind of Cold War thinking that greeted the launch of the
Marshall Plan was already in the air in 1946. It found further expression in
Novikov's despatches on the Marshall Plan in June 1947, which analysed
US foreign policy along the same lines – a view which the Anglo-French
proposals in Paris appeared to vindicate. It seems likely too that Novikov in
his despatches was voicing what he presumed were Molotov's views and
that the Soviet foreign minister tended to share the view of US policy
articulated by Novikov. Molotov's annotations on the 'Novikov telegram'
indicate that this was the case and when Novikov was recalled to Moscow in
July 1947 he was given the task of producing another document, this time

on the Truman Doctrine and the Marshall Plan. Novikov's conclusion in this document was that Marshall aid was part of an American plan aimed at the worldwide encirclement of the USSR and the construction of an aggressive bloc directed against it. Molotov considered the document very useful.

A second influence on the change in Soviet policy that needs to be taken into account concerns the genesis of the Cominform and the role played by Tito and Yugoslavia in the left turn in the policy of the International Communist Movement in September 1947.

The decision to found a new coordinating centre for the international communist movement, to replace the Comintern which had been abolished in 1943, was made by Stalin around the same time as the rejection of the Marshall Plan. The Marshall Plan apart, the move was inspired, it seems, by concerns regarding the policy of the West European communist parties and their relative independence from Moscow, and by opposition to cooperation between its East European allies without Soviet involvement. The Cominform may also be seen as an outgrowth of internal bureaucratic developments in the Soviet communist party – including the creation of what was to become the International Department of the CPSU – designed to replace the defunct organizational structures of the Comintern.

As far as Soviet foreign policy is concerned there are two points of particular interest concerning the inception of the Cominform. First, it appears that the political line enunciated by Zhdanov at the founding conference in September 1947 – the ideological line of Soviet foreign policy in the period that followed – only emerged gradually in summer 1947. It seems, for example, that the two-camps thesis only found its way into Zhdanov's speech late in the drafting process.[41] This indicates that the Soviet political and ideological response to the Marshall Plan, as embodied in the Cominform, was very much an improvised one.[42]

The second point of interest concerns the role of Tito and the Yugoslav communist party in this improvisation. As Swain has recently argued, the establishment of the Cominform and the political line it proclaimed represented the acceptance/adoption by Stalin of the Yugoslav critique of the popular front line of the European communist parties in the immediate postwar period. This policy was denounced at the Cominform conference and the Yugoslav delegates led the attack on the idea of a parliamentary, non-Soviet road to socialism involving alliances with non-communist parties and groups and which envisaged a prolonged transition from capitalism to socialism. The alternative was class war, a militant popular front from below and the implementation of the most radical socialist measures possible in the shortest possible time. It was a view that Tito had been advocating and practising since the time of the war.

Following the Marshall Plan débâcle Moscow shifted its ideological view in this leftist direction.[43]

The final factor that needs to be taken into account when examining the Soviet policy shift in 1947 is the impact of internal Soviet politics. This is a highly vexed and still undetermined issue,[44] but it does seem that in the early postwar period there were tensions and conflicts within the Soviet leadership and within Soviet policy between ideological 'moderates' and 'radicals', between those who thought detente with the West possible and those who thought conflict inevitable. It seems to me also to be true that these moderate vs. radical contradictions were sited within Soviet ideology as well as constituting a battleground between different individuals and factions.[45]

One of the climactic moments in this internal debate came on the eve of Moscow's Marshall Plan decisions. In May 1947 Varga came under attack from hardliners over a book that he had published in 1946. In this book Varga had argued that as a result of economic, political and social changes during the war the character of Western capitalism had changed. Politically, the most important changes were the greater role of the state in regulating capitalism and its economic crises and the enhanced role of the left in political life. Varga's critics argued that capitalism had not changed its spots and that its crises and their political expression in aggressive tendencies remained a fact of life.

This debate was a harbinger of an internal ideological shift and mid-1947 marked the beginning of a retreat by Varga and others on the proposition that capitalism had changed in nature as a result of the war. This retreat went in parallel with other hardline ideological shifts and with the change to a more militant stance in Soviet foreign policy in 1947–8.[46]

*Conclusion: ideology and the Soviet origins of the Cold War*

To sum up, what seems to have happened in summer and autumn 1947 when the USSR embarked on its Cold War against the West was a coalescence of three trends in Soviet policy and politics: a return to Marxist–Leninist ideological orthodoxy internally; the triumph of a leftist trend within the international communist movement; and the acceptance of a hawkish interpretation of US foreign policy.

The role of the Marshall Plan in this process was that, coming on top of the Truman Doctrine and other negative developments in postwar Soviet–Western relations, it confirmed Moscow's worst fears about the prospects for collaboration, negotiation and agreement with the West. What the Marshall Plan seemed to signify was the final failure of what can be called an integrationist strategy in foreign policy – the political and economic integration of the USSR and its zone of influence into a wider European and international constellation. With the coming of the Marshall Plan, that kind of integration, it seemed to Moscow, was only possible on the basis of giving up vital Soviet positions and interests in Eastern Europe.

The alternative to integration was separation, isolation and consolidation within the sphere of influence that had been gained as a result of the war. That essentially was the choice made by the USSR in autumn 1947. Like the United States, the Soviet Union chose to abandon diplomacy and the search for cooperation and agreement and to seek instead to protect its interests by independent manoeuvring, the gathering of strengths and the judicious deployment of its power.[47]

Historically, the decision against integration and in favour of isolation was not an unusual one. It was the choice made in the 1920s when the doctrine of socialism in one country was adopted.[48] It was the choice made in 1939 when the integrationist strategy of the collective security period was abandoned in favour of the Nazi–Soviet pact. And it was the choice made at the time of the Hitler–Molotov conference in Berlin in November 1940 when Stalin refused integration into a German-dominated Europe and an Axis-dominated world.[49]

There is also another comparison to be made between the turn in Soviet foreign policy in 1947 and the radical shifts in policy of previous years: the extent to which each was compounded by the limits and possibilities of Soviet ideology.

The Soviet turn to Cold War in autumn 1947 was at one level simply a response to perceived threats and conditions that called for a strengthening of Moscow's position, particularly in Eastern Europe. At the same time this turn in Soviet policy took a peculiarly militant and ideological form – the delineation of a world split into two camps, the demand that states and peoples decide which side they were on, prognostications of an attack on the USSR, the imposition of a rigid Soviet model of socialism and revolution on both Eastern Europe and Western communist parties. To an extent all this was just a matter of perception, calculation, belief and, perhaps, expediency. However, a role was also played by the dynamics of the discourse in which political positions were discussed, formulated and acted on.[50]

Soviet ideology, like any other, was more than a set of beliefs. It was also a language of political communication – a set of terms, concepts and validating assumptions which constituted the public discourse through which individuals spoke to each other. This language presented its adherents with a set of resources – acceptable arguments and formulations – which they could deploy in political debate about policy and action. Those resources of communication were subject to interpretation, emphasis and change, but they imposed definite limits on what could be said if the speaker wanted to be listened to.

The case of the Soviet turn to Cold War appears to be an instance of a new course of policy and action that had to be discussed, presented and legitimated within the relatively narrow range of terms and concepts available within Soviet ideology at that time. The effect of the processing of policy through ideology was, instead of a simple adaptation to a more defensive and anti-Western posture in foreign relations, the adoption of a radical, aggressive ideological posture. Given the existence of a discourse that denoted capitalist hostility to the USSR, the inevitability of war and conflict in an imperialist world, and the universal validity of a single, Soviet model of revolution and socialism, such an outcome was highly likely.

However, it was not inevitable. As we have seen, in the early postwar years Moscow's policy and action drew on other elements of Soviet ideology. Ideology as discourse is a resource which individuals can choose to deploy in a variety of ways, even, indeed, to transform the meaning and use of existing terms and concepts. Were it otherwise it would be impossible to explain the history of change in Soviet ideology, most notably the ideological revolution of the Gorbachev years.

Ideology, moreover, has many different uses and results in many unexpected outcomes. A striking example in this respect concerns one of the sequels to Moscow's rejection of the Marshall Plan. The Soviet rejection was followed by the launch of the so-called Molotov Plan – the signature of a series of bilateral trade treaties between the USSR and Eastern Europe. This marked the beginning of the processes that led to the foundation of Comecon in 1949. Stamped on the character of Comecon and the ensuing history of attempted socialist economic integration in Eastern Europe was the ideological nature of the Soviet rejection of the Marshall Plan. Moscow formally rejected the Marshall Plan because, among other things, it proposed central direction of European economic development and limitations on national economic sovereignty. Moscow's objections on these grounds were subsequently embodied in Comecon's character and purpose and all Soviet efforts in the postwar period to amend the essentially national-based character of the organization ended in failure. The USSR's East European allies were able to resist socialist economic integration with the USSR for a variety of reasons, including the utilization of Moscow's own national-ideological arguments against the Marshall Plan. To make reference to a recent reinterpretation of the history of West European economic integration by Milward, it may be that in rejecting the Marshall Plan in the way it did Moscow helped save its communist allies from socialist economic integration and thereby contributed in no small way to the strengthening of the nation-state in Eastern Europe.[51]

NOTES

[Reorganized and renumbered from the original.]

1. W. Loth, *The Division of the World, 1941–1955* (London, 1988), chapters 6–7.

2. E.g. W. Taubman, *Stalin's American Policy: From Entente to Detente to Cold War* (New York, 1982), chapter 7.

3. The interpretation and conclusions of the present article are commensurate with those of S. D. Parrish, 'The Turn to Confrontation: The Soviet Reaction to the Marshall Plan, 1947', in *New Evidence on the Soviet Rejection of the Marshall Plan, 1947: Two Reports*, Working Paper no. 9, Cold War International History Project, March 1994. Parrish's work is based on direct access to a number of important archival documents.

4. An earlier version of this article was presented to the annual conference of the British International History Group, University of the West of England, September 1993. It was produced with financial support from the Arts Faculty Research and Development Fund, University College Cork.

5. *Foreign Relations of the United States 1947* (hereafter *FRUS*), vol. 3, section on 'The Marshall Plan', and T. Paterson, *Soviet–American Confrontation: Postwar Reconstruction and the Origins of the Cold War* (Baltimore, 1973), pp. 207–14.

6. *French Yellow Book: Documents of the Conference of Foreign Ministers of France, the United Kingdom, and the U.S.S.R. held in Paris from the 27th June to the 3rd July 1947* (hereafter French Yellow Book), pp. 18–19.

7. *Pravda Ukrainy*, 11 June 1947 (in *FRUS*, pp. 294–5); K. Gofman, 'Mr Marshall's "New Plan" for Relief to European Countries', *New Times*, 17 June 1947.

8. M. M. Narinsky, 'SSSR i Plan Marshalla: Po Materialam Arkhiva Prezidenta RF', *Novaya i Noveishaya Istoriya*, 1993, 4 (April), p. 12. For an English-language version of this article see Narinsky, 'The Soviet Union and the Marshall Plan', Working Paper no. 9, Cold War International History Project, March 1994.

9. French Yellow Book, pp. 20–1.

10. On the failure of the Foreign Ministers Conference see A. Werth, *Russia: The Post-War Years* (London, 1971), chapter 12.

11. See A. Resis, *Stalin, the Politburo, and the Onset of the Cold War, 1945–1946*, The Carl Beck Papers in Russian and East European Studies no. 701 (University of Pittsburgh, 1988); D. Allen, *The International Situation, 1945–1946: The View from Moscow* (Centre for Russian and East European Studies, University of Birmingham, 1986); G. D. Ra'anan, *International Policy Formation in the USSR: Factional 'Debates' during the Zhdanovshchina* (Connecticut, 1983), chapter 12; W. G. Hahn, *Postwar Soviet Politics: The Fall of Zhdanov and the Defeat of Moderation, 1946–1953* (Ithaca, 1982), chapter 1.

12. See Stalin's replies to questions by Eddie Gilmore (Associated Press), 22 March 1946, Alexander Werth (Sunday Times), 17 September 1946, and Hugh Baily (United Press), 23 October 1946 and interviews with Elliot Roosevelt (21 December 1946) and Harold Stassen (9 April 1947). For some summaries and discussion see Werth, pp. 142–7 and 250–2 and Ra'anan, pp. 124–9.

13. Russian foreign policy archives, cited by M. Narinsky, 'Soviet Foreign Policy and the Origins of the Cold War', in G. Gorodetsky (ed.), *Soviet Foreign*

*Policy 1917–1991* (London, 1994), p. 107. See also Parrish, pp. 7–8, who quotes a similar statement by Stalin recorded in an American foreign policy document.

14. Cited by Werth, p. 250.

15. The memo was drawn up by Varga following a request from Molotov in early June and was submitted to the Soviet foreign minister on 26 June. Its circulation list included Stalin and other Soviet leaders, as well as Molotov. For a detailed summary and discussion of the memo see Parrish, pp. 16–18.

16. Erofeev also noted that Molotov was a supporter of this position. In regard to Molotov, Parrish, p. 14, argues that his underlinings of the text of Marshall's speech indicate that the Soviet foreign minister viewed the Marshall Plan mainly in terms of American economic interest in staving off a postwar depression in the US.

17. See Parrish, pp. 17–18.

18. Novikov was in favour of participation in Marshall Plan discussions on tactical grounds: 'Our attitude to the "Marshall Plan" and to the conference of the three ministers should, I suppose, be one of seeking a decisive role in work on a programme for the rehabilitation and development of the national economies of European countries … Our participation in work on the programme would prevent the realisation of the American plan of subjecting Europe and forming an anti-Soviet bloc.' Telegram, Novikov to Molotov, 24 June 1947.

19. According to Parrish, p. 22, in a covering letter to Stalin, Molotov noted that these instructions were 'insufficiently worked out'.

20. On Anglo-French proposals see French Yellow Book, pp. 25–37.

21. Molotov's speech: French Yellow Book, pp. 38–42. Molotov's two speeches at the Paris conference are also reproduced in V. M. Molotov, *Problems of Foreign Policy* (Moscow, 1949), pp. 459–70.

22. Ibid., pp. 43 and 49–50.

23. See *FRUS*, pp. 296–301, for Western reports that indicate a relatively benign Soviet negotiating posture during the early stages of the conference.

24. French Yellow Book, pp. 58–61.

25. See *FRUS*, pp. 304–5.

26. Telegram, Vyshinsky to Molotov, 30 June 1947.

27. French Yellow Book, pp. 60–1.

28. Ibid., pp. 69–71.

29. See Parrish, p. 19, who cites replies from Warsaw and Prague to Moscow's telegraphed instructions to its ambassadors of 22 June.

30. S. Anderson, 'Poland and the Marshall Plan, 1947–1949', *Diplomatic History*, 15, 4, Fall 1991.

31. S. D. Kertesz, *Between Russia and the West: Hungary and the Illusions of Peacemaking, 1945–1947* (1984), pp. 243–9.

32. Parrish, p. 26.

33. On this episode see K. Kaplan, *The Short March: The Communist Takeover in Czechoslovakia, 1945–1948* (London, 1987), pp. 72–3.

34. See Werth (who cites Ripka's memoirs), pp. 266–8 and *FRUS*, pp. 319–20. In relation to Poland, according to the memoirs of Winiewicz, the Polish ambassador to the United States, it was his reports that convinced Warsaw to reject the Marshall Plan, not Moscow's veto. Winiewicz argued that the Marshall Plan had political as well as economic objectives and that no communist country would

be voted aid funds by Congress anyway. There was also apparently concern in Warsaw about the possibility of German participation in ERP and about the potential effect of the Marshall Plan on Polish reparations from Germany. (See Anderson, op. cit., pp. 476–9, but note that Anderson himself argues that Poland rejected the Marshall Plan on orders from Moscow.) Also of interest are Jakub Berman's brief comments on Polish and Soviet hesitations regarding rejection of the Marshall Plan in T. Toranska, *'Them': Stalin's Polish Puppets* (New York, 1987) pp. 297–9 and Werth's account of his conversation with Hilary Minc in August 1947 (pp. 275–6).

35. In connection with this general point see the documents and articles in the various bulletins and working papers of the Cold War International History Project.

36. M. McCauley, *The Origins of the Cold War*, doc. 27, p. 124.

37. A. A. Zhdanov, *The International Situation: Report made at the Conference of Nine Communist Parties held in Poland, September 1947*, pamphlet, n.d. For summary and analysis of the Zhdanov speech see Werth, chapter 14 and Parrish, pp. 35–8.

38. Molotov, *Problems of Foreign Policy*, pp. 483–93, and compare with Molotov's speeches in this volume before the Marshall Plan episode.

39. The 'telegram', together with various commentaries, is published in *Diplomatic History*, 15, 4, Fall 1991. The text was handed out by a Soviet archive official at a meeting of Soviet and American historians in Washington in July 1990.

40. On the background to Novikov's despatch see the commentary by Mal'kov in *Diplomatic History*, 15, 4. Molotov's underlining and annotations of the document are indicated in the text published in *Diplomatic History*, 15, 4.

41. See Parrish, p. 36.

42. This point is also made by Parrish, pp. 35–6.

43. G. Swain, 'The Cominform: Tito's International?', *The Historical Journal*, 35, 3, 1992. On the change in communist politics and policy in both Western and Eastern Europe following the setting up of the Cominform see P. Spriano, *Stalin and the European Communists* (London, 1995), chapters 22–4. Also D. Sassoon, 'The Rise and Fall of West European Communism', *Contemporary European History*, 1, 2, 1992.

44. See Hahn, Ra'anan, Resis and Allen; also T. Dunmore, *Soviet Politics 1945–53* (London, 1984).

45. There is a similar argument over Soviet foreign policy in the 1930s. See G. Roberts, *The Soviet Union and the Origins of the Second World War: Russo-German Relations and the Road to War, 1933–1941* (London, 1995), chapter 1.

46. Varga's book, *Izmeneniva v Ekonomike Kapitalizma v Itoge Vtoroi Voiny (Changes in the Economics of Capitalism as a Consequence of the Second World War)*, was published in September 1946. A number of chapters from the book and associated articles were published in 1945–7 in the journal edited by Varga, *Mirovoe Khoyaistvo i Mirovaya Politika (World Economics and World Politics)* (see nos 1 and 9, 1945 no. 6, 1946 and nos 3 and 8, 1947). The May 1947 discussion on Varga's book was convened by the Institute of Economics and the political economy department of Moscow State University. The discussion was held in three sessions on 7, 14, and 21 May and the stenographic transcript of what was

said was published as a special supplement of Varga's journal in November 1947. Opinions differ as to who came out best in the debate: Hahn, pp. 84–93, argues that Varga got the better of the hardliners, whereas Ra'anan, chapter 6, stresses the success of Varga's conservative opponents. In any event the sequel to the discussion in 1947–8 was the closure of Varga's journal and the marginalization, although not the complete suppression, of Varga's views.

47. In this connection one can refer to the following definition of Soviet foreign policy under Stalin during the Cold War: 'messianic in its world view, limited in its geographical and functional scope, pessimistic in its evaluation of situations, parsimonious in its acceptance of costs and risk.'

48. See T. J. Uldricks, 'Russia and Europe: Diplomacy, Revolution and Economic Development in the 1920s', *The International History Review*, 1, 1, 1979.

49. See Roberts, *The Soviet Union and the Origins of the Second World War*, op. cit.

50. The following paragraphs were prompted by J. Schull, 'What is Ideology? Theoretical Problems and Lessons from Soviet-Type Societies', *Political Studies*, XL, 1992 and 'The Self-Destruction of Soviet Ideology', in S. G. Soloman (ed.), *Beyond Sovietology* (New York, 1993).

51. See A. S. Milward, *The European Rescue of the Nation State* (London, 1992).

# STALIN'S DICTATORSHIP IN THE FINAL YEARS

The 'Age of Dictators' is a description often applied to the 1930s. It is not inappropriate to a time when democratic government held on only precariously, mainly in the extreme west and north of the European continent. But what does it mean? What exactly is a dictator? How does a dictator dictate? The styles of the Great Dictators – Hitler, Mussolini, Stalin – differed greatly, not to mention that of the Little Dictators – Pilsudski (Poland), Franco (Spain), Horthy (Hungary) and others. Recent accounts have portrayed a hands-off, 'lazy' Hitler. Mussolini's rule always had an element of buffoonery completely absent from that of Hitler or Stalin. Franco is usually thought to be more military authoritarian than fascist. Above all, Stalin's style of government has been both controversial and shrouded in obscurity. Public aspects of his rule – especially the grotesque cult of his personality which reached insane proportions by 1949 – and his firm personal grasp of the political situation were not in doubt. We also know that he did not use his position to acquire any material benefits for himself or his family. Power was his driving force not wealth or pleasure. Like Peter the Great, he ruled with a firm grip but he subjected himself to the same rigid discipline he expected of others. If, during the war, he was at his desk twenty hours a day, he expected the same from his minions and woe betide them if they fell short of expectations.

However, there were many questions. Was Stalin's power absolute? If so, at what point did it become so? As late as 1932, he was defeated on his proposal to have the oppositionist Riutin executed. But even in his last years he was busy shuffling institutions and changing their names, sizes and functions in order to maintain his grip. In the war years, although he expressed his opinions, he left strategic proposals to his generals. Unlike Hitler, he rarely imposed his own view on them. It is evident, though not often remarked on, that his immediate entourage tended to stay with him for long periods of time and even when he broke with them politically, like Marshals Voroshilov and Budennyi following the initial defeats of 1941, they were kicked upstairs and not into the gulag. However, apart from some useful but not entirely reliable defector accounts of the 1930s, we have not been able to pierce the veil of secrecy.

Now, however, even though large quantities of full Politburo (the key Soviet ruling body, akin to the British Cabinet but a party rather than state institution) minutes remain secret, it has been possible to piece together more about Stalin's method of government. Unsurprisingly, Stalin was very much a hands-on ruler who could not, in the final analysis, be opposed. Nonetheless, within certain parameters, he did depend on people speaking their minds. He often resolved issues between contending factions rather than simply dictated his will in the caricatural style of a fairytale despot. He even took a ten-week holiday in 1945 to recover from his war exertions, a habit he had indulged up to 1937. Given the level of communications of the time, although he still continually checked up on what was happening, there was some room for manoeuvre among the ruling group. Exactly how much we now know much better thanks to pioneering work on the 1930s and to the work of Yoram Gorlizki on the postwar period. This work does not fully answer all the questions but it does give us a much better basis for understanding how decisions were made at the highest level of the Soviet Government.

Before turning to Gorlizki's detailed account we should remind ourselves of the broader context of the postwar years. Soviet priorities were twofold, recovery and security. We have talked about the international aspects of the latter in the previous item. However, the security situation did affect internal events. As the Cold War developed, so links with the outside world became increasingly suspect and, following the old Stalinist principle that it was better to be be 'safe' (that is, imprison the innocent) than to be 'sorry' (that is, let one guilty person escape), a new darkness of arrest and exile descended on the country. It was accompanied by a renewed ideological clamp-down fronted by Andrei Zhdanov. Literary, cultural and philosophical norms were tightened up. Socialist realism and orthodoxy, tinged with an increasing dose of populist Russian chauvinism, were rigidly applied. Leading intellectuals were publicly pilloried, the most prominent being the poet Anna Akhmatova, the writer Mikhail Zoshchenko, the film director Sergei Eisenstein and the composer Dmitrii Shostakovich. The height of internal purging was reached in 1948 with the still murky Leningrad Affair in which a Politburo member and leading economic planner, Nikolai Voznesensky, and others were arrested. Several were executed. It is also possible that, at the very last, Stalin was preparing another purge based on the 'Doctors' Plot', a supposed conspiracy of Kremlin doctors aimed at killing Stalin. The fact that several, though by no means all, of the accused were Jewish raised the spectre of a possible antisemitic element to the purge. However, that remains speculative as Stalin died before any such outcome could be clearly detected. Be that as it may, here, too, security concerns were part of the issue since, after initially supporting the establishment of an Israel which appeared to undermine British imperial influence in the Middle East, Soviet policy had swung firmly behind the Arab cause when it was realized that Israel was more a front for burgeoning American interests in the Middle East. Anti-zionism emerged. For many it was a cover for a more visceral antisemitism but they cannot be simply equated in that way. Many Jews retained positions of great responsibility in Stalin's Russia even while others officially deemed to be zionist, were being arrested.

The question of security did not only mean relations with the west. After more than twenty-five years as the world's sole communist power, the emergence of the Eastern European satellites and, even more, the more independent communist revolutions of Tito in Yugoslavia and, from 1949, that of Mao Zedong in China, created opportunities, responsibilities and expenses. Yugoslavia was excommunicated, so to speak, from the communist brotherhood mainly because Tito appeared to be trying to develop a Balkan federation of communist states which would create a possible counterweight to the Russian-dominated movement. Mao's China was also a mixed blessing. In reality, Moscow exerted no authority over Beijing but it was assumed to do so especially by western policymakers who conceptualized a monolithic Soviet bloc. The East European 'empire' was also a drain on resources. Soviet policy towards its new allies was divided between the desire to exact tribute from former enemy countries, Germany in the forefront, and the need to build up friendlier relations with the local populations.

Here, security was intertwined with the other main theme of Soviet policy, recovery. In this domain the difficulties were legion. As we have seen, destruction of the country was unbelievably extensive. Outside help in overcoming it was nullified by the division of Germany, which took the more prosperous west of the country beyond the reach of any reparations, and Soviet exclusion from the Marshall Plan. Its internal resources were meagre. The call on them for the humanitarian purpose of restoring homes and lives to its citizens clashed with the imperative need to counter the enormous global military preponderance of the United States which appeared to threaten the USSR. Miraculously, recovery was taken in hand. Famine on a mass scale was avoided, though there were severe local shortages in 1947. Heavy industry recovered. Cities were painfully rebuilt. Conditions were harsh in the extreme with meagre food rations and cramped accommodation, but by 1951 something approaching normality had been achieved.

In 1949, Soviet military researchers had produced an atomic bomb. Taken together, all these developments made the world a more complex and, from the Moscow perspective, a much more dangerous place. Where, in the interwar years, the USSR had been fairly isolated, at least until 1933, it now became intimately linked to America by potential enmity and to China, South-East Asia, Eastern Europe and Yugoslavia by ambiguous 'friendships'. Globalization was well-advanced. Resources to deal with all these issues were scarce and knowledge of the outside world dangerously sketchy, even among the Soviet elite. The world was a powder keg. From Berlin to Korea crises deepened. By some miracle, it did not explode but the Soviet leadership had to face a world of unparalleled complexity. We still only have a partial idea of how they did it. Gorlizki's work leads us to some unprecedented insights but also raises issues that will need much further scrutiny.

## 9    Yoram Gorlizki: 'Stalin's Cabinet: the Politburo and Decision Making in the Postwar Years'

Over the 1930s the Politburo was pummelled into an instrument of Stalinist rule: what once had been a crucible of political struggle had turned, by the Second World War, into a tractable committee of Stalin's friends and accessories.[1] No longer hemmed in by formal procedures or protocol, the cabinet was recast to fit in with Stalin's personal habits and work rhythms. After the war, the cabinet adapted still further to the leader's needs and requirements. From October 1946 the formal Politburo elected at the XVIII Party Congress in 1939 practically ceased to function. The enlarged formal sessions of old, to which Central Committee members and other party officials were invited, had given way to small, loose-knit, kitchen cabinets which were at Stalin's beck and call.[2]

Nevertheless, even at the height of Stalin's dictatorship the Politburo continued to perform a distinct organizational role. By contrast with the Council of Ministers, the Politburo carried out a discrete set of institutional responsibilities which included control of foreign affairs, security matters and organizational issues. For the duration of Stalin's rule these questions remained firmly within the Politburo's domain. In addition, the Politburo also attended to high order party matters. In view of Stalin's control over his Politburo colleagues it may be wondered why the dictator should have persisted with the Politburo at all. Why was Stalin not drawn to a purely dictatorial system of executive rule which, governing in his name, would have dispensed with the Politburo altogether?

The present article examines this question by looking at the functions served by the postwar Politburo. It begins by looking at the internal dynamics of the Politburo and suggests that rather than one Politburo there were in fact a variety of distinct 'politburos' in the late Stalin period. Despite this diversity, each 'politburo' was deployed by Stalin to lock his colleagues into a system of collective responsibility; each offered a flexible yet reliable system by which the dictator could bind his peers. In the second part, the article moves on from the internal dynamics of the Politburo to look at its external relations. Whereas internally the Politburo was fluid and pliable, externally it projected an image of stability and order. The article suggests that a political system as hierarchic as Stalinism required an image of unity and authority at its apex. The Politburo, it argues, served this purpose well. In the third section, devoted to the last six months of Stalin's rule, the article looks at the Politburo as an agency of 'Bolshevik' leadership. Despite Stalin's importance, even at the height of his dictatorship the Soviet system never freed itself entirely from a deep-seated Bolshevik tradition of party 'democracy'. At times, such as the XIX Congress of October 1952, Stalin himself turned to this tradition in order to kick-start the political system. It was at this point that the Politburo, now substantially reformed, assumed a specific party leadership role. The article concludes by suggesting that after the XIX Congress, one of the 'politburos' under Stalin – the Politburo without Stalin – was given a decisive impetus.

*Internal dynamics*

*Composition of the Politburo.* It was some months after the war, and the formal dissolution of the State Defence Committee (GKO) on 4 September 1945, when the Politburo began to resume peacetime operations.[3] Formally the Politburo continued in much the same vein as it had left off before the war, with a virtually identical membership and a similarly modest workload. At its meeting of 29 December 1945 the Politburo resolved to meet every other Tuesday for a short time, from 8 pm to 9 pm. Apart from Andreev, who was absent, the meeting of 29 December was made up of the same Politburo members elected at the XVIII Congress in 1939: Voroshilov, Zhdanov, Kaganovich, Kalinin, Mikoyan, Molotov, Stalin and

Khrushchev. The candidate members of 1939, Beria and Shvernik, were now joined by Voznesensky and Malenkov, who had been coopted as candidate members in 1941.[4] In the coming years the ranks of the formal Politburo swelled as a succession of candidates – Malenkov and Beria in March 1946, Voznesensky in March 1947, Bulganin in February 1948 and Kosygin in September of that year – were raised to full membership.

Although it did not keep to the schedule set out on 29 December 1945, the full Politburo did convene with some regularity over the coming months, with sessions on 19 January, 4 March, 13 April and 4 May 1946.[5] Meetings of the Politburo, however, tailed off following the session of 3 October 1946; over the rest of Stalin's reign there were only two further formal, enlarged sessions of the Politburo, on 13 December 1947 and 17 June 1949. The official Politburo in fact came to be overshadowed by the regular conferences of a narrow 'ruling group' which met up routinely in Stalin's office. The composition of this circle, sometimes known as the 'select group' or the 'close circle', differed markedly from that of the formal Politburo. Excluded from the ruling group were those Politburo members who had either fallen foul of Stalin or who were cut off from the ruling circle for reasons of location or ill-health. For some time Stalin's suspicions had fallen on Voroshilov, Andreev and, to a lesser extent, Kaganovich, all of whom were, despite their formal membership of the Politburo, not privy to the proceedings of the ruling group in the aftermath of the war; others excluded were the head of state, Mikhail Kalinin, who had long suffered from ill-health and who died in 1946, and Khrushchev and Zhdanov, both of whom were stationed outside Moscow.[6] Although the composition and style of operations of the ruling group deviated, sometimes markedly, from those of the *de jure* Politburo, to the extent that most resolutions issued in the name of the Politburo in the late Stalin years were determined by this group, it may be thought of as a 'second' or '*de facto*' Politburo.

With six of the nine full members of the Politburo excluded, the ruling group at the war's end consisted of a small core of Politburo members who had also served on the State Defence Committee (GKO). Of this 'quintet' (*pyaterka*) three, Stalin, Molotov and Mikoyan, were full Politburo members while the others, Malenkov and Beria, were candidate members. From early October to mid-December 1945 Stalin took a holiday in the south, leaving the affairs of state in the hands of a 'quartet' (*chetverka*) of Molotov, Mikoyan, Malenkov and Beria.[7] Stalin kept closely informed of the decisions of his colleagues and grew quickly impatient with their performance, especially that of Molotov. On coming back to Moscow in December Stalin lessened his dependence on the 'quartet' and altered the balance of forces within it by adding a new member, Andrei Zhdanov, so that, with Stalin, the 'quintet' had now become a 'sextet'. At the same meeting of the Politburo, on 29 December, Stalin also sought to formalize the activities of the ruling group by endowing it with a title, 'the Commission of External Affairs at the Politburo'. Notwithstanding its title, the Politburo 'Commission' by no means confined itself to foreign affairs. Rather, it served Stalin as a procedural ruse for bringing together the ruling group. On 3 October 1946 Stalin did away with the pretence that the Commission was concerned entirely with external affairs by signing a Politburo resolution which allowed the Commission to engage with questions of 'domestic construction and internal policy'. Stalin also widened the membership of the group by determining that 'the head of Gosplan comrade Voznesensky be added to the sextet and that henceforth the sextet be known as the septet'.[8] In the following year the Commission was further consolidated with the addition of Nikolai Bulganin on 5 March 1947 and Aleksei Kuznetsov on 17 September 1947 so that the septet had now become a 'novenary' (*devyatka*). Finally, the vacancy within the novenary created on 31 August 1948 by the death of Andrei Zhdanov was filled three days later by Aleksei Kosygin.

Alongside the formal Politburo, which in effect ceased to function in the autumn of 1946, meetings of the ruling group were held frequently and the bulk of Politburo resolutions were in effect in its hands. Whereas 'neither the Central Committee, nor the Politburo ... worked regularly', Khrushchev recounted later, 'Stalin's regular sessions with his inner circle went along like clockwork'.[9] Indeed, one draft Politburo resolution on the organization of leadership meetings of December 1948 made no mention of the formal Politburo at all while it accorded the 'novenary' a fixed time, every Wednesday, in the leadership's schedule. Yet while Stalin bestowed on the ruling group shape and continuity by attaching to it titles (e.g. the 'Commission for Foreign Affairs') and numerical epithets (i.e. 'quartet', 'quintet' etc.) he refrained from encumbering it with rules and procedures. One of the great advantages to Stalin of an informally convened leadership group was its flexibility. For one thing, membership of the full Politburo was not a prerequisite for entry to the group. A succession of leaders, including Malenkov, Beria, Voznesensky and Bulganin, gained admission to the group many months before their formal accession as full members of the Politburo. Stalin hence unilaterally elevated colleagues without having to go through the tedious formality of having them 'elected' as full members of the Politburo by the Central Committee. Stalin could also expel members from his group with unseemly ease. This became a particular advantage in the wake of the Leningrad Affair, at which point membership of the ruling group became quite convoluted. Stalin began to whittle down the 'novenary' in the spring of 1949 with the removal of the disgraced Voznesensky and Kuznetsov, and later in the year of Kosygin, partially filling the gap with the rehabilitated Kaganovich. Tracing the contours of the 'leading group' thereafter is something of a puzzle, as it must have been not least for members of the ruling group themselves. Unbeknown to themselves, Mikoyan and Molotov were unceremoniously axed from the ruling circle towards the very end of Stalin's reign.[10] Having grown from a 'quintet' in 1945 to a 'novenary' in 1948, by the very end Stalin's core leadership had once again been reduced to a rump 'quintet' consisting of Malenkov, Beria, Bulganin, Khrushchev and the tyrant himself.[11]

In addition to the formal Politburo and the Politburo's standing 'Commission' of 'quintets', 'sextets' and so forth, there were still other informally convened groups which passed resolutions in the Politburo's name. In the postwar period some decisions, especially those on cadres at the very highest levels, were reached in minute caucuses consisting of no more than four or possibly even three members of the leadership. Thus, for example, the decision of 4 March 1949 to remove Mikoyan and Molotov as ministers of foreign trade and foreign affairs was reached by a supreme council of Stalin, Malenkov, Beria and Bulganin.[12] A minority of Politburo resolutions were even formulated and signed by Stalin alone.

By stark contrast, some sessions of the 'leading group' were convened without the leader at all. It is these meetings which are of greatest interest since they were to set the pattern for high-level interaction within the ruling group after Stalin's death. In the first autumn after the war, Stalin obtained leave from his Politburo colleagues to take a 10-week break in the south from early October to the middle of December. Whilst out of Moscow Stalin left the affairs of state in the hands of a quartet of Molotov, Mikoyan, Malenkov and Beria. Stalin received daily reports on events in Moscow and was quick to stamp his authority on the 'quartet', and especially on his own stand-in, the hapless Molotov, by first forcing the other three to gang up on Molotov and then by extracting a humiliating apology from the latter for what Stalin regarded as his unwarranted independence of action. A year later, again while away in the south, Stalin deployed similar tactics against another erstwhile Politburo member, Anastas Mikoyan. In the years that followed, especially after his seventieth birthday in December 1949, as Stalin spent longer stretches outside the capital, he became reliant on manipulating, cajoling and overruling his cabinet colleagues from afar.[13]

There is little evidence that, in meeting without Stalin, the Politburo gained any freedom of initiative. Many decisions formally approved by the Politburo in Moscow in Stalin's absence were in fact carefully monitored and vetted by the leader. On 1 November 1949, for example, a 'quintet' of Malenkov, Molotov, Beria, Kaganovich and Bulganin – without Stalin – issued a Politburo resolution setting up a commission to consider allegations against the Central Committee secretary G. M. Popov. On 4 December a 'sextet' of the same group now joined by Mikoyan – but again excluding Stalin – approved the conclusions of the commission on Popov. Although these decisions were formally reached without Stalin, a closer examination reveals that it was Stalin who first set in motion the inquiry in a letter from the south of 29 October and that Malenkov's later amendments to the resolution were all dictated by Stalin. Similarly the sacking of Men'shikov, Mikoyan's replacement at the ministry of foreign trade, on 4 November 1951 was passed as a Politburo resolution in Stalin's absence by a group of six Politburo members. Again, however, a reading of the memoir literature suggests that the decision was made entirely by Stalin while the leader was in Sochi and that, notwithstanding their own reservations, the cabinet were merely implementing Stalin's wishes. On other occasions Stalin simply rejected and overturned the decisions of his cabinet colleagues. Thus Stalin greeted a draft Politburo resolution of 19 August 1950 not to send a delegation to Romania, which had been unanimously agreed by the rest of the cabinet, with a terse message, rendered by Poskrebyshev as: 'Instruction to send the delegation'.

Some have attributed to the new leaders-in-waiting a conspiracy to pull Stalin away from the levers of power. Evidence for such a thesis is slender indeed. Yet the experience of routine meetings without Stalin over a number of years provided a firm footing for decision making after the dictator's death. Members of the group acquired independent knowledge of the machinery of policymaking and of the nature of collective cabinet responsibility. Even where collaborative decision making in effect came down to jointly trying to read Stalin's mind or anticipating his shifts in mood, these cabinet sessions provided the leadership with valuable experience of working together and of operating as a collective. The speed with which this Stalin-less cabinet swung into action on hearing of Stalin's illness – even issuing organizational directives before the dictator's death – indicates a level of common understanding and initiative among the leaders. The operational unity of the ruling group was confirmed by the alacrity with which the group was reconstituted as a cabinet after Stalin's death.[14] Thus a 'third' politburo, one without Stalin, acquired sufficient momentum and coherence to negotiate the gulf represented by Stalin's death with minimum disruption. Of the various politburos under Stalin it was this which best anticipated the decision-making dynamics and policy directions of the post-Stalin cabinet.

After the war Stalin experimented with a variety of organizational forms for the Politburo. This diversity and the diminutive proportions of the smaller politburos enabled Stalin to convert his cabinet into a responsive and flexible instrument of rule. In its most rudimentary form the Politburo comprised a small coterie of Stalin's favourites who were skilled at reading the dictator's mind and implementing his wishes with a minimum of fuss.[15] These narrow and informal Politburo meetings were

freed from the schedules and procedures which hamstrung the official or
*de jure* cabinet. In the company of a small circle of colleagues, all of whom
were well-known to Stalin and to each other, there was all the less reason
to follow the inconvenient and time-consuming protocols of formal
Politburo sessions.

*The Politburo and decision making.*    An abiding pre-*perestroika* image of
decision making in the late Stalin era is of policy issues of national
importance being discussed over interminable late-night dinners as Stalin's
aide, Poskrebyshev, went round the table collecting signatures off half-
drunk party and state leaders.[16] The archives are silent on the state of
mind and sobriety of the country's leaders at Stalin's drinking sessions.
What they do confirm is the absence of guidelines for putting issues on the
agenda or of rules for decision making and conflict resolution. Most
decisions, especially on 'political' – as opposed to 'technical' – questions
turned simply on Stalin's position, or expected position, on a given matter.
Indeed, it was precisely in order to free the Politburo from tedious rules
and formalities that the cabinet adopted the more manageable form of a
small 'Commission' whose proceedings depended in large part on the
personal chemistry between Stalin and its members. This lack of even a
rudimentary formality is perhaps most keenly expressed in the absence of
transparent or commonly agreed methods for minuting and commu-
nicating decisions.

Proceedings of the Politburo were not stenographically recorded or
professionally minuted. Instead, decisions were noted down by the head of
the special sector, Poskrebyshev, or, in his absence, by a member of the
Politburo's inner circle. Stalin routinely entrusted the task of formulating
and writing up Politburo decisions to Georgii Malenkov. Many first drafts
of Politburo resolutions in the late Stalin years are in Malenkov's hand.
Thus, for example, the text of the controversial resolutions to dismiss
A. A. Kuznetsov as Central Committee secretary on 15 February 1949 and
to sack Molotov as minister of foreign affairs and Mikoyan as minister of
external trade on 4 March 1949 were written up by Malenkov, as was the
Politburo resolution of 15 April 1950 to appoint Malenkov himself to
the Buro of the Presidium of the Council of Ministers. In some cases,
Politburo resolutions were relayed down the phone. Thus, for example, at
12.15 pm on 12 June 1949 Malenkov dictated to a secretary at the special
sector a Politburo resolution appointing Tevosyan deputy chairman of the
Council of Ministers. At other times Poskrebyshev would receive long lists
of orders, often scribbled down, which he would be asked to draw up as
Politburo resolutions.

For the most part the relative formlessness and procedural indeterminacy
of decision making was compensated for by the need for one indispensable

ingredient: Stalin's consent. Thus, for example, on 21 January 1950 Poskrebyshev received a list of draft Politburo resolutions from Marshal Vasilevsky which, the latter tellingly assured Poskrebyshev, 'has been confirmed by comrade Stalin'. Vasilevsky, it seems, did not even deem it worth mentioning that the decision had been taken at a joint meeting also attended by Molotov, Beria, Bulganin, Malenkov and Mikoyan. Similarly, a draft Politburo resolution 'On the refutation by TASS' of 6 June 1952 was accompanied by a short missive from Vyshinsky to Poskrebyshev: 'Comrade Poskrebyshev please draw up this resolution. Comrade Molotov tells me that it has been confirmed by comrade Stalin. Vyshinsky.'

These ill-defined procedures for drawing up Politburo resolutions were sometimes exploited by members of the leadership. So long as they had obtained Stalin's permission, members of the ruling circle could authorize Politburo resolutions directly, without having to go to the trouble of consulting other members of the cabinet. This was especially true of those low-key issues, such as permission to invite or to send overseas delegations, which the Politburo nevertheless regarded as its prerogative. Thus, for example, it was in this area that on 21 January 1950 Molotov sought Stalin's permission for a set of 21 Politburo resolutions which, 'by virtue of their clarity do not demand, it seems to me, special discussion'.

For the most part, however, Stalin insisted that all members of his inner circle ratify Politburo resolutions. The precise form of ratification was a matter usually determined by Stalin himself. As in the 1930s one of his preferred means was 'by correspondence' On 6 February 1951, for example, the minister of foreign affairs, Vyshinsky, requested of Molotov that 12 questions be voted on by correspondence. 'Comrade Stalin', he wrote, 'has agreed that this type of question may be resolved in this manner.' Obtaining Stalin's consent was at all times the main obstacle to getting a Politburo resolution passed. Nevertheless, Stalin still clung to the notion, inherited from the 1930s, that key decisions receive unanimous support, even if this incurred the inconvenience and delay of having a draft circulated by courier to all members of the Politburo for their signature. The frequency of correspondence votes indeed begs the question of why Stalin should have gone to the length of consulting all other members of the leadership when all knew that it was Stalin's opinion that mattered.[17] Certainly, once Stalin had given the green light to a Politburo resolution it was unthinkable that another member of the committee could have opposed it either at the meeting itself or, where the decision was voted on by correspondence, by refusing to put his signature to the proposal. In view of Stalin's tight grip over the Politburo it may be wondered why the Politburo should have stuck so rigidly to protocol by going through the time-consuming formalities of seeking the opinions of other members of the committee by conducting a vote.

One reason for this insistence was Stalin's need to bind his co-leaders in a system of collective responsibility. Stalin used correspondence votes and Politburo meetings to 'test' the loyalty of his inner circle. The formal device for achieving this goal was to force cabinet colleagues to sign Politburo resolutions, even after the event, thus making them jointly accountable for state policy. Less formally, Stalin would use Politburo meetings as occasions to spring awkward questions on unsuspecting colleagues and then to check their reactions.[18] Politburo meetings thus evolved into an amalgam of formal devices (the demand for co-signatures and correspondence votes) and personalized modes of control (throwing surprise questions and soliciting early opinions on controversial matters) through which Stalin could manipulate his colleagues. The Politburo thus became indispensable as a tool for controlling the leadership.

The Politburo also served a social function for Stalin. By most accounts Stalin was a lonely man who craved company. Much of his time with Politburo colleagues was spent sitting through Westerns or endless dinners marked by a conspicuous lack of policy-oriented discussion. In its increasingly informal settings and style of operations, the postwar Politburo satisfied Stalin's need for social interaction: here the country's ruling group doubled up as Stalin's social circle.[19]

Yet there were also other reasons why the outward 'form' of Politburo decision making was maintained. Internal relations within the Politburo were fluid and sometimes fast-changing. Authority and status within the Politburo depended on access to the leader, on gaining Stalin's trust and confidence. As Politburo members knew to their cost, Stalin's trust could vanish suddenly, without notice. Depending on the state of one's relations with Stalin, normal hierarchies might be quickly inverted. Thus even Poskrebyshev, who was no more than Stalin's aide, was known to shout and to 'snarl viciously' at Politburo members who had lost Stalin's confidence.[20] Outside the ruling circle, however, the Politburo had to project an image of stability and order. Here, in striking contrast to its internal reality, the Politburo was a symbol of steadfast authority.

*External relations*

*The Politburo and the party-state.*    Although it served as a general cabinet, the Politburo was also the chief executive committee of the party. In view of the long intervals separating party congresses and Central Committee plenums after the war, the party leadership functions of the Politburo became all the more important. This was especially so in the late 1940s when the governmental machinery, the Council of Ministers, led by some of the most senior politicians in the country, had seen its work become better organized and more systematic.[21] As the party's *de facto* chief executive committee, a robust Politburo was needed as a symbol of Bolshevik leadership and specifically, as a mechanism for keeping an increasingly authoritative Council of Ministers in check.

The division of responsibilities between the Politburo and the Council of Ministers was fairly clearly drawn in the postwar period. On 8 February 1947 the Politburo passed a resolution 'On the organisation of the Council of Ministers' which assigned most economic policies to that body but reserved for the Politburo all decisions relating to the ministry of foreign affairs, the ministry of external trade, the ministry of state security, most currency issues, and all questions relating to the ministry of the armed forces. In addition, the Politburo continued to exercise powers that had been in its remit by tradition. The first of these, exemplified not least by the February resolution itself, was administrative reorganizations. For most of the late Stalin period the Politburo amalgamated, divided and renamed a multitude of state and party organizations. As the party's supreme executive agency, the Politburo also took the most important decisions on appointments. The Politburo controlled all key state and ministerial assignments, while promotions to supreme party posts, including those of Central Committee secretary and republican first secretary, all came before the Politburo and were issued as Politburo resolutions.

Normally members of the Politburo had a clear understanding of what fell within the Politburo's jurisdiction. The dividing line between the Council of Ministers and the Politburo was not, however, always clear-cut. On occasion, the Politburo was moved to reassert its jurisdiction over contested policy areas. More significantly, the rather convoluted route for deciding some issues, especially those voted on by correspondence, allowed decisions to be 'intercepted' by members of the Politburo and taken to other venues for resolution. On 20 August 1947 an item on sending 44 athletes to the students' Olympiad in Paris came before the Politburo. The first Politburo member to consider the matter by correspondence was Beria, who requested that the issue be transferred to the Council of Ministers. The Buro of the Council of Ministers then rejected the Politburo draft, resolving instead to send five observers including, on Beria's insistence, 'a comrade from Abakumov'. Thus, as a consequence of the overlapping membership of the Politburo and Sovmin, an item which, strictly speaking, had been within the Politburo's brief was in fact decided by the latter.

Stalin was well aware of the growing systemization of affairs at the Council of Ministers. In order to keep that body in check he frequently made use of the Politburo's powers of assignment and reorganization. Another tactic, used prolifically towards the end of Stalin's reign, was to issue scathing resolutions condemning 'departmentalist' practices within the ministries. The Politburo thus served as an important counterweight to an energetic Council of Ministers apparatus. In addition to shaping the decision-making powers of non-party institutions, however, the Politburo exercised numerous leadership functions within the party itself. One of these consisted of dealing with the steady flow of work from the party's own central bureaucracy. Far from atrophying, as some commentators had once believed, the activities of the Central Committee apparatus flourished in the postwar years.

*The Politburo and the Central Committee apparatus.* In its relations with the party apparatus the Politburo was supreme: as a matter of course, party officials accepted its authority without question. Yet in view of its numerous other commitments – overseeing defence, state security, foreign affairs and administrative reorganizations, as well as keeping the leader company – the Politburo sought to free itself of its more mundane party responsibilities. In the long run the Politburo's attempts to curtail its own party-based duties, for example by strengthening the powers of auxiliary agencies such as the Orgburo (Organization Bureau), proved to be futile, however. One reason was that the bureaucratic system continued to throw up demands for authoritative guidance that could, in the end, only be satisfied by the ruling cabinet. In such a context, no attempt to delegate authority to subordinate committees could have been entirely successful.

The first major reorganization of the Central Committee apparatus took place in the wake of the Central Committee meeting of March 1946, which replaced Andreev and the deceased Shcherbakov with A. A. Kuznetsov and G. M. Popov, who now joined Malenkov and Zhdanov as secretaries at the Central Committee. On 13 April the Politburo adopted a resolution on the Orgburo and secretariat which assigned responsibilities among the new secretaries and attempted to define the relative powers of Orgburo and secretariat, something the leadership had never found it easy to do.[22] The spring 1946 reforms consolidated the power of the Orgburo. The April resolution confirmed that while the secretariat would confine itself to cadre issues, the Orgburo, which would now meet weekly, would exercise broader leadership tasks.[23] In order to meet its new workload, membership of the Orgburo was increased from nine members to 15. The sudden expansion of the Orgburo marked both its growing weight within the Central Committee apparatus and a loosening of Malenkov's grip over affairs there. These tendencies were reinforced over the following months when, on 4 May, Malenkov was ejected from the secretariat (to be replaced as Central Committee secretary by Patolichev) and, on 2 August, when Zhdanov took over the chairmanship of the Orgburo from Malenkov. A Politburo resolution on the latter date declared that, henceforth, the Orgburo would be the 'leading agency' of party-organizational work and that it would have the right to 'issue leading directives' on party matters.[24]

The new elevated status of the Orgburo heralded a fresh relationship between itself and the Politburo.[25] In assigning new 'leadership' functions to the Orgburo, the Politburo resolution aimed to relieve the Politburo itself of lesser responsibilities. In fact such a rationalization addressed a genuine concern within the party bureaucracy. Pressure on the party's top committees had been building up since the end of the war. Demobilization had brought with it an upsurge in the personnel-assignment functions of the Central Committee, while the campaign for ideological discipline, which reached a head in 1946, entailed a revitalization of the Central Committee's agitprop functions. The rise in workload at the Central Committee generated issues which, in the absence of meetings of the Central Committee, had to be addressed by the party's executive committees. Rather than taking such questions, especially those of an 'organizational' nature, to the Politburo, many were now siphoned off to the new beefed-up Orgburo. Unburdened of a good portion of its everyday party-based tasks, the Politburo could be left to concentrate on 'political' issues and be better able to slot in to Stalin's nighttime routines. The Orgburo, by contrast, would emerge as a surrogate Politburo devoted entirely to the most pressing and important party-organizational matters.

These arrangements did not, however, last long. The balance struck between the Orgburo and secretariat in 1946 was disturbed by the continued growth in cadre work at the Central Committee.[26] Moreover, the pre-eminence of the Orgburo, which had been a Zhdanov stronghold since the summer of 1946, was eroded with the decline in Zhdanov's own fortunes and his eventual death in August 1948. On 1 July 1948 Zhdanov's arch rival, Malenkov, was re-appointed party secretary. Soon the reinstated Malenkov was chairing sessions of both the secretariat and the Orgburo. Under a new schedule, the secretariat met weekly while the Orgburo convened only twice a month. An increasing share of party work was absorbed by the secretariat while the functions of the Orgburo were gradually eclipsed. These tendencies reached their apogee at the XIX Congress, which determined that the role of the secretariat be further increased, as a result of which the number of secretaries was doubled from five to ten. At the same time the Politburo and Orgburo were also reformed. In the previous years the Orgburo had been unable to perform an authoritative party-based role independently of the Politburo. In recognition of this fact the Politburo and Orgburo were now merged into a single institution.[27] With a total membership of 36 (25 members and 11 candidates), the party 'Presidium' was presented as the Soviet Union's new cabinet.

In terms of its internal mode of decision making and actual membership the Politburo in Stalin's latter years was a malleable institution shaped above all by the inclinations and preferences of the leader. To those outside the inner circle, however, the Politburo assumed an image of unimpeachable authority: Politburo members possessed supreme rank and status, Politburo resolutions took precedence over other commands, and the Politburo as an institution enjoyed automatic jurisdiction over the most important policy issues and cadre questions. Yet by the end of Stalin's reign the discrepancy between a Politburo which, in reality, had become jaded and undisciplined, and the considerable leadership functions which this body was expected to exercise, had become accentuated. It may have been for this reason that Stalin decided to modernize the Politburo. Thus at the XIX Congress the name, membership and operations of the Politburo were all fundamentally changed. This reorganization of the Politburo was more than a simple 'rationalization', however. The reforms of October 1952 underlined the cabinet's role as an agency of Bolshevik leadership. In fact, the creation of the new presidium resonated closely with the calls for 'party democracy' and the demands for increased accountability and collective decision making which were raised in the run-up to the party congress.

### Stalin's cabinet and the XIX congress

The XIX congress stimulated efforts to 'democratize' the party at all levels. Steps to promote 'internal democracy' within the party included more frequent meetings of the party rank and file, mandatory reports of the apparatus to full party committees and a host of protest votes against sitting party officials.[28] Such moves to reactivate party 'democracy' were twinned with steps to regularize the party's decision-making processes at all levels.[29] At the very highest tier, the Politburo and Orgburo were merged into the Presidium, with an enlarged full membership of 25 and 11 candidate members.[30] In contrast to its narrowly constituted predecessor, the new larger Presidium appeared to be more representative of the different sectors of the Soviet party-state and thus more open to outside influences. Underlining its claims to inclusiveness, the new Presidium embraced 12 (of the 13) vice-chairmen of the Council of Ministers, all ten Central Committee secretaries as well as the most important individual ministers, regional representatives and leaders of other key state and party institutions. One commentator has even suggested that the new Presidium represented an extension of the 'job-slot system – the principle that seats on the Central Committee were *ex officio* – to the Soviet cabinet.[31]

The full Presidium, however, met only once and never came to exercise regular cabinet-type functions. That position was taken by a newly constituted Buro of the Presidium, for which there was no provision in the new party statutes but which was set up at the Central Committee meeting immediately after the XIX Congress. Unlike the full Presidium, which was supposed to meet once a month – but in fact met only once, on

18 October 1952 – the Buro, according to a resolution of 10 November, was to meet once a week on Mondays. The composition of this inner group was close to that of the ruling group which had met in the previous two years, with the exception that two younger leaders, Saburov and, then, in a revised list, Pervukhin, were added. In meeting regularly, the new Buro regained some of the shape and consistency which had eluded the pre-existing, informally convened, ruling circle. With Stalin's health failing, the new Buro even met in his absence. Indeed, a second resolution, also of 10 November, openly made provision for this by indicating that, should Stalin be away, chairmanship of the Buro be rotated between Malenkov, Khrushchev and Bulganin. In fact, in its latter meetings the Presidium Buro may be regarded as a continuation of the third of the politburo variants identified in the first section of this article – namely the politburo without Stalin – and a forerunner of the cabinet that took over when Stalin died. The Presidium Buro also accorded with the prevailing spirit of the Congress period – again anticipating what would follow Stalin's death – by opening its proceedings to the scrutiny of subordinate party officials.

As with the Presidium, the role of the secretariat was clarified in the 1952 party statutes.[32] The reform of the secretariat mirrored changes taking place across the Central Committee. The appointment of Aristov, Mikhailov, Brezhnev and Ignatov as secretaries assured a rejuvenation of the Central Committee apparatus – something Stalin had apparently contemplated for some years. Moreover, with a doubling in the number of secretaries from five to ten, the secretariat began to handle more material, absorbing a considerable amount of workload from the old Orgburo, Notwithstanding a Presidium Buro decision of 17 November, which determined that the secretariat would meet once a week, with Malenkov, Pegov and Suslov chairing it, the vast amount of post-congress activities forced the secretariat to meet more often. With the Orgburo gone and the secretariat now taking over its everyday administrative duties, there was a clear-cut division of labour between a Presidium which addressed issues of 'political leadership' and a secretariat which handled 'administrative' matters.

One of the major innovations of the XIX Congress was the establishment of new cabinet commissions on foreign affairs, defence and ideology. The commissions, which were attached to the part Presidium, reflected a new turn in the organization of upper party-state structures. Each commission was headed by a senior party figure – Malenkov, Bulganin and Shepilov – and had other important party leaders as members. Significantly, the commissions signalled a loosening of ties between party and state. Whereas previously Politburo work had been regarded as compatible with service within the Council of Ministers – thereby underlining the view that the party and state were 'interlocking directorates' – a separation between the two hierarchies was now effected. A resolution of 10 November released

Malenkov from his work as deputy chairman of the Council of Ministers in order to let him focus on the new Presidium commission on foreign affairs, while on the same day Bulganin was released from his position on the Council of Ministers in order to allow him to concentrate on the new defence commission. The severance of their connections to Sovmin meant that these leaders were now tied exclusively to the Presidium and to its commissions. Further, in a symmetrical move which split the leadership in half, a resolution of 10 November 1952 assigned Malenkov, Khrushchev and Bulganin as chairmen of the Presidium Buro (in Stalin's absence), while chairmanship of the Sovmin Buro was allocated to Beria, Pervukhin and Saburov.

The evolution of the cabinet in Stalin's last months reflected broader developments within the Soviet party-state. Prime among these was the holding of the XIX Congress, which had direct consequences for the Politburo. Apart from its new name, the regular sessions of the Presidium Buro accorded with the new post-congress emphasis on 'collective decision making'. Further, and also in line with the new emphasis on party leadership, the establishment of the Presidium commissions and the transfer of senior leaders and of policymaking powers from Sovmin to party agencies signalled both the incipient separation of party and state hierarchies and, albeit more tentatively, the supremacy of the former over the latter. At the same time the oncoming succession also left its mark on the cabinet, which became less dependent on Stalin than it had been in earlier years and which, in line with Stalin's own wishes, accommodated a new generation of younger leaders, many of whom were from the provinces.

## Conclusion

For much of the postwar period Politburo meetings assumed the form of small gatherings in Stalin's office or at his dacha from which were excluded not only specialist third parties such as ministers or Central Committee members but even members of the *de jure* Politburo itself. Decisions at these meetings were rarely taken to a vote and, when they were, the preferences of absent members were registered 'by correspondence' after the meeting itself. Both the composition of meetings and the mode of decision making were determined above all by the dynamics of confrontation and exclusion which were Stalin's preferred methods of inter-personal control. The system of rule, however, never descended into a pure dictatorship where Stalin pursued policies in his own name, bypassing the Politburo altogether. In fact, Stalin approached the Politburo with a measure of caution and reserve. This applied not only to the outward mechanisms of Politburo rule (for example the procedures for electing Politburo members or for passing Politburo resolutions), which remained largely unchanged, but to the handling of Politburo members themselves. Despite frequently being excluded and manipulated by the leader, members of the Politburo under Stalin were treated relatively leniently.[33]

The ability of one capricious individual to determine the composition and to set the agenda of Politburo meetings accounts for the internal fluidity of the Politburo in the late Stalin period. Outwardly, however, the Politburo projected an image of solidity and order. One reason for this appearance of stability was that Stalin himself sought continuity in the Politburo's membership.[34] As much as he tested and intimidated his colleagues at close range, they were all known quantities and, collectively, the easier to control and to manage for that. Irrespective of their usefulness to Stalin, some Politburo members were also key figures for the political system as a whole. More so than anyone who perished during the Great Purges, leaders such as Molotov, Mikoyan, Kaganovich and Voroshilov were acknowledged as Stalin's comrades-in-arms and as architects of the Stalinist system. No attempt to discredit these leaders, even one instigated by Stalin, could have failed to weaken faith in the Stalinist system. Stalin himself intimated as much when he was forced to temper his attack on Molotov and Mikoyan at the October 1952 plenum of the Central Committee. 'He had to do so,' claimed Mikoyan, 'since, to the extent that all members of the Politburo and participants at the plenum knew us well, the plenum was flabbergasted by his attacks on the two of us.' Both Molotov and Mikoyan continued to carry out important functions not only after they had been sacked as ministers in 1949 but even after they had been condemned by Stalin in the autumn of 1952; indeed, the moment Stalin died both were immediately reinstated in the ruling circle. That this should have been the case is hardly surprising given that the personal authority of these hero-founders continued to be immense, and certainly exceeded that of the institutions which they headed.[35]

Yet the Politburo was more than the sum of its individual member-parts. It was also an institution in its own right. It was as an institution, with its own rules and expectations, that the Politburo enabled Stalin to bind his deputies into a system of collective responsibility. Moreover, the Stalinist system was sufficiently hierarchic and bureaucratic to require an image of stability and order at its summit. The outward institutional coherence of the Politburo was a source of authority for functionaries further down the hierarchy. In addition to being the leading executive committee of the party-state the Politburo was also, in the absence of meetings of the Central Committee or of party congresses, the ruling committee of the party. Even at its height, Stalinism had never become an unalloyed personal dictatorship, for it always contained a strong trace of Bolshevik ideology. At times, such as the XIX Congress, this ideology became more robust and the practices of internal 'party democracy' were revived. This had direct consequences for the organization of the party and its ruling committees. It was because of its claim to be more 'democratic' than any other institution that, at the time of the XIX Congress, party committees were elevated over institutions of the state. This, however, came at a price: the rise of party institutions was conditional on the resuscitation of 'collective decision making' within the party, a commitment that reached to the nerve-centre of the party's power. To the extent that three politburos had co-existed under Stalin – the expanded sessions of the *de jure* Politburo, the closed meetings of the inner circle and the Politburo without Stalin – it was to be a combination of this drive for collective decision making and the fact of Stalin's death itself that would allow the last of these politburos – the Politburo without Stalin – finally to come into its own.

NOTES

Reorganized and renumbered from the original.

1. Research for this article was generously supported by grant no. 00222676 from the United Kingdom Economic and Social Research Council. I am very grateful to my collaborator on the project, Oleg Khlevnyuk, for sharing his ideas on this topic and for collecting the archival materials. An earlier version of the article was presented at a conference on 'Stalin's Politburo, 1929–1953' at the European University Institute, Florence, March 2000, organized by Arfon Rees. I would like to thank the participants at the conference and Vera Tolz for their comments and suggestions.

2. In order to blunt the original charge that the creation of the Politburo might demote the rest of the Central Committee to a lower status, the VIII Congress of 1919 required that members of the Central Committee who were not Politburo members be given the right to attend and to participate in Politburo sessions, albeit without full voting rights. This set the precedent for the enlarged Politburo sessions of the 1920s and early 1930s. See Merle Fainsod, *How Russia is Ruled* (Cambridge, MA, 1963), p. 178.

3. It is worth bearing in mind that immediately prior to its effective dissolution during the war and its replacement by GKO the Politburo had met in full session only rarely. Thus, for example, it had met only twice in each of the two years preceding the outbreak of war.

4. Other participants at this session were the members of the Central Committee Bulganin, Kosygin and Shkiryatov, the candidate member of the central committee A. F. Gorkin, a member of the central auditing commission, Shatalin, and the head of the trade union organization, V. V. Kuznetsov.

5. In addition, there were two further meetings after the summer vacation, on 2 and 6 September 1946.

6. For a brief portrait of a senile and near-blind 'Old Uncle Kalinin' being chided and made fun of by Stalin in 1945, see Milovan Djilas, *Conversations with*

*Stalin* (London, 1962), p. 97. Zhdanov spent much of the war in Leningrad, while Khruschev was based in Ukraine.

7. There is a gap in Stalin's Kremlin visitors' book from 8 October to 17 December 1945.

8. There is a reference to this resolution in Khrushchev's secret speech.

9. See N. S. Khruschev, *Khrushchev Remembers* (London, 1971), p. 299.

10. For a description of how, much to Stalin's disgust, Mikoyan and Molotov turned up uninvited to meetings they had been told about by other members of the inner circle, see for example Khrushchev, *Khrushchev Remembers*, pp. 280–1.

11. For references to the 'usual five' see Khrushchev, *Khrushchev Remembers*, pp. 281, 307. Khrushchev appears to have taken Kaganovich's place in the inner circle later in 1950.

12. Stalin's practice of convening at his office select ad hoc meetings of like-minded Politburo members went back to the late 1920s.

13. From the collections of long-distance correspondence in the Stalin archives it is apparent that Stalin was out of Moscow at least from 8 September to 20 December 1946, 17 August to 16 November 1947, 8 September to 11 December 1948, 5 September to 7 December 1949, 6 August to 21 December 1950 and 11 August to 21 December 1951. Towards the end Stalin also saw fewer visitors in Moscow. In 1950 Stalin did not receive visitors in his Kremlin office for a five-month stretch, from the beginning of August to the end of December; the same was true of a seven-month period from August 1951 to February 1952. The meetings in Stalin's office also fall from 227 hours in 1949 to 120 in 1950, 94 in 1951 and 72 in 1952.

14. The first post-Stalin presidium announced on 7 March 1953 restored some figures, such as Molotov, Mikoyan and Kaganovich, who had been attacked (Kaganovich to a lesser extent) by Stalin in previous months. The full line up was Malenkov, Beria, Molotov, Voroshilov, Khrushchev, Bulganin, Kaganovich, Mikoyan, Saburov and Pervukhin. Zhukov suggests that the last ruling circle under Stalin consisted of Beria, Bulganin, Malenkov, Khrushchev, Saburov and Pervukhin; Khrushchev suggests that the ruling circle consisted of Stalin, Beria, Malenkov, Bulganin and Khrushchev (*Khrushchev Remembers*, pp. 281, 307).

15. This was especially true of Beria and Malenkov who, as a rule, never opposed Stalin and always tried to prevail on other members of the inner circle not to do anything which might infuriate the leader.

16. Djilas, *Conversations with Stalin*, p. 73, wrote: 'Unofficially and in actual fact a significant part of Soviet policy was shaped at these dinners' (also see p. 144). By contrast, Khrushchev does not overstate the sigtuticance of these meetings for policymaking. 'It's true', he averred, 'that sometimes state and party questions were decided, but we spent only a fraction of our time on those. The main thing was to occupy Stalin's time so he wouldn't suffer from loneliness' (Khrushchev, *Khrushchev Remembers*, pp. 298–301, p. 299). It should be noted, however, that Khrushchev is one leader who tends to play up the level of 'disorder' at the Politburo, possibly in order to absolve himself of responsibility for its more reprehensible actions. This tactic was especially significant at the height of de-Stalinization. Consider the following passages from Khrushchev's secret speech: 'Comrades may ask us: Where were the members of the Political Buro of the Central Committee? Why did they

not assert themselves against the cult of the individual in time? ... Many decisions were taken either by one person or in a roundabout way, without collective discussions. The sad fate of Politburo member, comrade Voznesensky, who fell victim to Stalin's repressions, is known to all. It is a characteristic thing that the decision to remove him from the Politburo was never discussed but was reached in a devious fashion ... The importance of the Central Committee's Politburo was reduced and its work was disorganized by the creation within the Politburo of various commissions – the so-called "quintets", "sextets", "septets" and "novenaries"' (Khrushchev, *Secret Speech*, pp. 81, 83).

17. Correspondence votes applied to high-profile cadre decisions, such as the move to elevate Malenkov in August 1946 and to downgrade Molotov and Mikoyan in March 1949. The post hoc correspondence vote was also used to confirm decisions drafted by sub-groups with specialized expertise where the matter required urgent action. This was true of foreign policy matters, which were normally agreed jointly by Vyshinsky and Molotov and then sent to Stalin in the first instance before being forwarded to other members of the Politburo for ratification.

18. Both in his secret speech and in his memoirs Khrushchev recalled: 'Sometimes he would glare at you and say, "Why don't you look me in the eye today? Why are you averting your eyes from mine?" or some such stupidity.' Without warning he would turn on you with real viciousness.' See Khrushchev, *Khrushchev Remembers*, p. 258; also see Khrushchev, *Secret Speech*, p. 40. On another occasion, recounted by Mikoyan, Stalin reportedly ordered Poskrebyshev to accuse Molotov and Mikoyan of conspiring against the leader, so that Stalin might test their reactions.

19. 'The main thing [at those dinners],' Khrushchev recalled, 'was to occupy Stalin's time so that he wouldn't suffer from loneliness. He was depressed by loneliness and he feared it' (Khrushchev, *Khrushchev Remembers*, p. 299).

20. Examples may be found in Khrushchev, *Khrushchev Remembers*, pp. 274–5.

21. For more on this, see Gorlizki, 'Ordinary Stalinism', pp. 4–11.

22. Under the 1939 party statutes the Orgburo had been supposed to exercise 'general leadership of organizational work' while the secretariat was expected to carry out 'current work of an organizational-executive character' (Art. 34, in Graeme Gill, *The Rules of the Communist Party of the Soviet Union* (Basingstoke, 1988), pp. 172–3). Earlier statutes had not been any clearer. The party statutes of 1922 had stated simply that the Orgburo carried out 'general leadership of organizational work' and the secretariat 'current work of an organizational and executive character'. A Central Committee report of 1923 stated that appointments to the highest party positions came under the jurisdiction of the Orgburo whereas lower-level appointments came before the secretariat. See Gill, p. 120 (art. 25); and Fainsod, *How Russia is Ruled*, p. 182.

23. These included checking the work of regional and republican party committees and hearing their reports, taking appropriate measures where necessary.

24. By contrast, in a move which placed it in a directly subordinate position, the secretariat was entrusted with 'preparing questions for consideration by the Orgburo and checking implementation of decisions of the Politburo and the Orgburo'. The resolution also stated that the secretariat, in not having its own plan of work, would 'follow the workplans of the Orgburo and of the Politburo'. Whereas

the Orgburo was to meet no less than once a week, the secretariat would 'convene as deemed necessary'.

25. As with the relationship between the Orgburo and the secretariat, the dividing line between the Orgburo and the Politburo had never been clear-cut. Reviewing the relationship between the Orgburo and the Politburo on 29 March 1920, Lenin remarked: 'The practice arrived at was that it became the main and proper function of the Orgburo to distribute the forces of the party, while the function of the Political Buro was to deal with political questions. It goes without saying that this distinction is to a certain extent artificial; it is obvious that no policy can be carried out in practice without finding expression in appointments and transfers. Consequently, every organizational question assumes a political significance; and the practice was established that a request of a single member of the Central Committee was sufficient to have any question for any reason whatsoever examined as a political question.' Cited in Fainsod, *How Russia is Ruled*, p. 179.

26. The expansion of cadre work at the Central Committee was such that in a draft on the reorganization of the apparatus even Zhdanov recognized that 'concentrating the distribution of cadres under the leadership of one secretary' was not enough, and recommended as an alternative that 12 new cadres secretaries be appointed.

27. Although the Presidium is sometimes seen as a straight substitute for the Politburo, it was in fact successor to both the Politburo and the Orgburo. See Fainsod, *How Russia is Ruled*, pp. 216, 323.

28. See Yoram Gorlizki, 'Party Revivalism and the Death of Stalin', *Slavic Review*, 54, 1, 1995 pp. 5–9.

29. Thus, for example, plenums of republican and regional party committees were to meet once every two months, as opposed to every three months, and the plenums of district committees were to meet once every month instead of once every month and a half. Gorlizki, 'Party Revivalism, p. 7.

30. More explicitly than before, the new party statutes of 1952 made plain the leadership function of the Presidium over the Central Committee between Central Committee plenums. Article 34 of the 1952 statutes stated tersely that the Central Committee organizes a Presidium for leadership of the work of the Central Committee between plenums. By contrast, the 1939 and earlier statutes had stated only that the Central Committee organizes a Politburo for political work [and] an Organizational Buro for the general leadership of organizational work'. See Gill, *The Rules of the Communist Party*, pp. 47, 172, 193.

31. See Evan Mawdsley, 'An Elite within an Elite: Politburo/Presidium Membership under Stalin, 1927–1953', paper presented at conference on 'Stalin's Politburo, 1928–1953', European University Institute, Florence, March 2000, cited by permission, pp. 17–18. For more on the 'job-slot' system see Robert V. Daniels, 'Office Holding and Elite Status: The Central Committee of the CPSU', in Paul Cocks *et al.* (eds), *The Soviet Politics* (Cambridge, MA, 1976), pp. 77–95; and Evan Mawdsley and Stephen White, *The Soviet Elite from Lenin to Gorbachev: The Central Committee and its Members* (Oxford, 2000), pp. x–xi, 5, 41–50, 98–104.

32. Whereas the 1939 rules had stipulated that the secretariat engage in 'current work of an organizational-executive character' the 1952 version introduced the

broader formulation: '[The secretariat exists] for leadership of current work, chiefly the organization of verification of the implementation of decisions of the party and the selection of cadres.' See Gill, *The Rules*, pp. 172–3, 193.

33. Commentators have long noted the relative durability of Politburo membership and high survival rate in the postwar years. With the notable exception of Voznesensky no member of the formal Politburo was arrested or detained in this period. For the double argument that levels of attrition were lower in the Politburo than in the 'wider circles of the party elite' and 'that stability of [Politburo] membership was greater in the years of Stalin's fully developed despotism [i.e. 1939–1953] than in any other period ... in Soviet history' see T. H. Rigby, 'Was Stalin a Disloyal Patron?', in T. H. Rigby, *Political Elites in the USSR* (Aldershot, 1990), pp. 138, 141. Rigby reaches the conclusion (p. 141) that 'the durability of Stalin's inner clientele was truly remarkable'. Khlevnyuk also makes the point that even those, such as Molotov and Mikoyan, who were repeatedly harangued by the ageing dictator escaped his onslaughts unharmed and that, even after the attacks of October 1952, they continued to play an important role. By contrast, Khrushchev was 'convinced that [had] Stalin lived much longer, Molotov and Mikoyan would have met a disastrous end' (Khrushchev, *Khrushchev Remembers*, p. 310).

34. The formal Politburo was dominated by figures such as Molotov, Voroshilov, Kaganovich, Mikoyan, Andreev, Malenkov and Shvernik whom Stalin had known since the 1920s; most of the other members, such as Beria, Bulganin and Khrushchev, he had known since the early 1930s. These were leaders whose loyalty Stalin had repeatedly tested and whose strengths and weaknesses the leader knew inside out. Apart from the unfortunate Voznesensky, the only new recruit was Kosygin. These points are made in T. H. Rigby, *Political Elites in the USSR*, pp. 141, 143.

35. Indeed, as the former diplomat Oleg Troyanovsky recounts, the main consequence of Molotov leaving the ministry of foreign affairs was not that Molotov's stature should have diminished but, rather, that the institutional weight of the ministry itself should have fallen away. He writes: 'After the replacement of Molotov by Vyshinsky [in 1949], who was not a Politburo member, the role of the ministry in determining the course of the Soviet Union in international affairs noticeably decreased, and became all but ancillary' (Troyanovsky, *Cherez gody*, p. 166).

# VII   Some Reflections on Stalinism

## STALINISM AS A CIVILIZATION

One of the most influential volumes on the Stalin years published in the 1990s was Stephen Kotkin's *Magnetic Mountain*. In it, he looked at the epic struggle to build a new city in the middle of nowhere, the city of Magnitogorsk (Magnetic Mountain). Having completed a detailed empirical account of the construction of the city, its achievements and its disasters, Kotkin concluded his study by reflecting on the new city as a microcosm of the civilization being constructed in the USSR. While Professor Kotkin's reflections are all the more poignant in the light of the collapse of Soviet socialist aspirations in 1991, he also points out that the issues did not solely affect the Soviet way of thinking. The Soviet project of building a new, better society arose from a deeply European Enlightenment impulse to perfect humanity. The author not only compares Magnitogorsk to Thomas Campanella's *City of the Sun*, a seventeenth-century utopian conceptualization, but, perhaps more surprisingly, to its immediate model, Gary, Indiana. Gary was also seen, as Kotkin argues, as a model city for modern American civilization. How ironic it should have been consciously taken up by the Soviet planners as a partial blueprint for their own showpiece of Soviet civilization. These multiple ironies give Professor Kotkin scope for a series of post-Soviet reflections on the meaning of high Stalinism.

### 10   Stephen Kotkin: 'Stalinism as a Civilization'

Although the Communist revolution may start with the most idealistic concepts, calling for heroism and gigantic effort, it sows the greatest and most permanent illusions.

Milovan Djilas[1]

In the 1930s, the people of the USSR were engaged in a grand historical endeavour called building socialism. This violent upheaval, which began the suppression of capitalism, amounted to a collective search for socialism in housing, urban form, popular culture, the economy, management, population migration, social structure, politics, values, and just about everything else one could think of, from styles of dress to modes of reasoning. Within a steadfast but vague non-capitalist orientation, much remained to be discovered and settled.

Did planning mean centralized decision making in absolutely all matters? Or could a planned economy also permit forms of direct, ostensibly market-like, relations between firms, which remained state-owned? In factories designed and partly built by capitalist firms and containing capitalist-invented technology, were there socialist forms of labour? If so, what were these forms and how did they manifest the purported moral superiority of socialism? In terms of the municipal economy, if there was no private property, would there be no trade? If there was such a thing as socialist trade, how was it to be organized? And what of the law? Was there a specifically socialist justice, and how were socialist courts supposed to function?

What did a socialist city look like? Did a rejection of individualism and commitment to collectivism mean that socialist housing should not be built to accommodate the family, or was the family compatible with socialism? What of socialist culture: did it signify workers writing poetry, or workers becoming 'cultured' by reading Pushkin? Should socialism permit popular entertainments, and if so, what kind? Was jazz socialist, capitalist, or neither? If capitalist, could jazz nonetheless be permitted, provided there were enough other cultural activities that were unambiguously socialist, whatever those might be? And, perhaps the most difficult question of all, could a socialist revolution create a new elite, and if so, was this just?

Of course, the Soviet regime was a dictatorship and on these questions, unconditionally binding decisions backed by the threat of coercion were handed down from Moscow, without discussion beforehand and with little opportunity to give direct voice to reservations afterwards. Yet, from the shopfloor production campaigns to nonprivate trade, from domestic living arrangements to organized recreation, the realization of socialism in practice involved the participation of people, affording ample opportunities for the circumvention of official strictures, spontaneous reinterpretations of the permissible cloaked by professions of ignorance, and myriad other forms of indirect challenges, as well as the discovery of unintended realms not envisioned by the decrees. No one except perhaps certain labour colony inmates with nothing to lose had a completely free hand to act as he or she saw fit, but even leaving aside calculated petty transgressions, living socialism according to the perceived rules made for its share of surprises.

Indeed, one of the most striking aspects of life in the Magnitogorsk of the 1930s was the constant effort to name and characterize the many surprising, as well as mundane, phenomena encountered in daily life, and then explain their relation to socialism, from the machinations of the shadow economy to the endless search for political enemies. New categories of thinking suddenly appeared, old ones were modified; nothing stood still. This inescapable tangle of discussion and explanation was made especially complex given the periodic shifts in policies and laws, sometimes of 180 degrees, such as the reversals on abortion and divorce in the mid-1930s.

Abrupt policy changes have usually been taken as evidence that, contrary to the regime's claims, there was no single ideology, and that in general, ideology had less influence over the shape of events than other, 'more practical' considerations. To argue thusly, however, is to overlook both the process of searching for socialism, rooted in an 'ideological' rejection of capitalism, and the enormous commitment of resources by the regime to maintain a single ideology and relate all events to that ideology, a struggle that the inhabitants of Magnitogorsk had no choice but to take part in. Life in the USSR under Stalin was enveloped not merely in constrained experimentation but in perpetual explication where neither mistakes nor reversals could be admitted, and where socialism, understood as non-capitalism, served as a universal point of reference.

Further misunderstandings surround the shift on abortion and the family in the mid-1930s because it was accompanied by a conspicuous revival of the Great Russian past, hitherto anathema. These developments (in combination with the rehabilitation of the Orthodox Church during the Second World War) have been interpreted as constituting nothing less than a 'great retreat' from the original goals of the revolution, if not a counterrevolution.[2] But the proponents of the great retreat interpretation of Stalinism fail to consider that there was no comparable 'retreat' on private ownership of land and the means of production or on the hiring of wage labour, whose absence was seen as the defining characteristic of socialism. It was in this unwavering repudiation of 'exploitation' that the USSR's claims to have brought about a civilization distinct from capitalism were grounded, whatever the other vacillations.

At bottom, the notion of a great retreat has always been based on the assumption that 'true' revolution and an imperial state are inherently incompatible, an historically indefensible tenet. From the beginning of the revolution, Great Russian domination coexisted uneasily with the striving for a multinational identity, a tension exacerbated by the circumstance that socialism was, in the language of the day, built in one country. By and large, however, the great retreat interpretation removes consideration of the fate of the revolution from that geopolitical context. Soviet socialism formed part of the same historical epoch as Nazism and fascism, against which it was locked in a deadly competition.

In that light, the strengthening of the family and the promotion of Great Russian nationalism are better appreciated as, on the one hand, part of the groping for an understanding of what constituted socialism and, on the other, as indicative of a strategic shift from the task of building socialism to that of defending socialism. This shift became noticeable with the anxious attention given to the civil war in Spain, where Hitler supported Franco's 'counterrevolution', and to Mussolini's imperialist war in Abyssinia. It was around this time, 1936, that socialism in the USSR was declared built in its foundations, and yet the external threat, rooted in what was called capitalist encirclement, appeared more menacing than ever.

This paradoxical combination of triumph and heightened vulnerability was used as one of the principal devices to stoke the terror of 1936–8, a bizarre episode that contemporaries struggled with little effect to comprehend and accept. Not even the enormously dysfunctional terror, however, proved capable of invalidating the USSR's claim to being a socialist society and therefore the fulfillment of October. Such a claim continued to make sense and motivate people the world over until the very end in 1991 – a circumstance that the historian may or may not find abhorrent but has no right to dismiss and every obligation to explain. One can argue that millions of people were ignorant or deceived. Or one can try to understand how so many people could have reasoned the way they did, holding apparently contradictory views, fearing terror yet believing that they had built, and lived under, socialism.

Inside Stalin's USSR, the appeal of socialism had several layers, including the prospect of a quick leap, not simply into modernity but a superior form of modernity, the corresponding attainment of high international status, a broad conception of social welfare and a sense of social justice that was built into property relations. Despite the long, vicious political struggle for power, rampant opportunism and careerism, and the violence and hatred that were unleashed, the USSR under Stalin meant something hopeful. It stood for a new world power, founded on laudatory ideals, and backed up by tangible programs and institutions: full employment, subsidized prices, paid vacations for workers, childcare, health care, retirement pensions, education and the promise of advancement for oneself and one's children.

To be sure, life in Magnitogorsk and around the USSR was characterized by gradations of commitment – particularly in the willingness to suspend disbelief. Put another way, belief in Soviet socialism, as in all matters of faith, was never without ambivalence, confusion and misgivings. Even the truest of true believers appears to have had regular bouts with private doubt. But few could imagine alternatives. Nor was anyone encouraged to do so. Sealed borders and censorship did their part – especially considering that Soviet censorship was not merely the suppression of information, but also the hyperactive, indefatigable dissemination of certain kinds of information, as well as the inculcation of specific ways of understanding that information.

That such activist censorship proved effective need not be seen as solely a matter of manipulation, however. To be effective, propaganda must offer a story that people are prepared at some level to accept; one that retains the capacity to capture their imagination, and one that they can learn to express in their own words. As we have seen, the process of articulating the sanctioned vocabulary and values of the new society in one's own words was far from entirely voluntary, linked not merely to access to food and housing but to one's safety and the safety of one's relatives. But the presence of coercion, subtle and unsubtle, does not mean the absence of a high degree of voluntarism any more than the holding of genuine ideals precludes the energetic pursuit of self-interest.

Even when they found a niche in the new society, the inhabitants of Magnitogorsk did equivocate and evade, cry and curse – and with good reason. Constantly told that in material terms much of the promise of socialism remained in the future, they were compelled to endure enervating bureaucratic indifference and arbitrary repression. Only the most dogmatic refused to acknowledge the hardships, as well as the staggering waste, corruption, recourse to intimidation and widespread fear. But no matter how suspect matters might come to seem, the contrast with the apparent progress made since the tsar and, above all, with the recognized evils of capitalism – unemployment, exploitation, endemic economic crises, and imperialism – was available to quell even the deepest of doubts.

It needs to be recalled, moreover, that in the 1930s a parade of authoritative foreigners willingly came to the USSR, making pilgrimages to shrines such as Magnitogorsk, denouncing capitalism and praising socialism. Volumes were spoken, too, by the trumpeted borrowings undertaken by socialism's friends, and preemptive imitation by its foes, in Europe, the United States, Japan, and elsewhere. Whether within the framework of parliamentary democracy or under an alternate model of overt authoritarianism, the aim of achieving what the USSR had apparently achieved by way of national purpose, economic development and overcoming class divisions preoccupied the world community in the interwar period. Socialism addressed real problems and seemed to offer real solutions. As long as capitalism was mired in crisis, socialism retained a powerful appeal.

Some sixty years after Magnitogorsk was founded, the writer Veniamin Kaverin recalled a visit he had made to the famous construction site as a youth in 1931. He recalled having been bowled over by the speed with which the factory and city were rising in the wide-open steppe. In retrospect, though, he also claimed to have been overwhelmed at the time by the sight of starving women, the wives and widows of the thousands of peasants deported to Magnitogorsk and forced to live in tents through the winter. 'The cemetery grew faster than the steel works,' Kaverin now wrote, confessing that back then, having seen 'the direct connection between the growth of the cemetery and the growth of the steel works, I tried not to see this connection – and, it came to pass, I walked the construction with closed eyes.'[3]

In 1931, Kaverin walked the construction not with closed eyes but with eyes eager to gather in the promised new world. And that new world, centred on the technologically advanced factory, was easy to see. Decades afterwards, when he came to question his once firmly held beliefs, Kaverin did so by remembering what he had in fact seen with his own eyes. The same history in the making that filled him with hope and a powerful sense of progress – his progress, the country's progress – subsequently filled him with shame for his country and himself. Kaverin expressed the dynamic whereby Soviet socialism unravelled: insight came, disillusionment set in, repentant confessions were made – not by everyone, to be sure, but by many, very many.[4]

The widely remarked disappointment in Soviet socialism reveals what had once been a powerful faith; to become disillusioned one had to have believed in the first place. And the greater the belief, the greater the disillusionment. Feelings of guilt were often so powerful that they became the basis for a fervent opposite reaction – no doubt in large part because socialism as a faith was also a source of identity. The story of socialism was nearly indistinguishable from the story of people's lives, a merged personal and societal allegory of progress, social justice and overcoming adversity – in short, a fable of a new person and a new civilization, distinct because it was not capitalist, distinct because it was better than capitalism. This was socialism's original strength; it also turned out to be a crushing burden.

Soviet socialism collapsed from within, but it did so because it existed as an anti-world to capitalism. It was from capitalism that socialism derived its identity and against which it constantly measured itself. Over the long haul, however, socialism proved incapable of meeting the challenge that it had set of besting capitalism. At a certain point, the competition with capitalism – in military technology, in living standards, in ideas about politics and society – began working to the disadvantage of the USSR. This dynamic, which in a different form had helped precipitate the downfall of the tsarist regime and the onset of the revolutionary process, impelled the Soviet regime on a path that also culminated in that regimes dramatic self-liquidation.

Veniamin Kaverin did not say what induced his re-remembering of incidents he once willingly suppressed, but a changed perspective on the outside world – capitalism – probably played a critical role. For many, it was this altered context that enabled, even demanded, a reassessment of socialism and their own association with it. That reevaluation naturally focused on the icons of the new world. Magnitogorsk, what many had reasoned would 'be the best propaganda for socialism', turned out to be effective propaganda against socialism – but effective propaganda all the same.

Under socialism there was little room for neutrality. It demanded spiritual commitment and constant affirmations of that commitment, even when people felt ambivalent, indifferent, or hostile, and even after socialism's claims of surpassing capitalist civilization had become seriously strained. By adopting a confessional mode and using personal experiences to evaluate the legitimacy of their country's political system, Kaverin and others were following the same procedures they had learned as youths, only with the exact opposite result: socialism as a matter of faith, but now the loss of faith; autobiography as politically meaningful, but now delegitimizing.

In the almost six decades between Kaverin's visits to Magnitogorsk, evaluations of the baseline for measuring socialism – the outside world – changed; so did the ability to make such evaluations. Part of this could be attributed to the increased availability of information, part to a heavy-handed but nonetheless humanistic education that promoted *both* outright falsehoods *and* a real commitment to the truth; a vision of merciless class struggle *and* of universal good.

In the Magnitogorsk of the 1930s, more than forty thousand people were enrolled in full- or part-time education programs, ranging from beginning and middle schools, regular or technical high schools, and institutions of higher learning (such as the Mining and Metallurgical Institute and the Pedagogical Institute) to so-called workers' academies (*rabfaks*). Another twelve thousand individuals were enrolled in literacy courses, part-time trade courses, or night school (with an additional several hundred students at a school for classical music).[5] Virtually everyone in the city who could study was studying.

Magnitogorsk schools suffered from chronic problems with facilities.[6] Only a handful of the almost forty elementary schools were located in what were designated as permanent buildings; the rest were housed in broken-down barracks that lacked not merely adequate classrooms or laboratories but heat and running water. Furniture, such as desks and chairs, was in critically short supply, as were books and paper. Owing to delays in planned construction and repairs, each September classes invariably started late – but they always managed to get underway.[7] What ensured the onset of each school year despite the daunting obstacles was the devotion to education, one of the primary values associated with the new world that Magnitogorsk incarnated.

Curriculum combined the basic – reading, writing, and arithmetic – with a very strong emphasis on civics and politics. Students were trained in what was called the 'spirit of socialism', by which was meant the traditions and myths of a revolutionary legacy inherited and advanced by the USSR. This inculcation of the spirit of socialism was supposed to carry over even to technical subjects (on which great emphasis was placed). First-year students of the Mining Institute, for example, were accused of being culturally illiterate for not knowing the dates of the French revolution, or when fascism began. They were also taken to task for not reading the 'classics' of Marxism.[8] But these students had to know the same science that 'capitalists' studied and used, not to mention the novels of Tolstoy and the music of Tchaikovsky.

In the processes of socialization the greatest attention and resources were bestowed upon Magnitogorsk's youngest pupils, who in addition to class-time activities participated in a countrywide children's organization known as the 'Pioneers', where civic training in the spirit of socialism was especially pronounced.[9] Aspirations for this next generation were high. One concerned pamphleteer complained that in a Magnitogorsk kindergarten, the children did not know what a shock worker was, who Voroshilov was, or what was meant by the term *kulak*. By the end of their education, however, every one of these pupils could be expected to have been taught all this – and much more, including the sometimes condemned but mostly admired values of European civilization and its 'highest achievements', as well as native values and forms of sociability that pre-dated the revolutionary speech.

It was taken for granted by the above pamphleteer that information about Magnitogorsk kindergartens should be broadcast, not only so that the situation there could be 'corrected' but because the whole world should know. Such missionary zeal in the propagation of the minutest details of the city's life recalled the example of Magnitogorsk's famous American predecessor, Gary, Indiana. When Gary was founded during the first decade of the twentieth century, contemporaries engaged in shameless boosterism, replete with poetry, and began immediately to collect documents on the city and its factory, in part to sell land, but also with the aim of rearing the present generation in the spirit of the values Gary supposedly represented, and passing these values on to the next generation.[10]

What Magnitogorsk and Gary shared was a sense that they constituted not merely a single city, however important, but an entire civilization, *and* that their civilization could rightfully lay claim to being the vanguard of progressive humanity. It was no accident that Gary became the model for Magnitogorsk, for after the revolution in the Russian empire there was an enormous amount of admiring discussion of the United States as the world's most advanced civilization, and of a kind of 'Soviet Americanism' as history's next stage.[11] This Soviet cult of America – a young, dynamic country that appeared to have made itself – took many forms, from the worship of industrial technology to a sense among large segments of the population that they had inherited from the Americans the mantle of civilization and enlightenment, even as their envy and imitation persisted.

Many of the large number of Americans who made pilgrimages to the USSR after the revolution, John Scott among them, enthusiastically confirmed this passing of the torch from the United States to the USSR. Their interest in Soviet socialism demonstrated yet again that socialism in the Soviet Union took shape as, and for a long time remained, a deeply felt aspiration, much like the so-called American dream – only ostensibly far better. But most of these foreign champions of Soviet socialism came to reject their admiration. Several became avid adversaries, tirelessly warning against the dangers of socialism's allure while becoming strident about the superiority of American civilization and adamant in their refusals to acknowledge any positive influence of Soviet socialism on themselves or their country. Such repudiations from outside, much like the earlier affirmations, eventually found an eager audience among once true-believing Soviet citizens, including Veniamin Kaverin. The circle became complete, ironically concealing the full extent of interconnectedness and reciprocal influence.


In the world after 1991, Soviet socialism may seem little more than a bizarre nightmare best condemned and forgotten, or if remembered, then only as a cautionary tale about political despotism and dangerous ideas. But even though it was rooted in a rejection of capitalism, the story of the USSR needs to be recognized as an integral part of the course of European history.

At the very least, Europe and the United States are complicit in the Russian revolution. It was, after all, the senseless war among the Great Powers that provided the indispensable context for the all-important politicization of the tsarist army, the seizure of power by conspiratorial revolutionaries and the legitimation of transcendental socialism as an alternative to death and destruction. Moreover, Lenin and other exiled members of the Bolshevik conspiracy had been provided refuge in various

European capitals and were able to return to Russia from Switzerland only through the maliciously intentioned assistance of the German high command. Remember, too, that although the revolutionary authorities had been compelled to cede enormous territories to the Germans at the risk of internal collapse, the entrance of the United States into the war on the side of the allies turned the tide against the Germans, allowing the Soviet regime an opportunity to rebuild the Russian empire.

During the Civil War, ineffective military intervention in Soviet Russia by Britain, France, the United States and Japan provided an important impetus for the establishment of Bolshevik hegemony over the revolutionary process. During the 1920s, the Germans provided critical technical assistance to the USSR, including to the Red Army. During the 1930s, a veritable 'Who's Who' of leading capitalist firms, the originators of the culture of Fordism, advised and aided Stalinist industrialization. Above all, what we call Stalinism was consolidated in the USSR against the background of, and as an answer to, the Great Depression that spread throughout the advanced capitalist countries, as well as the aggression that coincided with it.

In the end, though, the main reason that the USSR needs to be reincorporated into European history is that Stalinism constituted a quintessential Enlightenment utopia, an attempt, via the instrumentality of the state, to impose a rational ordering on society, while at the same time overcoming the wrenching class divisions brought about by nineteenth-century industrialization. That attempt, in turn, was rooted in a tradition of urban-modelled, socially oriented utopias that helped make the Enlightenment possible. Magnitogorsk had very deep roots.


In the early part of the seventeenth century, Tommaso Campanella (1568–1639), a Dominican friar from near Naples, composed what may perhaps be regarded as the quintessential urban-modelled, socially oriented utopia. It took the form of a dialogue between an inquisitive innkeeper and a garrulous Genovese sailor (one of Columbus's crew), who has purportedly returned from a wondrous place known as 'the City of the Sun'.[12] At the time Magnitogorsk was being built three centuries later, this dialogue was mobilized as part of the efforts to situate the Russian revolution historically, a goal that in retrospect can be seen to have been perhaps even more successful than intended.

In a brief introduction to the Russian-language edition of Campanella's text that was reissued in 1934 (the first had appeared in 1918), the scholar V. P. Volgin placed the monk within what he identified as the tradition of 'communist utopias', singling out especially 'the absence of private property, the universal obligation of labour (which is considered a matter of honour), the social organization of production and distribution and the training through labour of the inhabitant'. Volgin might also have underscored the importance in the City of the Sun of the development and proper use of science, the vigorous efforts to ensure the welfare of the population combined with equally vigorous defensive preparations for the inevitability of war, the fusion of spiritual and temporal power in a kind of theocracy, the frequency of individual confession or self-criticism, and the assumption that state power rests on the nature of everyday life – all core aspects, as we have seen, of the society in which Volgin himself was living.

These were not the only remarkable parallels called to mind by Campanella's text that Volgin overlooked. In the course of comparing Campanella's work with Plato's and that of the early Christian fathers, for example, Volgin delicately touched on the idea of the undemocratic 'rule of the wise', but he did so without invoking the 'leading role of the Communist party'. Volgin also made no mention, not even indirectly, of the resemblance between Campanella's portrait of the supreme ruler, Sun, and the emerging cult of Stalin. What Volgin did do, however, was to recognize a more than passing affinity between Soviet society and an avowedly utopian document in which social welfare was made the state's foremost duty and the key to its international standing.

However circumscribed the circle of people in the USSR who were acquainted with Campanella's work might have been, it was in effect the ideal of a City of the Sun – a city-based society engineered and regulated so as to ensure the utmost well-being, productivity, and hence state power – that served as the sublime vision from which the real-life Stalinist microcosm, Magnitogorsk, derived and into which it fed. Placing Magnitogorsk within the context of Campanella's text helps explain why a single Soviet city, especially one built in near-isolation at a previously almost uninhabited site, could serve as such a potent symbol for the self-proclaimed new civilization of socialism.

NOTES

[Reorganized and renumbered from the original.]

1. *The New Class* (New York 1957), p. 30.

2. N. Timasheff, *The Great Retreat* (New York, 1946). Virtually all English-language textbooks on the history of the USSR adopt Timasheff's line.

3. The date of the Magnitogorsk cemetery's founding remains mysterious, for initially the city had no cemetery. The first doctor on the site in 1929, desperately fighting an outbreak of scarlet fever, claimed he had wanted to establish one, but that a decision was instead taken to build a crematorium.

4. The Soviet émigré Lev Kopelev, a young enthusiast sent to facilitate the brutal collectivization process in the Ukraine, put it eloquently: 'I convinced myself

and others that the main thing had remained unchanged, that all our ills, malefacations and falsehoods were inevitable but temporary afflictions in our overall healthy society. In freeing ourselves from barbarity, we were forced to resort to barbaric methods, and in repulsing cruel and crafty foes, we could not do without cruelty and craftiness. ... Insight came later: it grew slowly and irregularly.' *The Education of a True Believer* (New York, 1980; originally published in Russian, 1978), pp. 122–3.

5. The Pedagogical Institute was initially organized as a night school, which opened in 1936. In 1938, it switched to daytime and took over the premises of a converted elementary school.

6. The Mining and Metallurgical Institute, for example, was located in a decayed barracks on the Ezhovka section of the Fifth Sector (initially it had been located in building no. 25 of Kirov district). In 1939 the institute had 680 students (including those studying at the *rabfak*), for whom there were thirty teachers, one professor, and five docents. Poor as its facilities were, the institute was far better off than the industrial trade high school. The latter had changed location four times in three years, and in 1936 was still without a permanent site. Founded in 1931, the trade high school graduated 420 students by 1938, at which time it had 260 students, 145 of whom attended at night.

7. In 1937 the city decided to accredit its elementary-school teachers. Of the almost 600 teachers in the city, 283 passed the test; another 231 retained the right to teach under the condition that they attend courses; 45 were to be reexamined, and 16 had lost the right to teach. The newspaper complained that only 97 teachers were enrolled in any courses. By 1941 the number of elementary-school pupils had declined to 21,801, by which time there were still approximately 600 teachers, or less than one for every 350 pupils. This ratio was actually a marked improvement over the situation of four years earlier, when the ratio was closer to one teacher for 500 pupils. Teachers also functioned as social workers. See the comments by John Scott on his wife, Mariia Scott, who was among the first class of twenty-odd graduates from the city's fledgling Pedagogical Institute and worked as a teacher in a school for the children of the dekulakized. Scott, *Behind the Urals* (London, 1973) p. 132.

8. The newspaper added that this was less the students' fault than the result of improper training, insisting that the country needed not just technical specialists but 'socialist technical specialists'.

9. The newspaper lamented the fact that of the 13,000 to 15,000 pupils of pioneer age living in the city, only 6200 belonged to the organization, but this was still a sizeable number and in subsequent years it would grow.

10. Gary's schools became famous under the direction of William Wirt, a pupil and disciple of John Dewey. Quillen, 'Industrial City', pp. 170–1 (one of the first school teachers was R. R. Quillen, evidently a relative of the author). See also Randolph, *The Gary Schools* (Boston, 1916), based on a visit in 1915. Gary schools were, of course, segregated. Neil Betten and Raymond Mottl, 'The Evolution of Racism in an Industrial City, 1906–40: Case Study of Gary, Indiana', *Journal of Negro History* 59, no. 1 (1974), 51–64. See also Arthur Shumway, 'Gary, Shrine of the Steel God: The City that Has Everything, and at the Same Time Has Nothing', *The American Parade* 3, no. 2 (1929), 23; and [Howard Harries], *The*

*Story of Gary, Indiana: An Illustrated Study of the Building of the Most Marvellous City on the American Continent* (Gary, 1908).

11. The eyewitness René Fülöp-Miller, writing that 'for the Bolsheviks, industrialized America became the Promised Land', offered several examples. Fülöp-Miller, *The Mind and Face of Bolshevism*, pp. 29–33. In his 1924 codification of Leninism, Stalin alluded to the combination of 'Russian revolutionary sweep' and 'American efficiency'. This talk, according to Mariia Scott, reached the countryside. See also Jeffrey Brooks, 'The Press and Its Message: Images of America in the 1920s and 1930s', in Sheila Fitzpatrick et al. (eds), *Russia in the Era of Nep: Explorations in Soviet Society and Culture* (Bloomington, 1991), pp. 231–52.

12. Tommaso Campanella, *The City of the Sun: A Poetical Dialogue*, trans. by Daniel J. Donno (Berkeley, Cal., 1981). Written in Italian in 1602, the dialogue circulated in manuscript until its publication in Latin in 1623.

# THE EMERGING PICTURE: SOME CONCLUDING THOUGHTS

The items in this collection have, hopefully, whetted the appetite of the reader to pursue further the emerging lines of enquiry into the Stalin years. Anyone wishing to do so will find no shortage of material of many kinds. The comments below focus on materials available to the English-speaking reader.

Among the most valuable types of publication are those which provide new information. Some of these are memoirs of people involved in great events. These include leading political figures like Molotov, whose memoirs have already been referred to, and another long-time foreign minister Andrei Gromyko, both of which have been translated into English.[1] Lesser participants in great events are also writing of their experiences. One of the first to appear was the book by Yakov Rapoport about the Kremlin Doctors' Plot, a murky affair mercifully cut short by Stalin's death after which the investigation was dropped.[2] One of the reasons why it had been published quickly, in reponse to Gorbachev's call that there should be no 'blank pages' in Soviet history, was because it had been written for the desk drawer in 1973. Items of fiction were similarly retrieved from desk drawers, including Vassili Grossman's great novel *Life and Fate* and Anatoli Rybakov's *Children of the Arbat*.[3] Many other memoirs came to light or were written and published in the new atmosphere. Among the most interesting were memoirs of the most secret of areas, Soviet nuclear and space programmes, which underlined that Stalin could make serious mistakes, none greater than cutting off the development of rocketry during the war.[4] Clearly accounts by individuals, while very welcome and interesting in getting behind the scenes and suggesting new perspectives, have to be treated with great caution and analysed very carefully. Also valuable and needing caution of a different kind are the collections of high-level documents from formerly secret archives which are being published. In the forefront of these are *The Road to Terror: Stalin and the Self-Destruction of the Bolsheviks 1932–1939* and *Stalin's Letters to Molotov 1925–1936*.[5] The danger here is that the great advances resulting from the partial publication of sources might be mistaken for new, definitive accounts when other important materials remain to see the light of day. Nonetheless, they provide unprecedented access to historical raw material which will be mulled over by historians for decades to come.

However, the majority of writings of the late 1980s, 1990s and early years of the new millennium are secondary analyses usually based on examinations of new evidence or offering interpretations stimulated by the dramatically new environment. Contrasting examples of general surveys of Stalin and his career are provided by the books of Robert McNeal and Edvard Radzinsky.[6] McNeal's book, published initially in 1988, was perhaps the last which could write in its introduction that 'Almost thirty-five years after his death we know the official file number of the Stalin papers in the Central Party Archive (*fond* 558), but that is all we know about this presumably vast store of information.'[7] Radzinsky's volume was, after Volkogonov's, one of the first to use more of the formerly hidden materials. However, no doubt understandably, as a Russian writer Radzinsky was highly conscious of his role as a breaker of taboos. He also had one eye on the best-seller markets and tended like other Russian writers of the period to prioritize anecdote and rumour (the more lurid the better) over analytical objectivity. The result was a widely distributed and readable biography but not always a first choice for objectivity. Similar considerations affected other early Russian accounts of more specialized areas. A combination of scholarship and sensationalism characterizes Viktor Suvorov's *Icebreaker*, an attempt to prove that Stalin was planning to take the offensive against Hitler in 1941.[8] The thesis has been roundly dismissed by western diplomatic historians, notably Geoffrey Roberts and Gabriel Gorodetsky.[9] An associated area in which new materials and possibilities of, for example, interviewing participants, have emerged is the history of the war. Several major contributions have been published in the west.[10]

Many other excellent accounts have appeared looking at the broad perspective[11] while a wide sub-genre of overviews of the rise and fall of the Soviet system – much of the focus of which falls, inevitably, on the Stalin years – has also evolved.[12] However, some of the most fruitful areas have involved study of more specialized topics. Important new studies have illuminated many themes. A new generation of detailed political studies focusing on the province as well as the centre has made considerable use of newly available materials.[13] Jeffrey Brooks has thrown new light on popular culture while there are highly informative studies of many other topics, notably the armed forces, nationalities policy, the terror and secondary figures like Vyshinsky, Beria and Ezhov.[14] This ever-expanding material has enriched our view. New fields of study have also appeared. Among the most interesting are Douglas R. Weiner's work on environmental protection[15] and David King's study of the highly-developed Soviet craft of doctoring photographs.[16]

The main thrust of this material, like that included in this collection, has been to add detail and complexity to our picture of the Stalin years. In many ways, the principal outcome has been the identification of a more dynamic and spontaneous society within the well-known parameters of control from the centre. Despite their great variety the selection of articles share some features. In the first place, the picture of Soviet society in the Stalin years is much more complex than most previous versions. The opening of some archives and access to key figures has deepened our knowledge in many areas. Soviet society in the 1930s contained many dynamic elements. We have seen this among doctors, atheist agitators, peasants, workers and parts of the bureaucracy. It was not a uniform society and the leadership had to respond to pressures. At the same time, the centre held a firm grip over key policies and their implementation. In this respect, the arguments of both totalitarians and revisionists have been superseded by a post-revisionist view borrowing from both traditions. The Soviet system was, undoubtedly, under firm central direction but within that direction there was considerable spontaneity and, even during the purges, the centre could be outmanoeuvred or even to a degree ignored by ordinary workers and peasants.

The picture of postwar society is not so clear. Most of the research since the Gorbachev years has focused on the twenties and thirties. We have far fewer studies of Soviet society from 1945–53. The indications we do have suggest a society much more rigid and cowed – through exhaustion and shortages as well as political repression – pursuing a grim, grey existence picking through endless bureaucratic obstacles to obtain limited resources of food, housing and other basics. There was, of course, no shortage of employment as the country turned its shoulder to the wheel of reconstruction. The nation's success, by the mid-1950s, in digging the Soviet Union out of its vast losses in the war and carrying the continuing burden of defence in the face of the hostility of the United States and NATO, with their far greater resources and endlessly expanding nuclear advantage, is one of the epics of Soviet history. But it was achieved at a great cost. Political repression appeared to be at its peak in these years. Returned war prisoners suspected of disloyalty and a dwindling band of German war prisoners rotting away in Siberia and elsewhere swelled the numbers, but even so political imprisonment was part of everyday life. It is in these grim years that Solzhenitsyn set his magnificent story *A Day in the Life of Ivan Denisovich* based on his own years in the gulag (1945–53) and his novel *The First Circle* which portrayed a situation one can scarcely imagine anywhere else, a scientific research institute, working on top secret projects, staffed entirely by political prisoners and controlled by secret police guards.

Outside the immediate camp system there were millions of forced exiles including the bulk of several national groups – including Chechens, Volga Germans and Crimean Tartars – who had simply been dislodged from their homelands and deported by the trainload because Stalin suspected their loyalty during the war. Better punish a whole group rather than let a single collaborator operate. This most absurd of Stalin's purges even led to fully operational, loyal fighting men being arrested at the front, where they were sorely needed, simply because they belonged to one of these nationalities. Opportunists, drifters and wandering victims of earlier purges took over their lands leaving a complex heritage which caused immense problems as protests became possible in the Khruschev and Brezhnev years. One and a half million people were displaced. True, this was a step short of Hitlerite extermination for unwanted nationalities but it did bring a large 'collateral' death toll as many were imprisoned and deported families struggled to make a living in new and hostile environments.

These years, rather than the thirties, probably fit the totalitarian model more closely. The grimness of the time – a consequence of purges, wartime regimentation, outside hostility in the form of the Cold War and shortages resulting from wartime destruction – was all the more disappointing for a society expecting some reward for its wartime sacrifices and victory. For the Soviet Union, as for Britain and France, the fruits of victory appeared more bitter than those of defeat tasted by West Germany and Japan which were the focus of massive American aid to re-build their capitalist economies before communism could seduce their inhabitants. In both cases the victors took on the main burden of defending these former enemies through forward bases and prohibitions and limitations on building their own armed forces. Freed of military expenditure, they came to dominate the expanding consumer markets of the west and enjoy economic 'miracles' that were much less spectacular for Britain, France and the USSR. Even the promise of relative cultural freedom in the Soviet Union, which began to develop in the war, was replaced by a massive clamp-down in 1947–8 in response to the Cold War. In this respect the two contending powers resembled each other by pursuing witch hunts. Zhdanov opened up a war against bourgeois influences, and the McCarthyite frenzy was turned on communist influences. The latter, of course, did not go so far in terms of its victims and was directed by a powerful lobby against the government and civil service rather than by them but the principles of both were strikingly similar. Mutual hostility was reinforcing hawkish, anti-liberal sentiment on both sides and the pattern that came to characterize the Cold War was established.

For the time being, then, we have an imbalance between the amount of scholarship on the early Stalin years and relatively little on the last, post-war years. Wartime, particularly its social and economic history as well as the strategic side, has been under steadily increasing scrutiny. There is obviously still a great deal of work to be done but the ongoing research of the post-Soviet period has already begun to illuminate many dark areas and even to change some of the wider contours of our view of the Stalin years.

## NOTES

1. V. Molotov, *Molotov Remembers: Inside Kremlin Politics, Conversations with Felix Chuev*, ed. A. Resis (Chicago, 1993); A. Gromyko, *Memories: From Stalin to Gorbachev* (London, 1989).

2. Yakov Rapoport, *The Doctors' Plot* (London, 1991).

3. Vasily Grossman, *Life and Fate: A Novel* (New York, 1987); Anatolii Rybakov, *Children of the Arbat* (London, 1988).

4. Ronald Z. Sagdaev, *The Making of a Soviet Scientist: My Adventures in Nuclear Fusion and Space from Stalin to Star Wars* (London, 1995); Andrei Sakharov, *Memoirs* (London, 1990). For a systematic account see David Holloway, *Stalin and the Bomb: The Soviet Union and Atomic Energy, 1939–1956* (New Haven, 1994).

5. J. A. Getty and Oleg Naumov (eds), *The Road to Terror: Stalin and the Self-Destruction of the Bolsheviks, 1932–1939* (New Haven, 1999); Lars T. Lih, Oleg Naumov and Oleg V. Khlevniuk, *Stalin's Letters to Molotov, 1925–1936* (New Haven and London, 1995). An important edition of Stalin's letters to his assistant Kaganovich in the 1930s has also been compiled by O. Khlevniuk, R. W. Davies, L. Kosheleva, E. A. Rees and L. Rogovaya but is currently only available in Russian with the title *Stalin–Kaganovich: Perepiska, 1931–36* (Moscow, 2001).

6. McNeal, *Stalin: Man and Ruler* (Basingstoke, 1988); Edvard Radzinsky, *Stalin* (London, 1996).

7. McNeal, *Stalin: Man and Ruler*, p. xi.

8. V. Suvorov, *Icebreaker* (London, 1993).

9. Gabriel Gorodetsky, *Soviet Foreign Policy 1917–91: A Retrospective* (London, 1994); Gabriel Gorodetsky and Alexander Chubarian (eds), *The Soviet Union and the Outbreak of War, 1939–1941* (London, 2001) and Gabriel Gorodetsky, *Grand Delusion: Stalin and the German Invasion of Russia* (New Haven and London, 1999); Geoffrey Roberts, *The Soviet Union and the Origins of the Second World War: Russo-German Relations and the Road to War: 1933–41* (London, 1995).

10. Antony Beevor, *Stalingrad* (London, 1998) and *Berlin: The Downfall, 1945* (London, 2002); Richard Overy, *Russia's War* (London, 1998); David Glantz and Jonathan House, *When Titans Clashed: How the Red Army Stopped Hitler* (New York, 1999); David Glantz, *Barbarossa: Hitler's Invasion of Russia, 1941* (London, 2001); David Glantz, *Zhukov's Greatest Defeat: the Red Army's Epic Disaster in Operation Mars, 1942* (Manchester, 2000).

11. Evan Mawdsley, *The Stalin Years* (London, 1998).

12. Martin Malia, *The Soviet Tragedy: A History of Socialism in Russia 1917– 1991* (New York, 1994); Richard Pipes, *Communism: A Brief History* (London, 2002); R. V. Daniels, *The End of the Communist Revolution* (London, 1993); Christopher Read, *The Making and Breaking of the Soviet System* (London, 2001).

13. Sarah Davies, *Popular Opinion in Stalin's Russia: Terror, Propaganda and Dissent 1934–39* (Cambridge, 1997); E. A. Rees (ed.), *Decision Making in the Soviet Command Economy, 1933–1937* (London, 1997); S. Fitzpatrick (ed.), *Stalinism: New Directions* (London, 2000).

14. Jeffrey Brooks, *Thank You, Comrade Stalin!* (Princeton, NJ, 2001); J. Arch Getty and Roberta Manning (eds), *Stalinist Terror: New Perspectives* (Cambridge, 1993); Arkady Vaksberg, *The Prosecutor and the Prey: Vyshinsky and the 1930s Moscow Show Trials* (London, 1990); Marc Jansen et al., *Stalin's Loyal Executioner: People's Commissar Nikolai Ezhov, 1885–1940* (Stanford, CA, 2002); Amy Knight, *Beria: Stalin's First Lieutenant* (Princeton, NJ, 1993); Robert Conquest, *Stalin: Breaker of Nations* (London, 2000, 2nd edition); Barry McLoughlin and Kevin McDermott, *Stalin's Terror: High Politics and Mass Repression in the Soviet Union* (London, 2002); Jurgen Rohwehr and Mikhail Monakov, *Stalin's Ocean-Going Fleet* (London, 2001); Tomas Polak and Christopher Shores, *Stalin's Falcons: The Aces of the Red Star* (London, 1999); Vladimir Papernyai, *Architecture in the Age of Stalin* (Cambridge, 2002).

15. Douglas R. Weiner *A Little Corner of Freedom: Russian Nature Protection from Stalin to Gorbachev* (Berkeley, Los Angeles and London, 2002).

16. David King, *The Commissar Vanishes: The Falsification of Photographs and Art in Stalin's Russia* (London, 1997).

# Bibliography

## 1. GENERAL WORKS

Acton, E., *Russia: The Tsarist and Soviet Legacy*, 2nd edn (London, 1995).

Andrlé, V., *A Social History of Twentieth-Century Russia* (London, 1994).

Arendt, H., *The Origins of Totalitarianism* (New York, 1951).

Brzezinski, Z., *The Permanent Purge: Politics in Soviet Totalitarianism* (Cambridge, Mass., 1956).

Cohen, S., *Re-thinking the Soviet Experience: Politics and History since 1917* (New York and Oxford, 1985).

Daniels, R. V., *The End of the Communist Revolution* (London, 1993).

Fainsod, M., *How Russia is Ruled* (Cambridge, Mass., 1953).

Friedrich, C. (ed.), *Totalitarianism* (Cambridge, Mass., 1954).

Friedrich, C. and Z. Brzezinski, *Totalitarian Dictatorship and Autocracy* (New York, 1956).

Gleason, A., *Totalitarianism: The Inner History of the Cold War* (New York and Oxford, 1995).

Hayek, F. A., *The Road to Serfdom* (London, 1944).

Hosking, G., *A History of the Soviet Union, 1917–1991*, 2nd edn (London, 1992).

Hosking, G. and R. Service (eds), *Reinterpreting Russia* (London, 1999).

Kenez, P., *A History of the Soviet Union from the Beginning to the End* (Cambridge, 1999).

Malia, M., *The Soviet Tragedy: A History of Socialism in Russia, 1917–1991* (New York, 1994).

Nove, A., *An Economic History of the USSR*, 3rd edn (London, 1992).

Popper, K., *The Open Society and its Enemies* (Princeton, NJ, 1950).

Sandle, M., *A Short History of Soviet Socialism* (London, 1999).

Schapiro, L., *Totalitarianism* (London, 1972).

Service, R., *A History of Twentieth-Century Russia* (London, 1997).

Suny, R., *The Soviet Experiment: Russia, the USSR and the Successor States* (Oxford, 1998).

Talmon, J. L., *The Origins of Totalitarian Democracy* (London, 1952).

Talmon, J. L., *Political Messianism: The Romantic Phase* (London, 1960).

Talmon, J. L., *The Myth of the Nation and the Vision of Revolution* (London, 1980).

## 2. SPECIALIZED WORKS

Alliluyeva, S., *Twenty Letters to a Friend* (London, 1967).

Andrlé, V., *Workers in Stalin's Russia: Industrialization and Social Change in a Planned Economy* (Brighton, 1988).

Axell, A., *Stalin's War through the Eyes of His Commanders* (London, 1997).

Bacon, E., *The Gulag at War* (London, 1994).

Barber, J. and M. Harrison, *The Soviet Home Front, 1941–45* (London, 1991).

Berger, J., *Shipwreck of a Generation* (London, 1967).

Bialer, S. (ed.), *Stalin and His Generals* (New York, 1969).

Carr, E. H. and R. W. Davies, *Foundations of a Planned Economy, 1926–1929* (London, 1969).

Carrère d'Encausse, H., *Stalin: Order through Terror* (London, 1982).

Caute, D., *The Fellow Travellers: A Postscript to the Enlightenment* (London, 1977).

Chamberlin, W. H., *Soviet Russia: A Living Record and a History* (London, 1930).

Chase, W., *Workers, Society and the Soviet State: Labour and Life in Moscow, 1918–1929* (Urbana, 1987).

Ciszek, W. S. J., *With God in Russia* (New York, 1966).

Cohen, S., *Bukharin and the Bolshevik Revolution: A Political Biography, 1888–1938 (New York, 1973).*

Cohen, S., *Rethinking the Soviet Experience: Politics and History since 1917* (New York, 1985).

Conquest, R., *The Great Terror: A Reassessment* (1st edn, 1968) (Oxford, 1990).

Conquest, R., *The Nation Killers* (London, 1970).

Cooper, J., M. Perrie and E. A. Rees (eds), *Soviet History, 1917–53: Essays in Honour of R. W. Davies* (London, 1995).

Davies, R. W., *The Industrialization of Soviet Russia*, 2 vols (London, 1980).

Davies, R. W., *The Soviet Economy in Turmoil, 1929–30* (London, 1988).

Davies, R. W., M. Harrison and S. Wheatcroft (eds), *The Economic Transformation of the Soviet Union, 1913–1945* (Cambridge, 1994).

Davies, S., *Public Opinion in Stalin's Russia* (London, 1998).

Deutscher, I., *Trotsky: The Prophet Armed, 1879–1921* (Oxford, 1959).

Deutscher, I., *Trotsky: The Prophet Unarmed* (Oxford, 1959).

Djilas, M., *Conversations with Stalin* (London, 1962).

Dunham, V., *In Stalin's Time: Middle-class Values in Soviet Fiction* (Cambridge, 1976).

Dunmore, T., *The Stalinist Command Economy: The Soviet State Apparatus and Economic Policy, 1945–53* (London, 1980).

Erickson, J., *The Road to Stalingrad* (London, 1975).

Erickson, J., *The Road to Berlin* (London, 1983).

Fainsod, M., *Smolensk Under Soviet Rule* (London, 1958).

Filtzer, D., *Soviet Workers and Stalinist Industrialisation* (London, 1986).

Fitzpatrick, S., *Education and Social Mobility in the Soviet Union, 1921–1934* (Cambridge, 1979).

Fitzpatrick, S. (ed.), *Cultural Revolution in Russia, 1928–1931* (Bloomington, 1978).

Fitzpatrick, S., A. Rabinowitch and R. Suny (eds), *Russia in the Era of NEP* (Bloomington, 1991).

Fitzpatrick, S., *Stalin's Peasants: Resistance and Survival in the Russian Village after Collectivisation* (Oxford, 1994).

Fitzpatrick, S., *Everyday Stalinism* (Oxford, 1999).

Fitzpatrick, S. (ed.), *Stalinism: New Directions* (London, 2000).

Franklin, B. (ed.), *The Essential Stalin: Major Theoretical Writings, 1905–52* (London, 1975).

Getty, J. A., *The Origins of the Great Purges: The Soviet Communist Party Reconsidered, 1933–1938* (Cambridge, 1986).

Getty, J. A. and R. Manning, *Stalinist Terror: New Perspectives* (Cambridge, 1993).

Getty, J. A. and O. Naumov (eds), *The Road to Terror: Stalin and the Self-Destruction of the Bolsheviks, 1932–1939* (New Haven, 1999).

Gill, G., *The Origins of the Stalinist Political System* (Cambridge, 1990).

Ginzburg, E., *Into the Whirlwind* (London, 1967).

Gleason, A., *Totalitarianism: The Hidden History of the Cold War* (New York, 1995).

Goldman, W., *Women, the State and Revolution: Soviet Family Policy and Social Life 1917–1936* (Cambridge, 1993).

Hahn, W., *Postwar Soviet Politics: The Fall of Zhdanov and the Defeat of Moderation* (Ithaca, 1982).

Harrison, M., *Soviet Planning in Peace and War* (Cambridge, 1985).

Harrison, M., *Accounting for War: Soviet Production, Employment, and the Defence Burden* (Cambridge, 1996).

Harrison, M. (ed.), *The Economics of World War Two: Six Great Powers in International Comparison* (Cambridge, 2000).

Harrison, M. and J. Barber (eds), *The Soviet Defence Industry Complex from Stalin to Khrushchev* (London, 2000).

Hoffman, D., *Peasant Metropolis: Social Identities in Moscow, 1929–41* (Ithaca and London, 1994).

Holloway, D., *Stalin and the Bomb: The Soviet Union and Atomic Energy, 1939–1956* (New Haven, 1994).

Khlevniuk, O., *In Stalin's Shadow: The Career of Sergo Ordzhonikidze* (Armonk, NY, 1995).

Khrushchev, N., *Khrushchev Remembers*, 2 vols (London, 1977).

Knight, A., *Beria: Stalin's First Lieutenant* (Princeton, 1993).

Kopelev, L., *The Education of a True Believer* (New York, 1980).

Kotkin, S., *Magnetic Mountain: Stalinism as a Civilization* (Berkeley and Los Angeles, 1995).

Kuromiya, H., *Stalin's Industrial Revolution: Politics and Workers, 1928–32* (Cambridge, 1988).

Lampert, N. and G. Rittersporn (eds), *Stalinism – Its Nature and Aftermath: Essays in Honour of Moshe Lewin* (Armonk, NY 1992).

Levi, P., *The Truce* (London, 1987).

Linz, S. (ed.), *The Impact of World War II on the Soviet Union* (London, 1985).

Lukkanen, A., *The Religious Policy of the Stalinist State – A Case Study: The Central Standing Commission on Religious Questions, 1929–1938* (Helsinki, 1994).

Mandelstam, N., *Hope Against Hope* (London, 1970).

Mandelstam, N., *Hope Abandoned* (London, 1974).

Medvedev, R., *Let History Judge: The Origins and Consequences of Stalinism* (London, 1971).

Molotov, V., *Molotov Remembers: Inside Kremlin Politics, Conversations with Felix Chuev* (ed. A. Resis) (Chicago, 1993).

Overy, R., *Russia's War* (London, 1998).

Rees, E. A., *State Control in Soviet Russia* (London, 1987).

Rees, E. A. (ed.), *Decision-Making in the Stalinist Command Economy, 1932–37* (London, 1997).

Rigby, T. H., *Communist Party Membership in the USSR, 1917–1967* (Princeton, 1968).

Rigby, T. H. and P. Reddaway (eds), *Authority, Power, and Policy in the USSR: Essays Dedicated to Leonard Schapiro* (New York and London, 1980).

Rosenberg, W. and L. Siegelbaum (eds), *Social Dimensions of Soviet Industrialisation* (Bloomington, 1993).

Samuelson, L., *Planning for Stalin's War Machine: Tukhachevskii and Military-Economic Planning, 1925–41* (London, 2000).

Schapiro, L., *The Communist Party of the Soviet Union* (London, 1963).

Scott, J., *Behind the Urals: An American Worker in Russia's City of Steel* (Bloomington and London, 1973).

Serge, V., *Memoirs of a Revolutionary*, trans. and abridged by P. Sedgwick (Oxford, 1963).

Service, R., *Lenin: A Political Life*, 3 vols (London, 1985, 1991, 1994).

Service, R., *Lenin: A Biography* (London, 2000).

Siegelbaum, L., *Stakhanovism and the Politics of Productivity in the USSR, 1935–1941* (Cambridge, 1988).

Siegelbaum, L., *Soviet State and Society between Revolutions, 1918–1929* (Cambridge, 1992).

Siegelbaum, L. and R. Suny, *Making Workers Soviet: Power, Class and Identity* (Ithaca, NY, and London, 1994).

Solzhenitsyn, A., *The Gulag Archipelago*, 3 vols (London, 1974, 1975 and 1978).

Stajner, K., *Seven Thousand Days in Siberia* (London, 1988).

Stalin, J., *Problems of Leninism* (Moscow, 1945).

Thurston, R., *Life and Terror in Stalin's Russia, 1934–1941* (New Haven, 1996).

Todorov, T., *Facing the Extreme: Moral Life in the Concentration Camps* (London, 1999).

Trotsky, L., *The Revolution Betrayed* (London, 1937).

Trotsky L., *Stalin: An Appraisal of the Man and His Influence* (London, 1969).

Trotsky L., *My Life: An Attempt at an Autobiography* (Harmondsworth, 1975).

Tucker, R. C., *Stalin as Revolutionary, 1879–1929* (London, 1974).

Tucker, R. C. (ed.), *Stalinism: Essays in Historical Interpretation* (New York, 1977).

Tucker, R. C., *Stalin in Power: The Revolution from Above, 1928–41* (New York, 1990).

Tutaev, D. (ed.), *The Alliluyev Memoirs* (London, 1968).

Viola, L., *Best Sons of the Fatherland: Workers in the Vanguard of Soviet Collectivisation* (Oxford, 1987).

Viola, L., *Peasant Rebels Under Stalin: Collectivization and the Culture of Peasant Resistance* (Oxford, 1996).

Volkogonov, D., *Stalin: Triumph and Tragedy* (New York, 1988).

Volkogonov, D., *Lenin: A New Biography* (New York, 1994).

Ward, C., *The Stalin Dictatorship* (London, 1998).

Ward, C., *Stalin's Russia*, 2nd edn (London, 1999).

Zaleski, E., *Planning for Economic Growth in the Soviet Union, 1918–1932* (London, 1980).
Zaleski, E., *Stalinist Planning for Economic Growth, 1933–1952* (London, 1980).
Zhukov, Marshall G., *Reminiscences and Reflections* (Moscow, 1974).
Zubok, V and C. V. Pleshakov, *Inside the Kremlin's Cold War* (Cambridge, Mass., 1995).

# Index

Afghanistan, 12
Agapov, Boris, 77
Air Defence Command, 159, 160–1
Akhmatova, Anna, 191
Alliluyeva, Nadezhda, 3
Alliluyeva, Svetlana, 3
All-Union Automobile and Tractor
    Association (VATO), 76, 78, 80
Ammende, Ewald, 8
AMO (Moscow Automobile Plant), 80
Amtorg, 72, 79
Anti-Zionism, 191
Arendt, Hannah, 10
Armand, Inessa, 31
Austria, 145
Austria-Hungary, 66
automobile production figures, 81
Averbakh, Leopold, 102
Avtostroi, 73, 74, 75, 76, 77, 78, 79,
    81, 82
*Azbuka materi* (*ABC of Motherhood*),
    29

Bakhtin, Mikhail, 140
Bakunin, Mikhail, 18
Baltic States, 146, 162
Belorussia, 124–5, 147
Beria, Lavrenti, 153, 194, 195, 196,
    199, 201, 206, 209 nn. 14, 15,
    212 n. 34, 227
Berlin, Battle of, 147
Bevin, E., 172
*Bezbozhnik* (*The Atheist*), 44
Bidault, G., 172
*Black Book of Communism*, 16
Brezhnev, Leonid, 167, 205
Brzezinski, Zbygniew, 10
Budennyi, Marshal, 190
Bukharin, N., 1–3, 18, 41, 54, 55,
    67–8, 69, 118, 122, 140, 141
Bukhartsev, I., 47, 48, 53, 58

Bulganin, N., 194, 195, 196, 199,
    205, 206, 208 n. 4, 209 n. 14,
    212 n. 34

Campanella, Tommasso (Thomas),
    213, 222–3
careerism, 24–5
Carr, E. H., 11
Caspian region, 147
Caucasus region, 51, 85, 95, 147
Central Asia, 51
Central Committee of Communist
    Party, 44, 54, 55, 59, 75, 77, 78,
    82, 105–18, 195, 200, 202–5,
    207, 208 n. 2, 210 n. 22, 211
    nn. 25, 26 and 30
Chamberlin, W. H., 6–7
Chernov, 96–8, 101 nn. 16, 18 and 20
Chevrolet Motor Company, 73–5
children's homes, 32
China, 12, 67, 109, 169, 191, 192
church valuables crisis, 43
Churchill, Sir Winston, 8
Cleveland, Ohio, 75
Cold War debate, 169–70
collectivization, 55, 57, 83–6, 103
Comecon, 185
Cominform, 181
Comintern, 54
*Communist Manifesto*, 40
Communist Party Conference XVI
    (1929), 55
Communist Party Congresses
    **X** (1921), 43
    **XII** (1923), 43
    **XIII** (1924), 43
    **XV** (1927), 72, 91
    **XVII** (1934), 102
    **XVIII** (1939), 192, 193
    **XX** (1956), 111
    **XXII** (1962), 111